Look What I Found Underneath The Bed...

Look What I Found Underneath The Bed...

K. David

2007

Look What I Found
Underneath The Bed...

This book was only possible because of the ones who have walked by my side, at least part of the way, throughout this journey. I appreciate the support and positive energy from everyone as this project was unveiled. I respectfully thank the energy of those who are no longer with me in the physical realm. Last but not least, a special thanks to the energy I call "The Teacher" for literally going back into my past and showing me what to write next. Thank you, Michael, for everything.

PROLOGUE

You have crossed my path in every major city in this nation. You have passed by me on the highway on your way to school or work. How about that day we were both in line at the supermarket? I read the magazine behind you when the other shopper got into the express line with the full shopping cart. I pretended to read while you debated whether or not it was worth your energy to speak up.

We've all been there. We live in the same city. We live in the same town. We live under the same adverse communal conditions. We just choose to keep to ourselves. We assume we have nothing in common.

Well, that time is over. It's time to get to know each other. I think we've got more in common than we thought.

Statistics show that roughly 39 million Americans relocate each year, with the lion's share happening from May to Labor Day. And, a whole lot of those people use movers.

It is difficult to explain the day-to-day grind of this seasonal work. In listing their achievements, many movers will count summers completed, as opposed to entire years. Not surprisingly, most part-timers only last one summer. Yet, it didn't take me very long to see why some individuals chose this profession as a career.

Movers are often looked down on as foul-mouthed, dumb ogres and heaven knows what else. But there's more to the story. I wanted to give a voice to the professionals walking through your front door. In this book, you'll read accounts from the entire stretch of my thirteen summers as a mover—and counting.

The moving game tends to be much like walking onto a beach looking out at the sunset. It's gorgeous, until you realize after a few moments of the awe-inspiring yellow, orange and red that your feet are actually not on stable ground. You are sinking into quicksand. The trick is to keep from getting sucked down.

But first, a little about me. Not everyone gets the pronunciation of my name right: Kamaul, as in "come one, *come all.*" Say it with me: "come one, *come all.*" (Some people still don't get it.)

When I was growing up, I didn't have too many friends. Friends know almost everything about you and are there for you whenever you need them, and I didn't have too many of those outside my family. I don't tend to let too many people truly into my world. It's fair to say I have found comfort in being alone.

However, there has been a constant stream of unusual characters in my life, acting out some unbelievable situations. I am an accumulator of stories. Each and every story that I recreate here, each event, each drama, are all things I witnessed firsthand. Believe me when I tell you these stories don't need embellishing—truth *is* sometimes stranger than fiction.

My top three priorities are simple. First, the wellbeing of my family. Once that's taken care of, my next priority is being able to feed myself. I don't mean physically. What I'm hungry for is accomplishment. Staying hungry fuels the quest to better myself. Combined with a strong work ethic, this hunger motivates everything I set out to do. I don't set out just to make money, but I find that money comes with accomplishment. The third priority for me is the quest to fully comprehend the journey set before me.

I started my work life young, with a lot of energy, trying many different jobs. I wouldn't characterize myself back then as a "hustler," just because it sounds too negative. But there's no doubt about it, at first I went wherever the money was. Like machine wheels turning and churning against each other, I was always on the "grind." Some people refer to me as a workaholic. I guess it's pretty much the same thing.

My true quest, though, was to be good at whatever I did. My Uncle T. used to tell me, "Maulie, if you're good at whatever you do, the money will find you. That's because people are always looking for someone who can get the job done, physically and mentally."

So I worked to be good in all sorts of jobs:

- As a caddie at Franklin Park Golf Course.
- As a golf ball collector in the morning and as a watcher over the 14th hole at dusk at a miniature golf course in Dedham, where if you putted a hole-in-one you actually won twenty-five dollars.
- At a youth service cleanup in Cambridge.
- At a fast food restaurant.
- As a video arcade attendant.
- As a deliveryman in Amherst.
- As a security guard throughout New England.

I call those jobs my W-2 jobs. But there were other jobs, the ones where I made straight cash. I actually liked those the most. You could call me an "independent contractor" or a "mercenary"—I was willing to do work no one else would. Here are the hats I wore: knife salesman, courier, locksmith, plumber, lending institution, card player, pool player, cable installer, phone installer, mobile paging connector, food distributor, computer salesman, athletic sportswear salesman, personal trainer. To complete the resume, I was also a plain old middleman, receiving the nickname "HGI": "What you want, what you need—He Got It." And if I didn't have it, all you had to do was let me make one phone call and I'd get it.

Education was important, too. It made for a great cover in the grand scheme of making moves. I graduated from Boston Latin School, founded in 1635, making it the first school in the New World and still one of the top academic public high schools in the nation. I then attended the University of Massachusetts at Boston and earned a degree in economics.

I bought my first house and paid off my student loans by the age of 27. The thing I'm proudest of is that I never compromised my self-respect by trying, using, or selling any drugs in my years on the grind. I never even drank until 1998, at the toast celebrating my completion of the Boston Marathon in 3 hours, 21 minutes officially (3 hours, 15 minutes unofficially). I won't be content until I finish the Boston Marathon under three hours (but that's for future endeavors).

The summer I started moving, I had a goal I needed to achieve. Along the way I learned how to handle tough situations, and I'd remember those who had inspired me to get me through. I learned not to give up, and to believe in myself.

And then I thought I would never move anything again. Why am I still doing it? Somehow, it's gotten into my blood. Moving allows me to help people, to meet new people every day. I'm there when people are going through their biggest transitions. Getting a new job, disengaging themselves from their kids, leaving a house they've been in for 30 plus years. Sometimes I just say, "Do you need a hug?" And people have just broken down. I find it rewarding to be there to make their lives a little easier.

But first, I had to go through some serious training. In order to understand how far you've traveled, sometimes you need to go back to revisit your starting points. This is the story of my first summer as a mover.

STRUCK BY INSPIRATION

If you thought and agreed
That each one
Owes it to teach one
What happens if the anointed one falls?
Forgets the natural struggle, starts with a crawl.
Never finding a way onto both feet to stand tall.
How does the next generation succeed?

The new chant carries the weight with an old resolution.
If each one teaches many
They will in turn reach plenty
If we take heed to the simple math solution
We give our seeds the armament for the next revolution
Hoping the generations to follow are not raised disillusioned
Live by the chorus for the new evolution.

We are all teachers. . .start class.

Let me introduce you to a typical day in the longtime mover's life. Well, typical except for the part with the hammer.

Saturday, October 8, 2005 was a typical morning waking up in the city of Boston. In New England, it's no surprise to experience three of the four seasons in any given twenty-four hour stretch. That morning, I woke thinking someone was drumming the crown of my head with their fingertips in my dream. The wind made the raindrops rattle against the glass window above my head, waking me up before the alarm clock had a chance to sound. I woke up in a cold sweat. I wake up in a cold sweat early every morning.

I prepare for this day as I do every day. I turn on *Sports Center* before I lie face down on the living room floor. The cold floor against my skin is enough of an incentive to finish off my one hundred push-ups and one hundred crunches. The blood circulating through my body warms me up a bit. A hot bowl of oatmeal warms my body up a bit more while I sit naked on the sofa. One piece of fruit plus a glass of water adds enough sustenance to my body to get me through the morning.

I prefer the heat of the summer months while I'm doing this line of work. I don't dictate the seasons, but I can be prepared for the adjustments. I hate the mosquitoes biting, so in the summer I carry bug repellent in the door of my truck. I dislike my inner thighs becoming chafed, so I carry Vaseline and wear Calvin Klein boxer briefs. When my hands get dried out, I have cocoa butter hand lotion. If I perspire, I have a fresh shirt and deodorant in my knapsack. Most people I have had to work with over the years lean toward enjoying the crispness of the spring and the fall air. However, I still prefer the months of June, July and August. I guess it's because no matter how late in the day, the weather tends to stay relatively hot in the summer.

In October, black Calvin Klein boxer briefs and two pair of socks make up the first layer of clothes. The second layer is a loose pair of basketball shorts with a tank top. My outer shell is a baggie blue sweatshirt with a pair of nylon pants. I slip my feet into Timberland boots and grab my baseball cap to shield my head from the rain. I leave the house and now, "It's time to make the donuts."

As far as work goes, I can't say that I love what I do. However, I do respect what I do six days a week. I enjoy the different characteristics of the people at work. I also enjoy the interactions with the customers. I am a mover who has graduated to the position of crew chief. Being crew chief means I pretty much babysit four other grown men according to their number of celebrated birthdays. My goal for that day in 2005 was simple. I wanted to keep them focused long enough to complete the job without breakage or injuries.

When I got to work I noticed my first scheduled job was estimated for five men and three trucks. The estimation also had us working somewhere between eleven to thirteen hours. We would be moving from the seventh floor of a luxury apartment in Brookline and going to a custom-built house in Wellesley. My team for the day was Daam, Nitbu, Deuce, and F.T.

My number one rule on the job is to never lose control or give it away. Once that power has been relinquished, it can never be regained. The customers are always the X-factor in the sometimes simple equation of making a moving job a success or a day from hell. I've found that all customers have the tendency to want to dictate how the job should be done. "If you put everything from the living room on the truck first then you can take the boxes from the bedroom, which in turn will give me time to pack the bedding and then…"

Some customers over the years have called or written into the office to say, "The crew was absolutely great. They busted their behinds to beat the estimate and they were successful." But then they'll add, "But the crew chief pushed them too hard, like a drill sergeant, and the only time I saw them slow down to take a break was when they were going to lunch. You may want to suggest he lightens up on the guys. But the move was great. I'll call your company when I move again."

I don't make an appointment, six months in advance, to go to the dentist because I have nothing else to do. And when I'm there sitting in his reclined chair, I definitely don't tell the dentist what he should do inside my mouth.

After sitting me down with the super overhead light blinding me so much so that I truly can't open both eyes at the same time without the fear of permanently going blind, the dentist then asks the symptoms and stuffs a bunch of cotton balls in my mouth. I believe the cotton balls are used more as a tool to keep the patients from talking. So I shut the hell up when work is in process.

I'm not going to say this is always easy. Sometimes when I'm sitting there and the dentist is working over me I just want to say bluntly, "With all the chemicals and toothbrushes in this office, why does your breath always smell so tart?" But I can't, I have a plantation's worth of cotton balls in my mouth.

See, your home is my office—the place where I set up shop for my business day. I've come to understand that we as movers are taking into our possession these customers' lives. Their family's world is being entrusted to our hands, to nestle in on the truck to be reconfigured at the new residence. This task needs to be accomplished with stern and gentle hands. So let me do the job I was hired to do.

The Dracuts had actually bought a house on a corner lot a year prior, knocked it down and built their dream home from custom-cut ash colored stone. You are probably wondering how I know that every stone was custom cut. Well, it turned out that John and Barbara Dracut thought it would be the greatest idea to keep every unused piece of stone in the closet of the three bedroom apartment where they lived with their five children, along with every other sample stone shown to them by the various contractors. "We plan on creating a family walkway," Barbara told me in her nasally voice eight separate times.

I actually had the pleasure of meeting Barbara Dracut the day prior, Friday, October 7. She met us at the storage facility where everything was to be moved out. After everyone introduced themselves we proceeded upstairs to the storage unit.

I learned to establish my foot-drawn lines in the sand years ago. Honesty and tact have always proven to give the best results.

Allow me to give you a little insight into the established history of the four other individuals who were part of the Dracut move—Nitbu, Deuce, F.T., and Daam.

Nitbu Carmichael came back to Boston every spring to make enough money over the summer to then disappear back to one of the valleys in California, usually by the first week in November. He lived to snowboard. This pattern was also his method of recuperating after being diagnosed with cancer in his mid-twenties.

Nitbu came to our company the year after chemotherapy helped place the cancer in remission. I think he initially came back to see if he still had what it took to do the physical moving on a daily basis. As weak as he was that first spring, he was back in good form by June.

Because of his brush with cancer, Nitbu was meticulous about infection. He used baby wipes and sanitary napkins to wipe down every possible surface he might touch. Surprisingly, he never wore gloves. Nitbu was a good, but thick, mover. I say "thick" not as an insult to the man's mental capacity, but as a strike to his common sense. More than half of the homes we go to each day are in disarray. Some homes look as though they have never been cleaned. Forget about seeing dust bunnies—when a dresser gets moved away from the wall, you better hope you don't awaken something that's been living there as long as the customer has.

The first day Nitbu and I worked together, he asked after lunch, "Could you guys wash your hands before we go back to work? With me recovering from cancer, my white blood cell count is pretty low. I just want to be as safe as possible. Thanks guys."

I watched as everyone filed single person behind each other to the restroom. Everyone got up except me.

J-Woogie, a six-foot four-inch twenty-three year old from Maine who always looked a little perplexed, was the first team member back from the bathroom. He asked me, "You're not gonna wash your hands?"

"Nope," I replied.

This puzzled him more. Let me say it a little plainer—J-Woogie was lost unless he had a drink in his hand. He could have been a decent athlete, judging from his physical stature. But I gathered that his lust for alcohol placed a firm hand around his glass of potential.

As everyone else filed outside with the same puzzled look about why I had not washed my hands, I waited for the Nitbu to ask me again.

Sure enough, there it came. "Could you please wash your hands before we go back?"

My reply once again, "Nope!"

I could tell he was starting to get upset. So I explained in my own way. I walked everyone to the back of the last truck we had packed before lunch and asked, "What was the last thing we loaded onto this truck?"

It was hard to forget because most of us were still covered in the dirt and bark from the customer's wood pile. The pile had consisted of about four hundred pieces of wood we carried by hand to the truck. I kept extra T-shirts in the cab of my truck, just in case some people came to work unprepared. As I opened the back of the truck everyone simultaneously said, "Wood."

"Here's why I'm not washing my hands. First, we all busted our humps to load the wood. Afterwards, we looked around for soap to wash up, but there wasn't any. The customer had already packed her supplies away. So most of us simply resorted to using water to clean up as best as we could. But then I noticed Nitbu walk upstairs to the bathroom, closing the door for privacy. He came downstairs smelling all soapy clean.

"So, I'm not washing my hands because Nitbu is way too neurotic not to carry in his backpack a bar of soap he could have let the rest of us use. I know for a fact he has a bottle of liquid antibacterial soap. It would not have hurt him to give each of us a squirt or two. Nitbu's actions tell me he wants us to care about his situation but he doesn't give a second thought about us.

"The other reason I'm not washing my hands is I still have to take the wood off the truck. I know I will be covered by dirt and crawling animals on my front side the minute we start. We all will. We have to accept the fact that this is the job, and it is dirty."

Nitbu didn't like it, but there wasn't much he could say. I was the crew chief, the elder statesman of the team. Everything has to go through me.

See, my job is to do a good job for the company, enhance its reputation, and get the check from the customer. The crew's job is to do what they're told to get a paycheck. There's an inherent conflict of interest there. So, the person in charge has to stay in charge. Sometimes you show you're in charge with the little things, like washing hands.

Everybody that starts with a moving company thinks they know a better way to do things. They want to inflict their view of how it should be done on everyone else. But the formula in place works pretty well. Nitbu was just doing his thing, trying to change the world.

When everyone climbed back into the trucks after lunch waiting for me to lead the convoy, J-Woogie looked at me with a smirk and said, "Yeah, you know you're an ass."

"You know my motto," I replied straight-faced.

"What's funny is funny?" J-Woogie was smiling, nodding his head, exposing his front upper teeth in which the third tooth from the middle right was missing. The missing tooth made J-Woogie look like a hockey player who never missed the opportunity to smile.

"No, fool!" I exclaimed.

"Oh yeah, 'no one man is above the team.' "

"Exactly," I replied with a wink.

The truth is, it took me a while to become as blunt as I am. I had made the decision six years prior when I came to Marathon Movers in 2000 that I would be 100% honest with everyone who worked with me. I knew honesty would be respected even if my co-workers didn't agree with me. I knew it was truly not what I said, but *how* I said it.

Not surprisingly, I bumped heads with some co-workers and sometimes it got physical. For those who took me on, I always hoped for their sake that it didn't take too long to find another job after they healed up. I have been told I am a bit intimidating. I don't see it myself, but I guess that's why some people choose to hold their emotions in check when it comes to dealing with me. As everyone who knows me knows, if it's on my mind I have to get it off because tomorrow I may not get that chance.

This was Nitbu's second year moving with us, and his fourth summer in the moving game. I respected what he bought to my team. Ever since our initial hand-washing pissing contest, we worked well together on bigger jobs. I usually had him pack the trucks for me while I stayed in the house as the point man. As the point man, my responsibility was to keep everything moving so he could pack the truck without stopping. Plus, being in the house gave me the opportunity to establish a comfort and trust level with the customers.

My crew's initial contact with Barbara Dracut was a little unusual. We met her at her fifteen-by-twenty foot storage unit, where she had some extra disassembled boxes she planned to use for packing before we arrived at the condo the following day.

We loaded the boxes into her vehicle within five minutes. Then Barbara said, "This is everything I need. I'm going to go back home so I can feed the kids, do you mind?"

"That's not a problem," I replied. "Let's you and I just walk back down to the truck so I can double-check the address, and we'll see you in the morning."

As an afterthought once I'd confirmed the address, she said, "Oh, there is a heavy desk in there. Could you be careful? It took the last moving company five people to move it into storage. See ya tomorrow."

When I got back upstairs, Nitbu and Daam just kept shaking their heads. Twelve slabs of marble had been hidden behind multiple remaining crushed boxes. Four of the slabs were huge, standing at least seven feet tall and badly crated. Upon further inspection, most of the boxes, which were labeled "fragile—china," rattled louder than most baby toys. Under the damaged boxes stood a seven-foot steel and granite desk that must have weighed nearly nine hundred pounds.

It took us another three hours to load these heavy items. I went to the front desk to inform the storage attendant that Unit 264A was empty, and the gate needed to be raised so we could leave.

"Where is the unit occupant?" asked the middle-aged man from behind the counter.

"She left about five minutes after we got here."

"Well, they owe us money. They cancelled the credit card they were using to pay for the storage unit. They disconnected their phone line. Your company is not going anywhere without us receiving our payment. Unless you can get them on the phone, that truck is staying right here."

Great. I gave the attendant the contact number I had for the Dracuts. After a lengthy one-sided argument, the attendant passed me the phone.

I heard, "Hi, Mr. Mover, this is John Dracut. This jerk is pretty much busting my balls here. Is it possible for you to pay the balance since we are going to see you tomorrow anyhow? This guy is holding my balls pretty tight here."

All I could muster for a response was, "Are you serious?" I'm thinking, *If they can't afford to pay their storage, how are they going to pay for this move? What if they try to say we damaged those rattling boxes?* My street sense started to tingle even as I fronted the money for the storage bill.

The two other members of the team that morning were F.T. and Deuce. I refer to Deuce as my left-hand man. We have been close associates since our years at UMass Boston. We even sat side by side at our graduation ceremony in 1997. He was one of the first friends who jumped in to help me complete the Boston Marathon. Without question, Deuce has always been good people to me.

Shortly after we graduated, Deuce was determined to co-produce and distribute his rhythm-and-blues album, which I keep in my CD changer as motivation to this day. After he took the CD as far as it could go, he got a job at the Boston's Museum of Fine Arts as director of community relations. A few years later, he went back to school for a master's degree in art administration at Boston University. He had just graduated at the time of this story. Deuce had joined us at the moving company here and there for a few extra bucks throughout, but he made it a forty-hour-a-week gig while he was in school.

At 19, F.T. was the youngest man to work with us that summer. He had just graduated from Randolph High School when we hired him. As a rule, I generally don't work with new guys until they have a week or two to get in shape. I like to take a guy at that point to show him what my days are like. F.T.'s first day working with me is still vivid in my mind because of how the day unfolded. Keep in mind, I had no clue who this young man was, but since he and his friends had been working with us they heard stories about how long a day my jobs are and that I am a no-nonsense crew chief.

So lo and behold this one summer morning in June, it is already ninety degrees at quarter past six when I show up to the warehouse. I had been given permission by the company owner to create a gym overlooking the warehouse. Since I am usually the first person there, I unlock all the doors and turn up the music to get ready for my day. I like to ease into my workout, so I throw on a compilation CD that starts off with Earth, Wind, and Fire's "Keep your head to the sky" and ends with The Notorious B.I.G.'s "One more chance (remix)."

This morning I wanted to max out my bench press at three hundred and seventy-five pounds. My body weight is one hundred and eighty-five pounds, standing solid for my height of five feet and nine inches. My upper body has always been over-developed. I started routinely doing push-ups at the age of ten. Today the goal is to maybe push the weight up two or three times at the most.

At quarter to seven I heard two voices. I didn't care who they were, I just needed a spotter. Groove Theory's ultra sexy lead singer Amiel Larieux's voice filled the warehouse as their song, "Tell me" played, which meant I had two songs left before Biggie Smalls filled the warehouse. I wasn't wearing a shirt at the time because it was too hot. I was already sweating from the first thirty minutes of working out.

When I stood up to see who came into the warehouse I guess I was so focused on lifting the weight and getting it over with that I barked, "You two just drop your bags, come up here and spot me."

When they came up the ladder, I didn't even introduce myself as maybe I should have. Instead I blurted out , "Have you ever spotted weight before? No? Okay, you both stand on either side of the bar. I'm going to try to lift this up three times. Don't touch the bar unless you hear me say, 'Take it!' Okay?"

I would show these guys a thing or two about discipline. They knew I was the first one in there every day, putting my house in order and getting ready mentally and physically before the chaos starts. Since they were the youngest kids that summer, they hadn't yet figured out what I did up there every day. In general, only a few people will venture upstairs.

As the young men took their places on either side of the bar, I got into position and was feeling pretty good. I lifted the weight off the stand and lowered it to my chest where it pressed up against my right pierced nipple ring, which is my indicator to extend the weight back up as I exhaled. Time for the second attempt, bring the weight down to the nipple ring and exhale. For some reason I glanced over to the face on my right side and noticed a look of panic. In that split second I thought, "If this weight got too heavy could these two actually pick it off me?" I decided the answer was not worth the risk so I put the weight back on the stand.

I looked at both of the young men and said, "Thanks, but if either one of you stays up here more than two minutes then you have to finish working out with me."

It was funny watching them scramble for the ladder. F.T., in second place, turned to descend the ladder and asked, "How much weight was that?"

"Three seventy-five," was my reply.

"Why didn't you do the last rep?"

My response was "I still have to work today—I didn't want to exhaust myself." When actually the truth was these young guys had made me extremely nervous after that second attempt.

At seven o'clock when I finished working out, I checked in at the office. Scottish Jimmy threw me our paperwork for the day's job. I watched the four pages sail right over my shoulder and flutter like a hurt pigeon to the floor.

"You could have caught the fucking paper, asshole."

"Yeah, I could have," I said, using my T-shirt to wipe the sweat off my back, "but it's funnier to watch your punk ass walk over and pick it up."

Jimmy is as fiery as the ethnically appropriate color of his cropped hair cut, and he's good at his job. We'd both been at the company since it started five years ago. It's rare for us to work together on a job, even though this is our sixth summer together. When we are placed together, it usually means the office wants to impress the customer. The unspoken message is either 1) we are going to be short manned, 2) there is a lot of heavy furniture, or 3) we are being set up to beat the estimate so we'll have time that day for a floater. A floater is an additional job scheduled for the afternoon that has not been assigned to any specific crew but will go to the first crew back from their morning job.

As I walked over to the table to see who my crew was for the day, Jimmy yelled, "Them fuckers wants us to pull off a wee hat trick and carry Pampers, too."

When I first met Jimmy, as he would speak I would turn to the person next to me and ask, "What the hell did he just say?" That person would generally shrug their shoulders because they didn't understand him either. Even to this day I'm not sure if I couldn't understand Jimmy because of his paternal Scottish or maternal Irish brogues or because he just didn't really care if anyone understood him or not. But that warm June morning, I understood exactly what he meant.

This "hat trick" was going to be interesting. Jimmy and I had been requested by a local real estate agent to move her sister from Avon to Stoughton. The previous moving company her sister had used employed six men and three trucks, and it still took them fifteen hours. Our brilliant company had estimated the job could be done with five men, two trucks and within eight to ten hours, coming out of the second floor of a two-family house. The paperwork listed a sofa and two armoires that once at the new home would need to be hoisted through a second floor window because they would not fit up the stairs. It was clear to Jimmy and me that we would be under the microscope since the sister's move with the other moving company had been an unpleasant experience.

The dispatcher Michael (aka "The Golden Boy") helped us out some because he assigned Marion to my team. Marion was a solid set. He was what I like to call the "complete mover." Marion was a Romanian who was not afraid of work. When it was time to run, he could keep up with

Jimmy stride for stride. He would never shy away from carrying anything. Marion was six feet tall, with a full head of well-groomed hair and a slight five o'clock shadow that made him look rustic. At twenty-seven years old, he fulfilled the mover fantasy of many female customers. Marion could have easily been a Calvin Klein underwear model. I'm sure we had many customers that wished he would move them in his underwear or out of theirs. I personally liked the fact that Marion would work for hours and never complain about anything.

As I said before, the job was estimated for five men. Today I counted three names on the list under mine, *ergo*, we were short manned. Marion went outside to get his truck ready.

When I saw an unfamiliar name on the list, I looked at Jimmy a little bewildered. "Who is this F.T.? Have you worked with him?"

Jimmy turned to the group of new summer help. "Which one of you sorry looking little bastards is F.T.? Actually I don't care. All of you look like your still nursing from your mummy's third nipple. Which one of you little pricks is F.T.?"

Thankfully, I could tell none of the young men understood anything Jimmy said except the last line. The kid who had asked me about the weight of my bench press was the one whose head fell to his chest. His friends all exhaled knowing they had dodged working with me once again.

As F.T. stepped forward, Jimmy looked him dead in the face. "Are you even strong enough to carry your own ball sack? You carry your knapsack like a changing bag. What you got in that knapsack Luvs or Huggies? I'm not going to change you if you shite yourself. If you break one damn thing today I'm going to stop the truck and leave you in whatever town we're in you little prick." Jimmy was systematic in the way he would break rookies down.

I pointed at F.T. "Junior, you ride with me. Jimmy, you and Marion take the lead. We'll follow you guys."

Just as we were leaving, dispatcher Michael yelled, "There are two floaters today. I need you guys on at least one." No pressure.

When F.T. climbed up into the truck, it was time to go through my ritual of rules. Everyone had heard my rules speech at least one time.

"This is your first time working with me," I started in. "How has working with the company been so far?" He nodded. "Good, good. I need to know if you have prior engagements tonight before I put this truck into gear." He shook his head. "Good, good. I'm going to be honest with you. I have no idea what time our job is going to end today. We are going to stop soon at the convenience store. I suggest you buy enough liquids and food to hold you over until lunch. Are you used to eating around noonish?" He nodded. "You need to break your body of that habit. I know we will eat at some point today; I'm just not sure when.

"You're on my team today. That means we all go home at the end of the day together. I know you have probably worked with other crew chiefs who have a different style. I'm not going to tell you anything they taught you was wrong. I'm going to simply tell you to pay particular attention to my style and to Jimmy's style. We are the standard the company strives to maintain.

"My main focus since this company started was to bring home the check at the end of our work day. I have never ever come back without being paid. Some crew chiefs have been stiffed by customers refusing to pay, customers stopping payment on a check or simply bouncing a check. A bounced check has only happened to me one time. I rectified the situation personally the following day.

"On the job today, I will pack the truck. Jimmy will play the point man in the house. You and Marion will be situated between us. When we show up to the house and begin working, we will run boxes first. When I say run, it means run. When boxes get passed to you carry it, don't run it, to the next man creating a linked chain back to me. Once you hand off your boxes sprint back to the man ahead of you in the chain. He should then smack you with the box in your chest. It stings at first but you'll get used to it. Marion and Jimmy are fast, so whatever they prep in a furniture pad that you feel you can carry out to me yourself, just bring it.

"We are already short-manned on this job, and I can't let your inexperience be a liability. A chain is only as strong as its weakest link. You are that link today. So you actually have a key role. Keep your feet moving, and don't look like you don't know what you're doing. If the customer happens to ask you how long you been moving the correct response is, 'All my life.'

"We have exactly one hour to impress the customer. If all of the boxes are out of the house and at least a quarter of the furniture is gone, we will have created the illusion of opening space they have not seen in their home since the day they moved in.

"We're not going to ask you carry any dressers or sofas today because you are not ready yet. I need you concentrating on simply padding and carrying. No matter what, stay away from the toolbox even if you think you know how to take something apart. At the end of the day you will be surprised at how fast the job gets done. You're going to think that this job is actually fun with me.

"Most importantly, I have the best tip ratio out of every crew chief we have working. I get tipped every nine out of ten jobs. That means if you impress me with your work effort, you will pretty much raise your hourly rate by a couple of bucks. Are you cool with everything I talked to you about?" He nodded, still with me.

"Good, good. I know Jimmy's tough as nails but he has a lot to teach. But if the job gets too tough out there on any day, or if one of the other crew chiefs is too hard, come and talk to me and I'll defuse the situation."

We had pulled up to the convenience store. As F.T. got out of the truck, I could see the weight of being assigned with me vanish from his chest.

Jimmy walked up to my driver's side window eating Skittles and drinking Coke.

"How the hell do you eat that in the morning?" I asked.

"Breakfast of champions."

The scowl on my face displayed my disapproval. As he chugged down the last of his soda and pulled a Snickers bar from his pocket, he glared back at me and yelled, "You know I'm hyperglycemic, asshole."

"That's the second time you've called me that. I ain't gonna be too many more assholes today." Jimmy saw my raised left eyebrow and knew he was getting to me. So he smiled. I smiled back, sticking up my middle finger letting him know he was still number one in my book.

I knew the real reason Jimmy walked over to my truck. He was trying to be coy, but I knew what was coming.

"How much you want to bet the kid falls at least once?" Jimmy said with a head nod.

I replied, "I'll take that bet for lunch, because his sneakers were actually laced to the top. I bet my future tip he doesn't make it more than a week from today."

Jimmy scrunched his face. "I'll take some of that."

With one bet each against young F.T., we needed a tie breaker. One of us always had to win.

"I got it," I chimed in. "Let's go no lunch until after we pick up the paperwork for the second job. I bet fifty bucks the kid never makes it to the second job."

The passenger side door opened and F.T. stepped inside carrying his gallon of water, a transparent bag consisting of a multigrain bar, Gatorade, and a banana, and a blueberry muffin in his hand. Jimmy and I looked at each other and smiled. The young man had adequate sustenance to make it until the second job. The question was, would he?

When we did the walk through at the customer's house, Jimmy, Marion and I all wondered, "Where was all the furniture?" Apparently the customers had been coming and going to the new house so often they decided they might as well bring a few boxes with them on each trip. We were going to be done by noon. We would only need one truck.

By a quarter to eleven, I called Michael at dispatch from the truck. "We'll be done at the Stoughton offload in thirty minutes. We'll grab something to eat on the way to the second job."

Then Marion walked over and whispered, "I see blood on the floor. I think the new kid hurt himself."

As Jimmy appeared, I looked at him with palms facing the sky. "What's up? I gave him a chair to carry in and unpad. How is he bleeding?"

Jimmy deadpanned, "I told him that I've finished jobs with an ankle the size of a rugby ball and three different shades of color, no worries. I told him what he has is like a bug bite. I once worked a full week with a dislocated shoulder and a broken finger. No worries. He has to grow to get used to the pain."

I could see into the first floor half bath of the customer's house through the kitchen window. The customer was in there assisting F.T., which could only mean trouble.

"Marion, why is F.T. bleeding?" I asked, searching for a more logical answer.

"The customer had a pair of scissors on her desk. The kid was having a difficult time breaking the tape from the furniture pads with his bare hands, so he picked up the scissors and cut himself."

After hearing this, at first I thought like Jimmy did. "Let's finish the job. Put a bandage on it." But as I walked into the house, I saw way too much blood on the linoleum floor. There was F.T. in the bathroom, with a roll of paper towels under his right arm and a wad of dry paper towels over his left index finger.

"Are you all right? What happened?" Now I wanted to hear the answer from the source.

His reply was consistent with Marion's report.

"Well, let me see how bad you cut yourself."

As F.T. removed the wad of paper towels from his index finger, all I could think of was this kid shooting a water gun of free flowing blood over the sink into the wad of paper towels. Whoo boy. I asked F.T. to cover his finger once again and try to add pressure around the finger.

I calmly walked into the kitchen and asked the customer, "Could one of you please take him to the hospital? He did way more than cut his finger."

As F.T. left for the emergency room, I said, "Call the dispatcher if you need anything and let us know how you're doing."

Jimmy, Marion and I finished the first job, the second job and a third job as well that day. When we got back to the warehouse at eight o'clock, Michael the dispatcher was still in his office.

"How's the kid?"

Michael looked up at us three and said, "He called about a half hour ago to say he can't make it to work tomorrow. The doctor wants him out at least ten work days. He had to have stitches. But I guess he really called to ask if anyone found the tip of his finger so they could sew it back on."

Jimmy and I slowly shook our heads then started smiling, relieved. Worrying about the kid's welfare all day had left the three of us with very little to speak about. In the moving industry, everyone is only one injury away from being done. Every mover I know wants the chance to walk away from this game on his own terms, not be carried away never to return.

"Jimmy," I decreed, "my new nickname for the kid will be 'F.T.' Short for 'Fingertip.' I've never seen anything like that before."

Jimmy roared back, "How about F.T. for Fucking Turnip. You would have to be dumb as a turnip to cut clean through your finger with a dull pair of shears. That's just stupid."

As the four of us exploded into laughter something dawned on me. The kid had never made it to lunch.

"Hey, Jimmy, you owe me fifty dollars!"

Fast forward back to the Dracut house. By the time Nitbu, F.T., Deuce, Daam and I finished loading all three trucks, it was just after noon. The rain was starting to let up. Since we were in Brookline just around the corner from Beacon Street we all knew exactly where to eat—Anna's Taqueria.

Anna's Taqueria was an excellent Mexican quick stop eatery. I always get either the steak quesadilla or spicy pork super burrito. Today I was in the mood to buy both, with the plan to eat the steak now and take the super burrito to snack on. With three trucks to unload, we were guaranteed a long day. I relayed my thoughts about buying extra food to my coworkers, and everyone agreed.

Lunchtime for us is equivalent to halftime in a football game. We sit down and relax. We reenergize and hydrate our bodies. We recap and make adjustments to our plan of what needs to get accomplished at the new house, during that day's second half.

Unfortunately, it had slipped my mind that the college students were back. Boston's population increases about tenfold during the school year, because it has the highest concentration of colleges per square mile of anywhere in the country. Anna's sat between Boston College and Boston University right on a busy trolley line. The growing line outside the door at Anna's Taqueria reminded me it was that time of year. We noticed five people getting seats right away at the pizza shop a couple of doors down. They probably didn't have the patience to wait in the drizzling weather for good food, but we did.

Even still, as my crew turned to cross the street, Nitbu yelled, "Run, a trolley full of students are coming!"

We made the dash across the trolley tracks before the line at Anna's increased by twenty. When we finally got served, there was not a table available for love or money to accommodate the five of us. So four of us sat on the windowsill while Daam sat on his duffel bag on the floor. Our lunchtime break was a half hour, and we had consumed twenty minutes of it in line. We may have eaten uncomfortably, but it was worth it.

When we got to the Dracuts' new house in Wellesley, it was just after one o'clock. John and Barbara had purchased two adjoining lots. They demolished the two houses that were there and constructed an admittedly beautiful mansion. It just didn't look as though it fit comfortably in their neighborhood.

The other houses throughout the area were spread out quaintly with just enough backyard space for a play structure and plenty of room for children to run around inside white picket fences. Then, there was this behemoth of a house. I was reminded of the kid in some sixth grade class picture who is a foot and a half taller than everyone else, including the teacher. Whenever you show someone outside of your school the class photo, they think the student is either the teacher or the principal. Remember how awkward that picture looks? The Dracuts' house, although undeniably stunning, was that same monstrosity among its peers.

The Brazilian cleaning service was there when we pulled up in the trucks. We knew it was Brazilian by the bright yellow cars with the green company logos plastered all over and the national flag on the hoods. As F.T., Deuce, Nitbu and I approached the house for the walk through, I noticed we were missing one. His beat-up blue suede Pumas could be seen underneath the truck.

I cocked my head in that direction. "F.T., go tell Daam I said to come on."

I had made Daam ride with me to the new house as my navigator after we left Anna's Taqueria. Daam hated riding with me, and I wasn't particularly fond of him either. But he was efficient at reading a map book, and in the winding roads of Boston, that can save you serious time.

Since it had been raining all morning, I figured I could turn the heat on inside the truck on the way to help our clothes dry a bit. It took maybe three minutes of heat before the funky smell of bad garbage smacked me in the face.

"What the hell is that smell?" The question was rhetorical. We both could see the two holes in Daam's left sneaker displaying his sock. Daam's right sneaker tongue looked like a panting, salivating, injured dog.

"I thought I asked you to get rid of those stinking-ass sneakers," I said with a scowl while rolling down the windows. This would usually be enough for any other coworker to at least consider buying new footwear—but not Daam.

"I told you these are my favorite sneakers. I wear them everywhere. I got them from my mom. These shoes will last two more years easily."

Daam also hated riding with me because I had placed six no smoking symbols in the cab of my truck. Daam smoked like a fiend. Every opportunity that presented itself outside the view of the customer, Daam went for a smoke, even if it were just for a drag or two. As we all turned to watch F.T.'s boots hold a brief intervention with Daam's sneakers in between the wheels of the truck, it occurred to me I didn't see the Dracuts' cars anywhere.

As Daam and F.T. reappeared from behind the truck, the front door of the house opened. The general contractor appeared in the doorway with a box in hand.

"Mrs. Dracut requests that everyone who walks in the house wear these rubber booties over their footwear or takes their shoes off. I'll leave the box of booties here so you guys can put them on."

The contractor seemed to be cool enough. He was just following his orders and trying to cover his own butt. I just wasn't in the mood to go back and forth.

"Is it possible for the cleaners to move their cars so we can get our trucks in place?" I asked. "Once we get the trucks in place, I'll place pads and Masonite over the floors for protection. We'll place furniture pads on all of the banisters as well.

"Just so you know, there are three trucks with extremely heavy furniture to unload. If my guys are carrying a dresser in their socks or these rubber booties, they could slip and fall. If they slip and fall, they are going to put a hole in the floor or in the walls. I'll take the responsibility if something goes wrong. But we are definitely not taking our shoes off."

The contractor let the cleaners know to move their cars. Then he gave me some advice. "The Dracut wife is pretty crazy. They have been threatening to sue me over any and everything, so be careful."

The eight Brazilian women hurried to finish their work and gather their supplies. Half of those Brazilian cleaners were not the most beautiful in the face. But what made these women jaw dropping as we watched them coming and going was how their curvaceous figures were being held ever so tightly together by their tan pants and yellow pullover collared shirts.

Since the Dracuts had not arrived yet, the five of us stood at the doorway like a pack of wolves. We were motionless, watching, saying absolutely nothing, as each young woman walked past until they finally piled into the three yellow vehicles. It was at that moment when we all simultaneously looked up from the last closing car door with a smile on our faces and began waving goodbye.

That's when I heard Deuce say from my right side, "Those bodies. I mean, women have truly been blessed. God is good!"

I began to hum, shaking my head in affirmation, as the rest of our small congregation said, "Amen!" I continued to hum for inspiration as the newly appointed Reverend Deuce continued his sermon on the doorsteps.

"By the end of this week, I'm starting some classes to learn Portuguese. I'm going to learn everything possible about soccer, and I'm even going to call it football. I'm going to learn how to dance the samba. I'm going to get a Brazilian flag to hang on my car window to go with my new soccer jerseys. I'm going to move to Somerville. And I'm going to Brazil where I might just meet Miss Right."

Nitbu replied, "See if your future Mrs. has some cousins who speak some English. I don't have that much time to devote to the country of Brazil."

We all busted out laughing while continuing to wave until the last car could no longer be seen.

I tried the Dracuts several times, but each time my call went unanswered. After leaving the second message I told everyone to relax until the Dracuts got there. We could not offload into the house without knowing where the furniture should be placed.

Two hours of waiting gave everyone time to refresh. I did my paperwork and caught a quick nap. I figured Daam had inhaled enough cancer sticks to tide him over until tomorrow. I could see Deuce checking his email on his Blackberry since we obviously were not going home anytime soon. I couldn't see F.T. but I assumed he was relaxing like everyone else—correction, everyone except Nitbu.

Neurotic Nitbu had been keeping busy from the moment the eye candy masquerading as Brazilian cleaners drove away. He pulled out our broom, sweeping away every grain of sand and granite on the front walk. Mud puddles had formed on the walkway from the rain, so Nitbu took the contractor's hose and washed down the front walk, the driveway, the back patio and every other possible surface he thought we might traverse. The man simply had to clean.

At three o'clock the Dracut entourage arrived in six cars, delivering John, Barbara, their five children, eight more adults including a grandmother in her walker that pulled along an oxygen tank, and four additional children. My mind's eye predicted nine children running under our feet as we carried furniture around—simply an accident waiting to happen.

Another half hour transpired while the entire family received a grand tour, complete with blue booties on their feet. I finally approached John and Barbara and said, "It is just before four o'clock at this point. My guys are going to need some direction from you two as to where you want the furniture as they come into the house. I'm going to need at least one of you two by the front door at all times. There are more people here than I anticipated. By saying this, I am asking if the children can be centralized in the basement so they can run around freely. I don't want them to get hurt as my guys are moving furniture. The rest of your family members can watch out for themselves."

It always amazes me that no matter how often I tell, not ask, the customer to stay close by the door to give us direction while we unload, each customer still prefers to use this as the most opportune moment to start unpacking boxes of dishes, to hang pictures, and to assemble tricycles.

I'll know we're at that point when I start hearing my team call out, "I have a china cabinet here. Which wall do you want it to go against? Hello!? Can someone tell me where the barstools are going? Okay, how about the crib? Hello!!!"

I couldn't fault the other family members because John and Barbara kept disappearing. How was Grandmother supposed to tell us where to put things? You could tell she was preoccupied by the oxygen level in her tank. She would not dare waste her breath calling for Barbara. But the rest of us had no choice. "Barbara?"

It is always challenging to place furniture properly. Most customers figure the furniture from the living room of the old house will fit right into the living room in the new house. If a family is relocating from one apartment to another apartment, this theory might work. Moving from a house to a house, again this theory works. But when a family is downsizing or upgrading, it doesn't quite work. From big to small, the rooms in the new home may become a little congested, though it has been known to work. From small to big, things can become ludicrous.

Relocating from an apartment where the living room is at most two hundred square feet to a corresponding great room in the new house of one thousand square feet of open space with fifteen foot high cathedral ceilings, the theory simply does not work. No matter how the furniture is reconfigured, it is dwarfed by the grandeur of the room. The only solution is to buy more furniture.

I was longing for a summer night at this very minute, but I was two months too late. During the unload of the second truck, I went into the house to begin the reassembly of furniture. I was tightening up the last leg of the dining room table when I heard the truck roaring. Deuce walked into the dining room eating his cold burrito.

He said with full mouth, "Second truck done."

"Cool," I replied.

He sat his burrito on the floor as I gave him the head nod to help me flip the table over.

I asked, "How is the boys' morale holding up?"

"Well, it's almost eight o'clock. Everyone except the two of us had already eaten their second burrito while waiting for the Dracuts to show up. I would say they are all pretty hungry. The customers had six pizzas delivered about a half hour ago, and didn't offer up one slice. But Miss Barbara was nice enough to place paper cups next to the kitchen sink if your throat gets parched. Nitbu keeps talking about how heavy the granite and steel desk was, so the boys are getting cranky, too. Your boy Daam volunteered to switch the trucks so he could get one full cigarette smoked."

We headed toward the front door. An instant chill forced me to pull my shoulder blades together.

"When did the temperature drop?" It was at that moment I noticed that he was the only one wearing a sweatshirt. Deuce was methodical about being overly prepared for work.

Finishing the last bite of burrito, Deuce replied, "It dropped to thirty-seven degrees the second it got dark. Plus it started raining again about twenty minutes ago."

Time for the desk. I proceeded to the cab of my truck while my crew members opened the doors and set up the ramp. Turning on the rear truck spot lights, I changed from a tank top to a uniform blue T-shirt and grabbed the emergency bag from behind the driver's seat. I reached the back of the truck to find four sets of eyes focused on the massive steel desk. I walked up the front steps to the large cardboard bin that held the folded furniture pads.

"It is the fourth quarter, gentlemen!" I said, more energetically than I felt. "I know it's cold. I know it's been a long day. I know you're hungry. I can't do much about Mother Nature. If everyone promises to focus and give me everything you have left, I'll share my emergency bag."

All eyes were fixated on the bag as I dumped the contents onto the stack of furniture pads. The grins stretched from ear to ear as Gatorades, spring water, Power bars, pretzels, potato chips, caramel corn, honey buns, Gummy bears and Now-or-Later candies spilled out. It's moments like this that made me happy to be a boss.

Off in the distance, I overheard Barbara say to her sister-in-law, "I can't believe they're holding up our move with their pointless breaks."

"It just doesn't seem to me, Barbara, that it should take this long to move your house. I saw an exclusive report on either *20/20* (or was it *Dateline?*) where the movers charged, like, triple the cost of the original estimate. There are companies out there looking to rip off people like us."

My street sense started to tingle again. All I could think about since the day prior was them asking me to pay their outstanding storage bill. Sensing the pressure beginning to mount, I stressed to my team to proceed with caution.

I had decided the day before that the desk was too heavy to be transported as a single unit, so I removed the granite surface from the steel base. Granted, both pieces were still heavy as all hell but with myself and Nitbu moving the pieces I was confident things would go well. We moved slowly to remain surefooted, plus I had Deuce walk in front of us just in case. The steel base was set down in the proper place in the library. The moment after we set the granite top on the base, Barbara walked in.

"How did you carry the desk in with only two people? I told your office the previous moving company used five people." As she began to look over the desk, she cried out, "Where is the corner of the stone top?" As I bent down to examine the marble top more closely I did notice that a centimeter worth of the corner was indeed missing.

Barbara launched into a tirade. "This is a thirty thousand dollar desk! Now it's ruined! Get the owner of the company on the phone. You're going to pay for my desk!"

The customer is always right, except when they're not. I had been all too reasonable during this move. Now was the time to make my position clear. "Are you serious?" I retorted, as respectfully as I could. "Let me say this. Number one, if that damage had been fresh, the break would not look worn and smoothed over like someone previously attempted to repair it. Who's to say it wasn't damaged going into storage?"

I knew I had pushed her off balance, but she bounced back. "There was tape over the corner holding the chips in place so you couldn't tell.

Now the chips are gone, and the desk is permanently ruined. You need to call your boss immediately!"

Nitbu spoke up. "If the corner of the desk was previously damaged and you failed to inform us, we are not liable."

I knew we had won already, and tried hard not to show it. I put on my most gracious smile. "I cannot connect you to the owner of the company because he is not in the office at this time of night. If you would like to make an insurance claim for the desk, you will have to do that on Monday between the hours of nine to five. I can make note of the damage as you have stated at this point. I will also make note of the desk being chipped prior to our moving it. But we can go over all of this when I bring in the bill."

Barbara began to say in her nasally voice, "We are not paying..."

John intervened with an "Okay, it's getting late."

My smile by now was pasted on. I was absolutely pissed by the time I reached the back of the truck. No way was I leaving there without being paid. Nitbu and Deuce had already informed F.T. and Daam of what had transpired. The guys cursed the Dracuts under their breath while wondering what I was going to do. I had to rally the troops.

"Fellows, let's not give them any ammunition against us. We'll be done in a half hour. Let's just finish and go home." This was all I could think of to say to encourage my crew forward.

Nitbu and Daam held one of the badly crated slabs of marble while I grabbed the hammer. It just made more sense to remove the marble from the crate and then carry it into the sitting room since there wasn't much extra room indoors. With Nitbu to my left and Daam to my right, I used the hammer's prongs to try to pry the wooden slats away. I knew I was still fuming over the Barbara's "free move" because no matter how I tried, I couldn't free the marble.

Handing over the hammer, I said, "Daam, you are at a better angle than me. Pry the cross slats away."

On Daam's first swing with the hammer both Nitbu and I yelled, "Whoa! Watch how you swing that thing!"

Nitbu and I were still to Daam's left side holding the balance of the crate as Daam pried away. I wasn't looking at Daam when I felt the cold metal strike me just outside my eye socket around my right temple. Instantly gravity kicked in, sliding the hammer onto my nose.

"Are you serious, Daam?!"

Those were the only words I could muster as I held my face while waiting for the blood to flow. My temple began to throb and my face became flushed. The guys stood there speechless, eyeing my right hand to see if I would reach for the knife on my hip. But I never reached for my hip. When there was no blood after about five seconds, I just started to laugh.

You know in those movies where someone gets hit in the head with a hammer? They go down. They are bleeding. They pass out. They do not get up. Yet I was still standing there laughing. Deuce had inched behind Daam waiting for me to give him the signal to inflict the same bodily harm on Daam's head in retaliation. I waved him off. I couldn't stop laughing. I had never been hit in the head with a hammer before. Somehow, this was funny.

I took myself into the Dracut house and into the first floor half bath. The mirror showed me a large welt across the right side of my head and a red, sore nose. I emerged from the bathroom to see Daam standing there.

"I'm sorry," he said. "The hammer slipped right out of my hand."

I replied, "It's cool, Smokey. This was the first time I have ever been hit in the head with a hammer."

Then Barbara's sister-in-law appeared, looking for any fresh scars as she handed me an ice pack. I assumed she had been watching through the window and had seen the whole thing.

"Are you okay?" she asked. When I said yes, she continued, "Was being hit by a hammer the craziest thing that has ever happened to you as a mover?"

I replied with a quick, "No, not even close!"

She smiled back at me. Maybe she had a nice side after all. "It would make for interesting reading if you wrote down all of the craziest moments from your moving experience."

I stood there smiling, thinking maybe for a couple seconds too long. "Well, if I did tell the stories, I would have to start from the very beginning."

We left that day with our check, and me with a new nudge to get this story told.

TIME TO GROW UP

Opportunity is the only free ticket we get these days.
We travel on in search of the reasons why
We all walk our separate ways.
Trails we walk change along with the seasons.
Don't be too surprised
This is still New England.

Sharing full bottled Coke glasses
Didn't make me many friends.
So when I reached my teens
My eyes saw clearer through contact lenses.

Every stop on this journey
Is like a carved section of a totem pole.
Understanding the rooted base's stability
Becomes more reflective
To what the future may hold.
You can't prevent what you can't predict.

Those who were loyal to me from the foundation
They will be my life support to the end.
They're the one who understand after graduation
I will not be the one trying to buy the Benz.

I am a natural B.M.W.
I humbly ride the train every day.
How far?
Well, that is still pending
If the conductor gives me a transfer.
My grinding is more of a cleansing.

Material possessions hard to come by
Seemed to be handed to me to hold.
Items I was given
I turned around and sold

I've heard
Working men like me are hard to behold.
Don't listen to the hype
That you've read and been told.
However, the dough I'm looking to make
Won't mix well in a cake bowl.

How did I get involved with moving? Well at first, the primary motivation was money.

Prior to moving, I worked as a security guard. The position I held, "roamer," earned an additional $1.25 per hour over the $5 minimum to fill in shifts when other security guards called in sick or had to be "released" for being caught sleeping. So I signed on for $7.25 an hour, was given a pager and told to wait for the company to call. Once called, I could be asked to work all the way from eight hours up to a double shift. Once I reached the designated job site, I was relegated to perform the duties of whomever I was replacing. I was a flashlight cop without the damn flashlight.

One of the sites I frequently filled in at was a parking garage in Boston. From the seventh floor and roof top, I could see the lights illuminating Bean-town. In front of me to the north was the Boston Garden (now the TD Banknorth Garden), the home of the championship basketball team, the Celtics. To the left shined the golden dome of the State House and the high-rises of the city. To the right appeared the one-if-by-land-two-if-by-sea Old North Church in the North End and the waterfront of Boston Harbor. The Custom House loomed to the rear, displaying the time in yellow and blue lights.

At around one thirty in the morning on my first night on security, a Saturday in 1992, most of the cars were exiting the garage, so I decided to stand next to Mark's booth and talk with him through the Plexiglas. Mark's stutter wasn't bad until he had the uncontrollable urge to go to the bathroom. He was a sixty-two year old man from South Boston who stood six foot, two inches tall. A big man who weighed close to three hundred pounds, he wore the same blue pair of pants each time I had seen him over the past year. I can't confirm if Mark had more than two pairs of the blue pants. However, I can confirm I have seen the same stain, in the same spot on the right back leg more than four consistent days during the same calendar week. Mark attended to the line of cars as we talked. One car of three middle-aged men drove up to the booth.

The driver said to me, "Has anyone ever told you that you resemble the boxer Roy Jones, Jr.?"

Since no one ever had, I answered "Yeah, I get that a lot."

Mark grinned from ear to ear. I noticed for the first time his false teeth floating in his mouth. Every car that pulled up after that, he would blurt out, "D-D-D-Doesn't he looks like R-R-R-Roy Jones, Jr.?" Most men agreed. Most women, alas, do not follow boxing close enough to recognize the resemblance.

I stood there thinking, life is filled with irony. Here I had in front of me carloads of people who thought I looked like a boxer. For the first of very few times in my short life I found myself standing there with a warm inner feeling. A warm feeling of acceptance that has always felt foreign to me.

It didn't matter to me whether Roy Jones, Jr., was known as handsome or if he had an impressive physique. Just the simple fact that he was deemed acceptable regardless of his profession was enough for me. You see, I had always seen myself as that six-year-old little boy from 10 Castle Gate Road, Grove Hall, being picked on nonstop from the moment my parents brought me home from the optometrist.

It was easy to pick on the little boy wearing the oversized glasses. My biggest problem wasn't the fact the glasses were too big for my face, which they were. The real problem was that I was extremely near sighted. The thickness of my lenses sparked the nicknames, "Baby Glasses," "Blind Boy Fuller" and "Coca-Cola Kid" since they were as thick as the bottom of a glass bottle. After nearly ten years of being tormented about those glasses, I could only think of my outer shell as average, or less than.

But my nana, my father's mother, used to tell me differently. When I was small enough to sit on her lap, she'd say, "Maulie, your big smile is contagious. If you can get someone to smile back at you, it can actually leave them feeling vulnerable to happiness. No matter what anyone tells you baby, everyone wants to be happy. We just get so preoccupied by the daily lessons life hands out we forget how to smile like the child we once were. But your smile, baby, will help them remember to let the child out. They will smile back."

The women in the next car that drove up knew their fighters. There were two black and one white woman, probably in their mid-twenties, smiling like they just had a festive night out. This time when Mark blurted out his now-favorite phrase, it sparked more than just smiling.

"You do look like R.J.," said the prettiest of the three from the back seat.

"Tina, isn't Roy a Super Middle Weight contender with a lot of stamina?" All three girls simultaneously began laughing. I didn't get the joke.

But I knew the focus was on me since all three women were looking at my waistline. Or was it just below?

Tina was the sitting in the front passenger seat, so she had to lean onto the driver from her seat to be seen. Average in looks, she was clearly the bold and outspoken one in the trio. "So is your middle weight super, Roy?" All three women looked me over from head to toe still smirking.

I smiled back. I smiled because I was nineteen years old. I smiled because I had worked out hard in the gym an hour before I was paged and my body was still swollen from being stimulated. I smiled because when I left the gym I had to dress in that too tight uniform. I smiled because I had decided it was too hot this evening to wear underwear.

So there I stood in these snug uniform pants with the tuxedo stripe down the leg, commando style. These women had no way of knowing that I become aroused when a summer breeze blows. Flirting with me was the equivalent to turning a fan up full blast. My answer to Tina's question was clear without my having to say a word. The women watched as I grew in front of them. I made no attempt to hide what was happening. It's not in me to be ashamed of what nature has given me.

Tina showed her approval. "Damn, Roy! I guess you are a serious contender. You might have to move into the heavyweight category upon further review." She licked her lips. "You can definitely come home with me. I can make room in the back seat for you. My girls can go hop on the train. We can go test that stamina." Again laughter erupted from inside the car.

I kept right on smiling. "This is my first day working here. I'm trying to stay hired, not get fired."

Tina reached into her purse and wrote down her phone number. "Call me the moment you get off work tonight."

As the car pulled away, all three started to chant, "Roy, Roy, Roy," until their voices faded out in the distance. I handed Mark the paper with Tina's phone number on it.

"Aren't you going to call her?" Mark asked.

"Nope! You can call her. You can pretend you are Roy Jones, Jr. I am Kamaul."

On the second Thursday in March, 1993, ten minutes past eleven, the microphone hanging from the left shoulder of my shiny black vinyl jacket began to squawk. Cashier Mark needed his bathroom break. I was standing in the lot with garage manager Obet and cashier Zenich.

"R-R-Roy, have you seen the R-R-R-Russian?" Mark said with his customary stutter.

Zenich was the Russian, and he was standing right there. But I didn't feel all that cooperative. "First of all, Mark, my name is Kamaul, not Roy. If I can call you by your first name, why can't you ever call me by mine? Since you keep calling me Roy, tell me what's the Russian's first name and I'll see if I can find him."

Mark didn't answer my question about the Russian's name right away. At that very moment, eleven minutes past eleven, the other three of us were waiting, chuckling uncontrollably, as Mark contemplated his response. As the seconds turned into a full minute, I knew that Mark had to go to the bathroom so bad he must have thought just trying to say the name Zenich would be enough for him to wet himself. Zenich had just finished his shift as a parking garage cashier, where he usually worked the 3pm—11pm shift. Mark would always ask Zenich to watch his cashier booth before Zenich went home, so he could take fifteen minutes to go to the bathroom and return with a coffee, corn muffin and the early edition of the daily newspaper. Zenich sometimes felt that Mark took this nightly favor for granted because Zenich was not native to our shores. So when Mark called, we stood on the roof top of the parking garage right next to each other, laughing so hard we had to prop each other up.

Then we heard Obet say as he laughed, "I'm on my way now to give you a five minute break, Mark."

Five minutes until two every night, Obet walked out the first floor office to his car, started the ignition and cranked the heater to full blast. A New England winter is tough enough for those raised in the Northeast. Obet was from West Africa. March was officially winter, minus the snow, although spring was just around the corner.

Exactly at two o'clock, Obet locked up the safe and the inner office door. He gave me a head nod as his way of saying goodbye. He then left me with what remains in the office—a table, two chairs, and a punch clock for the garage employees—departing in his heated automobile.

I worked the parking garage periodically over my year in security. It wasn't bad. Like I said earlier, I was a flashlight cop without a flashlight. Instead, I was given a leather bound steel clock which hung from a strap.

The time piece easily weighed twelve pounds. My detail was to walk the premises, finding the keys attached to the far corner of the walls on each floor. Turning the keys in the clock entered the time onto a white ribbon strip inside the clock's body.

One night I was so bored I hung the clock around my neck, put on a pair of sunglasses, turned my hat to the side, folded the silver side of the gum wrapper in half and placed it over my teeth. For fifteen minutes I pretended I was Flava Flav of Public Enemy, dancing from side to side while my hands flailed to the sides of my chest. I sang "911 is a Joke," yelling out an occasional "Yeahhh, Boooy!"

I had become pretty social with the other personnel. Whenever I worked the parking garage, Zenich would walk the fifteen-minute tour with me. Each tour started at quarter past the hour. It gave us the chance to catch up with each other from the last time. Zenich and I both went to UMass Boston. Let me clarify, because we actually didn't take classes together. One night at work, I saw Zenich reading a continuing education catalog from UMass, so I asked what classes he was planning to take in the fall. Zenich informed me he wanted to transfer over from Northeastern University, but he found out that if he changed his major from engineering to accounting, none of the prior credits in engineering would transfer.

Zenich walked the detail with me that night before he went home.

"So how is UMass treating you?" I asked as we made our way to the second key on the rooftop.

"I like it much better than Northeastern. I get all of my school work done as soon as I read the course requirements. I bring all of my books here to work. I keep reading until Mark gets here. I get to pick up the—how do you say?—extra shift at the garage to make some more money."

"How is your new wife treating you?" I smiled as I waited for his reply.

"I buy a lot of food. She cooks it very nice like she was taught from her tradition. I like to eat good food from my tradition, my homeland sometimes. Anna says it stinks very badly when I cook. So I don't get to eat my own cooking very often."

I enjoyed talking to Zenich because he was honest and I could be honest with him in return. Zenich fell in love with the looks and nice personality of Tatiana, a Latina friend I had at UMass. My female friend worked inside the administration building in the financial aid department. When

Zenich was trying to transfer to UMass, I told him to go to the financial aid office, take a numbered paper from the door, sit down and wait for her to call his number.

Easy enough, right? Well, Zenich became overwhelmed by her beauty. The tone of her voice must have sedated his brain because he missed his number being called. Instead of taking another number from the door he simply sat there until no one was left to be helped. After he dropped my name, Zenich was assisted from the financial aid office down to the administration office, which also included a shapely young Latina woman. He found out which of his classes could transfer over successfully from Northeastern. More importantly, Zenich had fallen in love twice that day.

Feeling ever so grateful, Zenich decided to take my advice and send both young ladies flowers, just to say thanks. Zenich wanted to make a strong impression on the two ladies, so for the one in the administration office, he added a dozen long stem red roses and two tickets to see the musical *Cats*. My friend in financial aid received a dozen red roses and an invitation to dinner. Both offices were buzzing with the gifts of thanks. Unfortunately, they had both been delivered unsigned and without the at-tached phone number. The space cadet at the flower shop who wrote out the cards to the delivery person barely understood Zenich's accent, so he left the deliveries unsigned. So, the two ladies escorted one another to the dinner and the show.

Depleted and broken hearted, Zenich set his mind on meeting a La-tina and marrying her. He had only been in the United States for a little over two years and he wasn't that big on going out partying, but he met someone anyway. Soon Zenich told me about Anna, a very special woman from Venezuela. I was naturally happy for him. He told me they loved one another deeply and planned to be married very soon. I have never seen people fall in love that fast except in an afternoon soap opera. But who was I to say anything.

So I smiled, and Zenich relaxed. I asked to see a picture of his future missus. Instead of going to his wallet, I watched as Zenich reached in his backpack. Zenich pulled out a magazine with the title *South American Brides*. The magazine was already folded in half with a yellow highlight around several different women named Anna, Marie-Anna or Ann-Maria. I knew which "Anna" he chose after I saw the red heart around the description and the picture. The resemblance to Tatiana from the financial aid office was uncanny. Tatiana as well as the Anna in the magazine heavily favored a twenty-four year old Catherine Zeta-Jones with the addition of a nicer, rounder backside. Less than two months after seeing his bride-to-be in the magazine, Zenich and Anna were pronounced officially wed.

"Zenich, how is your Spanish coming along?"

"It is coming along pretty good my friend. I take your advice. I write out index cards with English words, Spanish words and sometimes with Russian words and tape them on everything. I place them on the chair. I place the index cards on the bathroom door. I even place cards on my body. When Anna sees index cards on my body, she knows it is the hour to make ficky-ficky."

Every time he used the expression "ficky-ficky" I could not contain a smile. It was good to see his American dream materialize. By this time, we were descending the ramp of level six to level five. The garage became dense with parked cars as we reached the lower levels.

"I went to file my taxes last Monday," I said. "After all of double shifts and holiday shifts I worked, I ended up grossing nineteen thousand dollars. You know Zenich, I wasted a year from my schooling to see what life in the real world would afford me. I spent all of my free time working so many hours that I never enjoyed myself this year. Now on top of that, I don't have much saved money from working this year, I owe the government almost eight hundred dollars in back taxes."

"This is not very good, my friend."

"You're telling me. So, no matter what happens during the summer you'll see me at UMass in the fall semester."

"This will be very good. We can go to the library and sometimes study together, too. Tatiana will be very happy to see you because she asks for you all the time. Sometimes I feel like I am a messenger for you. You must tell me the truth! You make ficky-ficky with my Tatiana?!"

As we both laughed at the fact Zenich referred to our mutual friend as *his* Tatiana. I responded honestly as I always did whenever he demanded an answer to the repeated question.

"My friends are my friends. No matter how beautiful. I was taught by my father 'You never shit where you eat.' Therefore I could never jeopardize a good contact. Plus I am definitely going to need a good friend in the financial aid office now that I'm going back to school full time.

"Plus Nina, the love in my world, is up in Amherst. I have been with her crazy territorial ass since junior year in high school. She looks for reasons to start fighting. I am not giving Nina, a.k.a. Baby Girl, a reason to cut me. I told you she carries a butterfly knife.

"Rule number one is never cross a woman who can pull a knife faster than you. I think her father gave it to her. Did I tell you she has two cousins at UMass Boston watching me like a hawk? They watch me so well you would think they were on a payroll."

IT'S TIME TO WALK ALONE

I knew this day would come and be mine.
Since there's no way to stop time,
I can't say that I'm surprised.
It has played over and over
Like a movie projector in my mind.
Each time I've viewed this scene
I knew the hardest part would be
Standing toe to toe,
Looking you eye to eye,
Holding all my emotions inside
As I say, Goodbye.

Goodbye this time doesn't mean
I'll be around tomorrow.
If I could reach down deep
Into my soul to borrow—
To give to you that part of me
Which would exclude you from
All future pain and sorrow, I would...
But it still wouldn't be enough.

When I began to crawl
There was always someone there
To make sure my path was safe.
When I learned to walk
There was always someone a half step behind
To make sure I didn't land on my face.
Today, the past is in the rear
And the future I had been moving towards,
Is now here.

I can't lie, nor pretend
I know what it is I'm in search of,
It's a mystery.
All I know is that my gut feeling is,
It's a part of me.
And my heart tells me,
It's the necessary key,
Which will unlock the door to my destiny.

I have to tempt fate,
I have to conquer all my fears;
Every last one I've grown to hate.
I have to prove to myself
I can make it on my own.
If I turn around now,
I may never go.
Just reassure me
I'll always have a place to call home.
But for now
It's time for me to walk alone.

Zenich and I had reached the fourth level when I told him the real reason I wanted him to walk the detail with me.

UMass Boston was my goal. I was in—now all I needed was the money. The dollar figure I had set in my mind was ten thousand dollars.

I decided when I came back home after my first year up at UMass Amherst that I would pay for my education from that day forward. My parents had sacrificed for my education for years. Although they never said a thing to me about it, I now felt strongly that I needed to relieve them of the financial burden. I could see that they were making the same sacrifices for my little sister's education. She is eight years younger than me, so for all that time, my mother still had to work two jobs. The money she earned at the second jewelry store job was her spending money. She trudged through the door after eleven o'clock four or five nights each week from working that second job, yet she never complained. I set my mind on easing her burden as soon as I could.

It was time for me to take the burden off and pay for myself. I had done some time at UMass Amherst after graduating high school, but that year had been a disaster. That's when I thought I would take a year off and earn the money for school in Boston. But nineteen thousand dollars earned but no savings later, I realized I had to get more serious.

Ten thousand dollars was what I needed to pay up front for the next year's tuition, plus my book fees. I had written the dollar figure on a slip of paper and placed it inside my wallet so it would be the first thing I saw whenever I went to pay for something. I wanted to stay focused on why I was so willing to sweat my butt off.

"I was hired at this moving company in Cambridge yesterday," I now told Zenich. "I start my first day of work at seven o'clock this morning. So I am leaving from here, dropping off my parent's car at their house in Cambridge, grabbing my pop's ten speed and biking down to the storage facility on Vassar Street. I'll be making ten dollars an hour cash, helping offload a shipment from California."

Zenich looked at me wide-eyed. "Ten dollars an hour cash is excellent my friend. I think you are strong enough to handle the work. I could never do the physical lifting. I have suffered from lower back problems since I was a teenager."

"I think my twenty-year-old body can endure the workload. I go to the gym and work out three days a week, no matter how busy my week is. And it's better than the money I'm currently making. Plus, Uncle Sam is getting cut out of the picture, at least tomorrow."

We made our way along the rows of parked cars. We were en route to the second key on the fourth level, when I grabbed Zenich by the arm and motioned for him to crouch down. Grabbing the microphone of the two-way radio, I spoke in my soft announcer voice. We were not on the PGA golf tour, but you might have thought we were.

"Good evening, gentlemen and Mark," I whispered thickly. "Faneuil Hall Parking Garage brings you another episode of 'Thirsty Thursday.' We ask that everyone listening in, please turn your radios up to level ten for your listening enjoyment as I turn my radio down to level two. We ask that no one interrupts tonight's broadcast with any questions or interruptions, Mark!"

The first time I heard the term "Thirsty Thursday" was as a freshman at UMass at Amherst. I didn't drink, so I observed the other students getting a head start to their weekend on Thursday. Most seasoned students arranged their schedules so their classes were only Monday through Thursday. They knew they would be so bent come Friday they would either end up missing or failing any classes that day. Working at the parking garage made it clear that "Thirsty Thursday" applied to the young working class as well. The Market Place nearby had close to ten watering holes. People were ready to let their inhibitions fly free by the time they walked back to their vehicles.

I continued my broadcast. "We are three cars away from a black Chevy Blazer with the headlights turned off. Exhaust fumes are escaping the vehicle. There are no heads to be seen as we make our way forward. We are now within one car of the subject vehicle. Wait a minute. Wait a minute...I do see movement in the back seat of the vehicle. We will take this opportunity to move in for a closer investigation."

Excited, Zenich grabbed my microphone. "I think they are making ficky-ficky!"

I snatched the microphone back. "I apologize for the comments made by my co-announcer. His color commentary was way out of line. Now back to our original program 'Thirsty Thursday.'"

"We are still crouched down. We have made our way to the tail end of the car. I take note that there is one black high-heeled pump outside of the vehicle on the passenger side. It does appear as if it may have been discarded in a moment of haste. We have music blasting from the inside, definite rock and roll. Since they cannot hear us, we'll let our music specialist comment briefly."

Still excited, Zenich grabs the microphone, "Yes the song is 'Paradise City' by Guns and Rose. We are going to see them making ficky-ficky!"

"Once again, I apologize for the exuberant comments made by my assistant. But now we will take a look inside the vehicle to see what is really going on."

At that moment Zenich got cold feet. He didn't want to look inside the truck. I, on the other hand, was fine with it. I had a badge, a radio and a clock. I was security. Looking inside the truck was my job. And damn it, I was going to perform my duties to their fullest extent.

Zenich had backed off a car or two away when I began to raise my head to window height. I saw the bare back of a young man, sitting on the floor of the truck and entertaining a young woman while she lay flat on the rear seat. She had her sweater off but alas had kept her lavender bra on. It was definite, the shoe outside the vehicle belonged to her. Her exposed bare foot rested against the window now. She opened her eyes to see me watching. She smiled and winked in my direction. It was at that moment that the young man jumped up. He must have felt my eyes watching him.

I knocked on the window. "Security! Buddy you can't do that here. You have to take this business home."

All I could make out over the loud music was, "I'm sorry, we're going to leave right away."

"Make sure it doesn't happen again, okay?"

It's always pretty funny to watch people scramble to get dressed under such conditions. Trying to put pants and underwear on in such a confined space was damn near impossible. Yet it only took seconds to get undressed.

The two-way squawked with Mark's voice. "W-W-What's happening guys? Y-Y-Y-Y-Y-You didn't c-c-c-continue!"

"Sorry, Mark, it was a false alarm. The couple was merely engaged in conversation."

"D-D-D-Damn!"

Zenich and I reached the last key on the second floor. The spot where the last key was overlooked the two cashier booths like a balcony allowing us to watch over the front of the parking garage. We leaned forward on the wall and continued our conversation.

"So check this out," I said. "I show up to the interview yesterday with my resume in hand. I was ten minutes early, so I waited for the prior interview to end. I was taken aback a little bit because the men that worked in the office on average stood around six feet, two inches. These were some big boys. That was surely the reason to name the company Big Barney's Moving Company."

"It sounds like you walked into the land of the giants," Zenich said laughing.

"Yeah, I know. Then an assistant led me into the interview room, where I shook hands with the opposite—this very short man standing less than five feet tall, wearing a white sports jacket and a black tie."

"You two were the dwarfs in the land of the giants." Zenich kept coming with the short jokes.

"That's how I felt. Except at least I was taller than this man interviewing me. I relaxed. I couldn't shake the image of Tattoo from Fantasy Island. Hold on—isn't that the black Chevy blazer about to leave?"

Zenich nodded. I grabbed the microphone. "Mark, here comes the black blazer that was on the fourth floor."

He radioed back, "I thought you said nothing was going on upstairs?"

"I may have understated what I saw." I loved to get him going.

"S-S-S-So what h-h-happened up there? W-W-W-Was she completely naked? Y-Y-You always leave m-m-me out, Roy!"

Zenich and I could see Mark getting agitated from where we stood

"See, this is why I didn't tell you everything, you pervert!" I retorted. "You are going to get so excited your damn false teeth are going to slip out of your mouth again. I don't want Obet blaming me for your teeth breaking. You know you are not the most handsome person with or without your teeth."

"Screw you, R-R-Roy." Even Mark couldn't help but smile.

Brucey the janitor chimed in the two-way radio. "Don't worry old man, I found a couple of magazines if you want to take a look."

"Thanks, Brucey. S-S-S-Screw you, R-R-Roy."

The black Chevy made the right hand turn to leave the parking garage. We leaned against the balcony wall. A moment passed as I gathered my thoughts back to the conversation of my interview.

"Okay, so Daniel, the dwarf with salt and pepper hair, starts to ask me questions about football because he sees it on my resume. I say I used to play. He assumes because of my physique I was playing up at UMass at Amherst. His eyes started to light up, like all of a sudden playing college football was the greatest thing. So I went along with his notion."

"Did you play college football?" Zenich asked a little confused.

"The last time I actually touched a football was when Boston Latin beat English in the Turkey Day game," I responded.

"So did you tell him that fact? You were no longer playing?"

"If Daniel asked me that question directly, I might have told him the truth. But I figured there was no reason to personally place a cloud over my interview."

Zenich shrugged, "You were probably right to say nothing more."

"I think it was the next question Daniel asked that determined I was to be hired. He asked me who did I like better. Tour of Power or Earth, Wind and Fire?"

"Who?" Zenich asked, showing his limited knowledge on rhythm-and-blues funk bands.

"I told Daniel 'The Elements' of the Earth, the Wind and the Fire was hands down a superior band. EWF had better vocals, horns, and lyrically told better stories in their music. We must have continued the debate for close to twenty minutes before we were interrupted by a knock on the door.

"And there I saw Tattoo's partner Mr. Roarke coming through the door all the way from Fantasy Island except without the white suit. He introduced himself as Barney Lynch. Mr. Lynch, a native of Ireland, easily stood six feet, eight inches tall. After Daniel told him I was a football player he hired me on the spot. Mr. Lynch said he liked to have solid athletes on his team. He preferred rowers because he personally rowed for Northeastern University. He was aware of rowers' solid work ethic. But he felt a good athlete was still a good athlete. He told me he was happy to have me on the team.

"They gave me a phone number to call each night after 6 to hear a message about what time everyone was scheduled to work for the following day. I just had to listen for my name. The number is an 800 number so there would never be a reason not to call. They call the message line the 'boating line.'"

"Why?" Zenich asked trying to make sense of everything I had told him thus far.

"To be honest, I didn't even bother to ask. The correlation must lie somewhere in the rowing world. I'm sure I'll find out more, if I last. I was happy to be hired on the same day."

It was ten minutes after midnight, almost time for me to walk my second tour of the night. Zenich was ready to go home.

"Zenich, I don't know how the moving job is going to work out for me. So, if I don't see you here anytime soon I'll definitely see you at UMass in the fall. Look around the financial aid office for me." We both smiled.

"My friend, you should stop by on one of these nights that you are not doing anything just to say hi."

Zenich was a good guy. I liked having his company at work, but that was at work. I was too "on the go" to foresee coming down to Faneuil Hall Market Place just to visit anyone.

"Yeah, I'll get down this way as soon as I get the chance," I nodded. But we both knew the next time we would see one another would be at UMass in the fall. So we shook hands good bye. I pressed the up button for the elevator. Zenich took the stairs to go down.

I could hear Zenich saying goodnight to everyone. Just as the elevator door opened I heard Mark's voice.

"R-R-R-Russian. C-C-C-Could you watch my b-b-b-booth for me. I have to go to the b-b-b-bathroom." I smiled as the elevator door closed.

Friday morning, 6:45, I stood outside of Metropolitan Storage facility on Vassar Street in Cambridge. I had actually taken in a good night of rest. Five minutes after Obet went home, I stretched out between the two folding chairs. I don't need much comfort to fall asleep. I can pretty much fall sound asleep standing up.

I did however wake up around four o'clock in the morning. I had to go to the bathroom. I snuck outside Mark's booth and watched him sleep for a minute. I waited until his mouth widened from his snoring before I banged on the Plexiglas booth.

"Mark, you want anything from the store?" I asked with a smile.

Mark lurched forward as his false uppers slipped from his mouth onto the steel countertop. Startled, his eyes focused on finding his upper teeth. Then his eyes focused on my face.

"Y-Y-You buying, Roy?"

"Hell no! I saw Obet give you a check yesterday."

"No. I d-d-don't need anything." He countered.

I went back into the office and fell asleep. I figured this was the best way to say "good-bye" to Mark.

A few hours later, I leaned against the wall of the storage facility, waiting. The morning air was crisp. I stood in the sun to stay warm, across the street from the rear of MIT main gymnasium. I couldn't help thinking how many times my friends and I waited near the big steel double doors until someone pushed it open to catch some fresh air. We would then sneak inside and play basketball all day long every Sunday.

I wore a pair of loose fitting jeans, with one T-shirt, one long-sleeved shirt and a hooded sweatshirt. I had thrown on my Air Jordan sneakers just to look stylish. That was the usual gear I would wear when helping someone move, namely my aunt Baye.

Baye is my mother's younger sister. Ever since I turned thirteen, she would ritually move at least twice every three years. Sometimes it was the rent, sometimes it was something else. There was always one reason or another. Baye never had her own car. She would call everyone with a car to shuttle her clothes, dishes and practically anything else that would fit. Most items were moved in heavy-duty green garbage bags, dishes included. Then she would reserve the smallest, least expensive truck the rental company had for the bigger items. The family moving liability rule is, "If it breaks, so what? You should have hired somebody." Moving Baye was a multi-trip, all-day affair.

Seven o'clock on the nose everyone else began arriving at the storage facility. The morning attendant for the storage facility unlocked the doors and turned on lights. An enormous tractor trailer sat at the nearby red traffic light, waiting to make the left turn. I hoped the long truck wasn't going to be for us, but in my heart I knew better.

A gentleman walked towards me wearing jeans, sneakers and a windbreaker. He was sipping from a Styrofoam cup with what looked like the paper tab from a teabag flapping as the wind blew. Here was at least one guy who was about my height and my age—not everyone working at the moving company was enormous.

"Did the moving company Big Barney send you?" I asked.

His voice had a foreign lilt. "Yeah, Mr. Lynch says I will get a good day's wages today. Me name is Eddie. Me friends call me 'Fast Eddie.'" He extended his arm to shake hands.

"My name is Kamaul. This is my first day ever getting paid to do this line of work. You have an accent, where you from?" I asked.

"I am a Donegal man." You could see the pride in his face as he held his chin a touch higher. "I am from the same town as Mr. Lynch back home in Ireland. I work on the family farm back home. This will be a first time for me doing this work as well. I figure if I can carry feed around on the farm, how bad can this be? Mr. Lynch gave me a work visa to come here and work for him over the summer. When the summer is over, I will go back to college and farm work."

The tractor trailer made the turn at the lights. We went inside the storage facility, where the attendant sat behind the counter.

"You boys come to help from Big Barneys?" We were nodding yes to the shirt and tie behind the desk. He was leaning, looking out the window. "This should be your driver here. The shipment is from California."

"So who pays us and at what point do we get paid?" I wanted to get an understanding of how this payment situation worked before the driver got out of the truck.

"The driver pays you boys ten dollars an hour from now, 7am, until the job ends. He is to pay you cash—don't except any checks."

The door chimed as the driver entered the facility. He had a look of urgency.

"Howdy. Where can I go drain the main vein?" he asked the shirt behind the desk.

The attendant pointed to the door with the male figure on it. As the driver walked past me, it smelled as though someone had just knocked over an ashtray. He was gone for about fifteen minutes. I was hoping he was washing his clothes but I doubted I would be that lucky. He emerged from the bathroom, tapping the upside-down Marlboro carton against his hand. He pulled out a cigarette and stuck it in his mouth.

"Are you two boys with me today?" he asked with the cigarette dangling from his lips. He was a loud and fast talker—I couldn't figure out if he was excited or if he was yelling. The only item missing was a Stetson hat and a pair of leather chaps to complete the cowboy style. Fast Eddie seemed to be a little intimidated.

"My name is Paul Cavanaugh. Everybody calls me P.C. Let me guess, you two are Ebony and Ivory? You can be Michael Jackson, and you can be the Beatle." He was making himself laugh which in turn made me smile. He pulled a lighter from his shirt pocket.

"My name is Kamaul, and this is Eddie."

"Ka-Who? I think it will be easier for me just to call you two Michael and Ringo. Boys, we need to push off. We are wasting the daylight here. We need to go to Commonwealth Avenue."

P.C. lit his cigarette as he started walking through the front door, Eddie and I following. Eddie opened the passenger door to climb in the big rig first. I grabbed onto the outside chrome handle pulling my body weight into the vehicle. It would be the last clean breathe of air that I inhaled for the next couple minutes.

There was no other odor than that of cigarettes and dirty clothes. It was obvious P.C. slept in his rig. The bed in the extended cab was unmade. Empty soda bottles and fast food cartons littered the sheets, which were definitely in need of a wash. I was just glad I was next to the door. I rolled down the window quick. I felt bad for Eddie as he pushed close to me trying to breathe in the fresh air from the rolled down window.

"So boys, how do we get to this 138 Commonwealth Avenue?" he asked while puffing out a cloud of smoke.

"Commonwealth Ave. is just over the bridge on Massachusetts Ave.," I answered with my right arm and head hanging out the window. "The lower numbers for Commonwealth Ave are all on the end towards the Boston Common, so stay in your left lane."

The Warrens were waiting outside their town home as the truck pulled up after a ten-minute drive. They had moved both of their cars to make room for us, but we still had to double park because the truck stretched at least five car lengths.

P.C. had informed us on the way over that the entire shipment belonged to the Warrens—all fifty-three feet of the truck. I had no clue how much fifty-three feet was until P.C. turned the handle opening the sardine can from the rear. Floor to ceiling this shipment was packed tight. If someone were accidentally locked in the back, they would suffocate within the hour because there was no room to breathe.

I stepped off to the right side of the truck to get a clear visual of the truck's depth. Eddie was taking off his jacket, gearing up. I laced up my sneakers and had a thought.

"P.C. how long did it take you to load this shipment back in California?"

"Well, those boys probably took close to nine hours," he answered.

"How many of those boys were there to load this truck?" My inquiring mind had to know.

"Let's see. Including the packer there were four loaders. I just handle the inventory." He said with a smirk on his face.

"So how long do you think will take for the three of us to unload this trailer?"

"What do you mean the three of us, Michael?" His refusal to use my name made my teeth grit. "I have to check off everything I put down for you and Ringo to carry up. I'll be on the truck all day long until we're finished. Come on now, let's get going. There are only so many daylight hours left." He brought down two boxes and turned his back on us to check off the stickered numbers placed on the side.

I turned to Eddie as we began walking up the flight of stairs, "This guy is really sticking this workload to us."

"We're bollixed!" Eddie exclaimed.

"Who are we?" I was confused. We started off the morning as Kamaul and Eddie. Then our names were changed to Michael and Ringo. I couldn't take another name change this early in the morning.

"'Bollix' is like saying, P.C. is shagging us. He's screwing us over. There should be at least two more blokes helping us. He knows we have to stick around for the day's wages."

Ah. "I'll put it to you this way, Eddie. I'll finish if you're willing to finish. There's no possible way either one of us can carry all of the stuff off his truck on our own. Let's promise to end this day together." With that said, the deal was sealed.

William and Wilma Warren were in their early thirties. They were a close replica of Malibu Barbie and Ken. We introduced ourselves, and we all walked up two more flights. The Warrens relocated to the third and fourth floor split-level condo from their prior home in Los Angeles.

The Warrens gave us a general tour for the furniture location. They asked if there were going to be any more people helping us since they were moving to the third and fourth floors without an elevator. As Eddie and I shook our heads no, William informed us that the van line company was charging him extra money for all additional flights over the second landing. I counted five landings in total. Eddie was right, we were bollixed.

Descending the steps, I counted seventy-four steps from the fourth floor to the sidewalk. It was time to take my sweatshirt off and "man up."

"Man up" to me means, I made this situation so I have to make it work. I had searched out the moving company to make more money than I did in security. I had a strong body that I worked in the gym, lifting weights and playing basketball. I challenged myself now to test out the only asset I brought to the table—me. The only thing standing in the way of getting paid at the end of the day was that huge truck load double-parked on Commonwealth Avenue. Time to "man up."

It took until lunchtime to get in a rhythm climbing those stairs. By 12:30, my T-shirt was so wet that when I pulled it from my back, twisting it created a stream of absorbed sweat trickling to the ground. I changed into my long-sleeved shirt since it was the only dry one I had left. I hung my saturated T-shirt on the cast iron fence outside to let it dry. It was the first time I'd ever generated white body-salt stains on my clothing.

The Warrens had ordered a couple of pizzas, so we went upstairs for lunch. I sat on the floor in the corner with the two slices of pizza and two glasses of water. My body wasn't so much hungry as needing to be hydrated. My hands were starting to get the shakes.

"Hey, Kamaul, are you all right?" Eddie whispered as I lowered the plate to the floor.

"I'm all right, my body just has to get used to the physical workout. I can't lie though—those steps are burning a hole into my legs. I feel like I have been on a stair climber in the gym for the last four hours."

Eddie nodded in agreement. "I'm hurting, too, but I set my mind to finish if you can finish. Can you finish?"

Listening to the words coming out of Eddie's mouth, I could hear the defeat in his voice. He was just waiting for me to decide to quit.

I lifted my head. I saw P.C. retrieving his second paper plate full of pizza slices. He ate without hesitation. Meanwhile, my body was battling to keep one slice of plain pizza down. P.C. stood there yapping it up with the Warrens, while I was struggling to remember my own name. Was I Michael, Ebony or Ringo?

"Eddie, no matter how hurt I may look, I won't quit on you." I said it just loud enough for the two of us to hear. The bond was sealed.

Once again I had to "man up." I let my mind reflect back to sopho-more year at Boston Latin School. Football had been the only outlet where

I felt comfortable. I felt unstoppable. I was slated to be the starting quarterback for junior varsity. I had the position hands down—until the first day of school.

Established in 1635, Boston Latin was the first public school in the new world. Graduates went on to college at Harvard since that was the first college in the new world (established 1636). Prestige and tradition has maintained Latin's credibility over the years. Every student in Boston takes the entrance exam to attend. Latin only takes those students who score the highest on the exam. There are only a small number of seats available each year for admittance.

On my first day of orientation at Boston Latin, we all assembled inside the auditorium. I had spent my first eight years of schooling in the parochial system. I was a fish out of water at this private-like public school. I read all the names in gold all around the auditorium: Franklin, Emerson, Kennedy, Bullfinch, Adams, and Quincy Adams to name a few. Men who had signed the Declaration of Independence, countless senators, architects, lawyers, and doctors. Some of these people make up a good portion of our history books. Each one of these people sat in these same seats. They were taught the same curriculum. They are now interwoven into school history as well as America's history. Who was I to be sitting there?

Shortly into the welcoming program, the speaker asked us to look to our left and then to our right. He noted that we should look closely at those faces again, since there was an excellent chance they wouldn't make it to graduation. As I looked to my left and right, in front of me and behind me, I realized I was the only African-American sitting among four Asians. They were all taking notes as the orator spoke. I started to think my odds were not looking good. Damn!

Latin has a summer reading list of about forty books. Each student had to read seven books and write reports to support those readings. The summer after my freshman year, I read and completed four reports. For the last three reports, I relied on CliffsNotes. These held all of facts but very little of the detail I needed to support the summarization of each chapter. Needless to say, I failed the summer reading requirement. I had to give back my football equipment until it was completed.

Two weeks later, I received the clearance to go back and play. Two weeks is a long time to be without the sport you have lived to play since you were nine years old. All of my teammates were happy to get me back. I just had to go to Coach Ramsey and get my equipment.

Coach Ramsey, the J.V. coach, always said what he felt. He was honest. He was the only black football coach Latin School had in the 1980s and 1990s. His greatest coaching tool was to force you to be honest with yourself. His greatest liability was he swore and yelled, but that was just his coaching style.

I walked up to the coach as everyone else was piling onto the field for practice. We didn't practice on a football field. We practiced on dirt and rocks. We practiced on the side of the school building. Oh, how I yearned to tackle someone so I could instantly get covered in dirt.

I was smiling as I handed over the note from my English teacher stating my summer reading requirements were in order and I was fully up to speed in my classroom work as well. He blew his whistle, which told everyone to start stretches. But not me. For me, it was time for a little talk.

"So, what you want to do now that you're caught up, K?" he asked.

"I want to play, Coach," I asserted. "I can help the team. I know we lost the first two games. I want to help turn things around."

"Why didn't you think about any of that over the summer?" His question threw me. "You came to this Latin School to get an education first. Most kids study their butts off to get the opportunity to get into this school. And here you are. You made it in. But over three months in the summer, you can't be bothered to do your required reading. Now you tell me you want to play football."

My heart was in my throat. "I know I messed up, Coach. It'll never happen again. I know I let you down."

"K, son, you didn't just let me down. You let down your parents because you have an opportunity at a school most black kids won't get. You let down your teammates because they've seen you as their leader since freshman year. You made a name for yourself amongst the coaches as one of the upcoming kids to watch. Now everyone is watching you dressed in street clothes, standing on the pavement, talking to me. Looking at your face, I would say you let yourself down, too."

I wanted to tell Coach how I truly felt as my chin sunk to my chest. I wanted to hold my head up and say that every day I woke up to go to this Latin School, I doubted I belonged here. I had never taken a foreign language prior to walking through the school doors. Now I'm learning Latin,

Spanish and Greek. I have literally three and a half hours of homework and studying each night. Most nights I don't finish my studying until well after the evening news goes off at 11:30. When you add in the football season, it's like throwing dirt onto the grave I'm lying inside.

The real reason I hadn't finished those reports was because I had ended up in summer school. Before Latin, I had never received a letter grade less than a C. But the third report card my freshman year looked like a stutter—D-D-D-D-D-C. By year end, I had pulled my grades up enough so I didn't get kicked out. However, I either had to pass summer school or repeat the entire year. So, I studied my hardest that summer. I just couldn't quite finish the additional load of reading and reporting on seven books.

The explanation was caught in my esophagus. I had nothing more to say as I held my chin to my chest. Shameful tears streamed down my cheeks.

"K, hold your head up, son," Coach said. "Can you maintain your school work while playing football?"

"Yes, Coach." I could barely hear myself speak.

"I know the English teacher gave you permission to start playing again, but I'm not giving you your uniform until you earn it. If you want to play for me, you will spend the next two weeks running. Show your teammates you truly want to be by their side. Go onto the field right now and jog until practice is over. You show me you're not a quitter, K. You prove it to me. If you can make it two weeks running on this field, I'll give you your equipment."

The challenge had been issued. When I first came to Latin, I didn't make any friends until the word got out I could play football. I couldn't fathom going back to being the nobody I was the day I walked into Latin School. I also knew I would never accept the shame of my teammates and the other coaches seeing me quit.

I didn't even change into my cleats. I just got out there and started running. I ran every day. On the tenth day, Coach finally told me I could stop.

Seventy-four stairs are a lot of stairs to climb even once. Doing it over and over again over the next four hours created some serious discomfort. My forearms started to lock up from the muscle spasms. My lower back began to stiffen. Most importantly, there was a fire kindling between my legs. The boxer underwear had been riding up my inner thigh for some time now, surpassing the irritation of the bunching of underwear in my butt. The friction of the sweat, the jeans and the rising underpants chafed my inner thighs.

I went into the bathroom of the Warren residence to see how bad the inner quad area looked. When I pulled my pants down, it looked as if some animal had been scratching away in there. I never seen shredded underwear before. I rolled the legs of the boxers up, making them as short as possible. This eliminated the cloth rubbing my skin raw anymore. Upon closer examination, I could see the skin on both sides of my inner thighs had been broken. I just had not started to bleed yet.

The Warrens had nothing in the medicine cabinets because the bathroom boxes had not come upstairs yet. The sun was starting to set. I had to do the best I could. I walked like a cowboy to decrease the friction burn.

Eddie and I didn't say much to one another. We were both in our own private hell. I could only think Eddie was wondering how things were getting along for his family back home. How much of a culture shock this must seem to him. Thinking of Eddie got my thoughts off myself.

It was almost nine o'clock when P.C. handed down the last of the items from the truck. Eddie volunteered to make the final trip up the stairs. I went inside the hallway to change out of my wet long-sleeved shirt. I had placed my T-shirt over the heating vent after lunch, so it was now toasty dry. After tugging on my sweatshirt and jacket, all I wanted to do was go home and nurse my wounds.

William walked down with Eddie and Wilma, and came over to me with an extended hand.

"Wilma and I just wanted to thank you and Eddie personally for all of your hard work," he said. "We know it was a tough job for just you two. Eddie told us that it is your first day as a mover. We are impressed you guys were able to do the same work in the same time that it took five men to do in Los Angeles."

I squinted at him. "I'm sorry. I'm confused. The driver told us it took them eight to nine hours to load your shipment while he did the inventory."

Mr. Warren replied, "Paul did do the inventory. But there were five of their workers loading the shipment, not including him. Every time we turned around they all had cigarettes in their mouths and were sipping coffee. It took them into the night to finish."

I could feel my blood starting to boil. Bollixed?! Was this the only justifiable phrase to express my feelings?

"Wilma has a gratuity for you. We gave Eddie his upstairs. We could tell your leg was in pain so we wanted to come downstairs instead of you having to come up. Thanks again."

I shook hands with Wilma as she handed me the white envelope. I felt like I was receiving an award but there was no one to snap the picture. But I had a big Kool-Aid smile on my face nonetheless. I felt so appreciated at that moment. I almost forgot about the pain.

Just then, P.C. marched into the front hall. "I'll be back down in about five minutes, Michael and Ringo. We can settle up at that point."

I don't know what got into me but at that very moment I just didn't want to take his abuse anymore. The scorpion in me was awake. I could feel my stinger rise up.

"Excuse me, Mr. Paul Cavanaugh." I waited until we made eye contact. "His name is Eddie, and my name is Kamaul. Not Ringo, not Michael. Not Ivory or Ebony. His name is Eddie, and my name is Kamaul. K-A-M-A-U-L. Ka-maul. Kamaul. I'm asking that you please address us by our names when you come down to settle up. Thank you."

P.C was stunned to learn that as far as I was concerned, the bullshit was over. To his credit, he just let it roll off his back. He didn't want to lose it in front of a customer. Eddie and I walked outside and waited.

We discussed the best routes to go home. I lived on Harvard Street in Cambridge. I figured I would just walk slowly down to Massachusetts Ave., and catch the #1 bus to Central Square. Eddie lived in Somerville near Sullivan Station, so I showed him where to hop on the train.

After about ten minutes, Paul Cavanaugh exited the building. "I owe you boys some money," he said. "I need to settle up so I can jump on the road to pick up a small shipment in Rhode Island tomorrow before I head back out west." He was all smiles. "If I subtract the time off for the drive over here and the time off for lunch, I owe you boys for thirteen hours."

I didn't care at this point. One hour less for what I had endured since seven o'clock wasn't breaking us. So I shrugged my shoulders. "Whatever."

"Thirteen hours at eight dollars an hour is one hundred and four dollars. Can I write you boys out a check?"

Three voices in my head all started to speak at once. I had to look down at the ground and shake my head just to stop everyone from talking. The first voice, the one I refer to as Beast, said, "If this dude writes us a check or pays us eight dollars an hour for our work, we are picking up a brick. We are busting out his windows. Then we're going to run as fast as we can." Then the next voice, the one I call Animal, said, "I ain't running from nobody! I'm gonna bust all his windows out first. Then this dude is catching an ass kicking for all that Ebony and Ivory crap this morning."

But it was the Voice of Reason that came out of my mouth. "P.C., first of all Eddie and I are not accepting any checks. We were told we were receiving cash at the end of this job. We were also informed we are to be paid an hourly rate of eleven dollars per hour."

"Hey, you boys are only supposed to get ten dollars an hour!" He exclaimed in surprise.

Gotcha! "So if we were supposed to get ten dollars an hour, why were you just trying to cheat us by saying eight?" I could hear my voice level rising.

"I..."

I cut him off. "We are also supposed to receive one dollar more per hour for each flight over the second floor. The majority of the items went to the third floor, which places us at the eleven dollar point. I calculate from the time you picked us up this morning until the last item left this truck, you owe us for thirteen and one half hours. I round our wages off at one hundred and fifty dollars each."

The two of us stared each other down, but P.C. broke first.

"I was going to give you guys one fifty anyways for doing a good job." He dug into his right pant leg pocket, smiling. He pulled out a bank roll of cash and peeled off one hundred and fifty dollars for both of us.

Eddie and I started walking away the second the cash was in our hands. Okay, I admit it—I walked a little slower than Eddie.

"Thanks for not giving up on me today, Fast Eddie."

He looked surprised. "How could I give up on you? I needed the day's wages today. I am dead broke. I had to borrow money to buy my cup of tea this morning. Thanks for getting us properly paid today. Two hundred and fifty bucks is way more than I thought I'd make today."

"You mean one fifty?" I corrected him.

"No. One fifty came from that bollix. The other hundred came from the Warrens."

In the midst of the drama, I had forgotten all about the white envelope from the Warrens.

Eddie and I shook hands before he made his way towards the train. I kept walking straight. I pulled out my money to enjoy one final tally—yep, two hundred and fifty dollars. Two fifty for a single day was a better intake than most drug dealers I knew. My step perked up as I calculated the potential out loud.

"Two fifty times five days a week equals a brand new job!"

That was my first day as a prostitute.

IN THE ARENA...

The games Caesars foresaw as entertainment
Has since been the yardstick to measure
Bravado, courage and machismo in many men.
But here it has become a daily ritual.
The true question remains,
How do you stop the bull when all he sees is Red?

Once inside the arena
There exist no boundaries.
There are no walls to vault over
There are no means of escape.
In there, the grounds run as far as
The sky may stretch its mighty arms.
In and out the sanctuary doors is merely
A temporary opportunity to rest.
The other opportunity is through the one door
Where human breath is needed no more.

As the matador disembarks
From behind the comfort of the sanctuary doors
And emerges onto the concrete grounds of the arena
The blaring horns commence today's games.

In the arena, the horns quiet all onlookers...
Eyes are magnetized to this figure
Much like fireflies are drawn
To the porch light on the darkest of night.

Aside from her shiny black boots and belt
And the silk scarf worn around her neck.
The garbs that drape her body
Is all of the same color.

From her full brim hat,
Which always shades her left eye
Just long enough to avoid eye contact.
It is her trademark Duster jacket which garnishes
Her most underlying curvaceous assets.
Yet her name is not Scarlet.

In the arena she steps forward…
No one knows her true name
She is known by the color she adorns.
The color the sun's rays highlight
Throughout her layered, shoulder length hair.
The only color that sends an uncontrollable
Rage of adrenalin in all bulls
They call her Red.
Yet the question remains,
How do you stop the bull when all he sees is Red?

The matador is always prepared
To defend herself with her universal weapons.
In her possession her armament is increased tenfold.
She is not intimidated by the intense burning
Sensations of the bull's stare,
Nor by the bulls snarls and flaring nostrils,
Not even by the stamping hooves
Before the bull begins his charge forward.

Anticipating an approach by the bull
The matador in one swift whirlwind motion
Removes her Duster and hat
Revealing her backless cat suit which hugs
Her body's flesh tighter than any anaconda could
Displaying every muscle and feminine curvature
Throughout her entire body
She is ready for battle.

As the bull rushes forward
He is caught off guard by the tornado like
Removal of clothing and her mesmerizing body
He realizes she is even more beautiful up close
His timing is off,
He misses his target.

Unfortunately for the bull, battling every day
Has made the matador's timing impeccable.
Her words pierce the flesh with precision accuracy
Forcing the bull to stumble.
The staggered movement is all that Red
Needs to deliver the final phrase
This is a direct thrust through the bull's heart.
"I have no tolerance for Bullshitting!"

As the bull drags himself away
Tail between his legs
Trying to remove his carnage from sight
He needs to go bandage his interior wounds
He needs to be alone to ponder
The precise movement in his attack where he was unfocused.
The horns blare as Red turns leaving her backside exposed
She puts on her Duster and her hat,
Exiting the concrete arena through the sanctuary doors.
She knows the bulls will never stop approaching
She knows the only way to stop the bull
Is simply one battle at a time.
So the crowd anxiously awaits another day in the arena.

It had taken three days for my inner thighs to heal. I had slept right through Saturday, only to awaken early Sunday morning not by an alarm but my own yells due to the spasms in my calf muscle and in my hamstrings. My father massaged out the leg cramps before he headed off to the gym Sunday morning to attend his back-to-back aerobic classes.

I'd been on the job for a week. Since that first day, I had been sent back to Metropolitan Storage to help two other road drivers offload, but the other jobs after my initiation day were mercifully not nearly as bad. The other road drivers didn't stress speed. They were content with just getting the job done.

I offloaded their trucks at my pace. I carried one box at a time. On the big pieces, like dressers and sofas, the road driver gave me a hand. I set a pace to maximize the number of hours for which I would be paid. I didn't work lazily; I simply stretched the hours to my benefit. I didn't make the two hundred and fifty dollars every day that I had originally calculated. Instead, I pulled in between one hundred and seventy dollars to two hundred and ten dollars, including tips from both the customers and the road drivers. Not as much as I initially thought, but definitely better than security.

This was going to be my first day working for Big Barney's, and I was looking forward to it. I hadn't been back there since my interview. I felt like a child en route on the first day of school. This time, however, I was properly dressed. I wore older sneakers instead of my Air Jordan's. I had on new, looser boxer shorts, basketball shorts underneath my nylon sweatpants and a hooded sweatshirt to combat the morning chill. I had on my green company T-shirt underneath my sweatshirt. I was ready.

The bike ride from my parent's condominium on Harvard Street to Big Barney's moving company was seven minutes. I was feeling refreshed today.

I dismounted the ten speed once I reached Big Barney's, making sure the bike was locked up before I walked inside. On the ground floor of the warehouse, which was also where Barney's green trucks backed into the loading bays, there were endless rows of gigantic wooden boxes stacked three high. I later found out this was where customer storage items were packed. I was the sole person in the building until 6:45 when the other workers started to show up.

When I asked, a slim, white guy in his mid-twenties changing from biking shoes into hiking boots pointed the way to the bathroom. He had long blonde dreadlocks that fell to the middle of his back. His directions led me up the main stairs, through a door and down a corridor—simple enough.

The stairway housed a collage of pictures and awards mounted to the walls. Walking through the doorway at the top of the stairs, I couldn't help but see the rows of photo albums, each with a stickered name of a particular worker on them. Instead of photos in the slots, the albums carried comment cards—feedback on the individual and the crew that moved them. There were easily fifty albums resting on the wall-mounted shelves. I wondered if I would ever get my own album.

Continuing down the corridor, I passed a window on the left where the entire inside of the warehouse could easily be seen. The number of men was starting to multiply downstairs. I figured I should stop wasting time. There were three doors on the right before the door with the male stick figure. As I passed the first door, I heard a stern voice.

This person spoke from his guttural area. The words vibrated in his throat before they became spoken words.

"Hello!?! Big Bird, do you hear what I'm telling you?"

I thought the person was speaking to himself, so I kept walking.

"Barney! You are going to go over to your safe. You are going to take out ten grand in cash. I want my money. Helloooo!"

"We don't have ten grand in petty cash to give you right now. I can make arrangements to get it for you in a couple of days." Barney's soft Irish brogue finally surfaced.

"What the hell do you mean a couple of days?" the voice fumed. "Hello?! If I wanted to wait a couple of days I'd ask you to write me out a check and I'd go to the bank. I want my money now or I'm just gonna start smashing your head against the desk. You can tell me what wood tastes like. I'm gonna bet, not like chicken! Then I'm gonna just keep smashing your head every time you give me one more of your dumb-ass excuses. When you finally pass out, I'm gonna steal your safe and spend the rest of the day prying it open." His laughing sounded like he was coughing.

Curiosity and the urge to go to the restroom were now moving my legs forward. I shouldn't have—I didn't really want to. But I couldn't resist taking a quick peek inside the office.

As I passed, I saw Barney sitting at his desk, his head drooping and his shoulders shrugged as though bracing himself for impact. I felt sorry for him because I knew the only thing worse than actually getting hit is the anticipation of contact. The prolonged anxiety is painful enough.

So did I interfere? Nope. Barney's would-be-assailant was a monster. If a rhinoceros were transformed into human form, it would be built like this man. Funny thing though, Rhino-man was an inch or two shorter than me. He was bald at the crown of his head. His blonde shoulder-length hair made him appear as though he walked into the barbershop demanding a reverse fade-away haircut—long on the sides, thin on top.

His blonde mustache extended over the corners of his mouth, halting just before it reached his chin. He had huge twenty-five inch flexed muscular arms. I smiled because I so desperately wanted to stop, point, and yell inside the office, "You know who you look like?" but I figured now wasn't the most appropriate time so I held it inside and kept walking to the bathroom. What was happening in Barney's office is called "grown man business." I had been taught long before never to stick my nose into other grown men's business. So I gave no thought to getting involved.

As I used the facilities, I thought, *Rhino-man is about to beat Barney's gigantic ass. The reenactment of David and Goliath has been taken to a new form. When did Goliath become the underdog?*

As I washed my hands, I tried to figure out just how fast I should walk back down the corridor. But then I found an exit sign outside the bathroom door pointing to a stairwell to my right. I figured my chances were better going this way. I came out at the far corner of the warehouse and followed the yellow line back to the numbered wooden crates again.

I counted about forty guys on the loading dock, bustling around getting their trucks together. Most of the guys were taller than me—about ninety percent. A handful of the older men standing about, were as wide as oak trees. Most of the younger guys were on the lean side of muscular. I was standing there with my back against the wooden boxes when I noticed Fast Eddie.

We shook hands.

"Kamaul, today is your first day here?"

"Yeah, I don't know what I should be doing now. Do I have to report to some main person letting him know I'm here to work?"

Eddie pointed to a two page list tacked to the cork board. "Everyone who heard their name last night on the outgoing message is listed on the wall. Both of our names are listed. You just have to wait for your crew chief to call you. Nobody calls me by my first name. On the trucks, they refer to me as the rookie. The seven of us waiting and looking out of place are all newly hired."

"I guess that makes us all rookies?"

Rhino-man appeared as I said this. When a man with presence walks into the room, all eyes gravitate to him. The moment he walked through the warehouse door, all eyes just locked on him. He wasn't paying attention to the command he had on his audience—he was counting a stack of greenbacks. He made his way along, counting. He cleared a path faster than Moses or any ambulance could have.

Appearing satisfied with his count, he smiled. As he made his way over near the seven of us rookies he stopped in front of the six foot, two inch young man with curly blonde hair.

"Hey, kid, turn around and pick up the pen on the floor for me!"

His guttural demand produced a quick response.

As the young man straightened up and handed over the pen, the handsome one continued, "What's your name, son?"

His voice cracked in reply. "Tommy Blake, sir."

"I like you, Tommy, I like you a lot," Rhino-man said with a wicked smile. "I could have gotten about fifteen cartons of cigarettes for you back in the joint. You would have made me a very wealthy man." His laughing/coughing vibrated throughout the entire warehouse. Everyone knew who Tommy Blake's new daddy was. Tommy looked like he wanted to go back to the orphanage and wait for another father figure to adopt him. Better yet, a single mother would do fine right about now. Unfortunately, Tommy knew he had no say in the matter. To all appearances, he had been chosen by someone who would love him in a totally new way.

The dreadlock man carrying his bicycle tire attempted to call my name. I was used to my name being butchered so I just proceeded forward.

"I'm Steve. You are working as the third man with me and Gordon today, with Gordon in the lead. I'm the push man inside the house. You're supposed to be the college football player on scholarship they keep talking about around here?"

I hadn't worked a day here yet and I already earned a scholarship. "I play a little bit."

Steve was sizing me up, "Let's go, rookie. It's time to see what you got."

As we made our way to the door, I overheard the guttural sound, "Tommmmy! You're working with Daddy today!" Such an evil laugh followed. I knew I wasn't the only person walking through the warehouse who felt bad for Tommy—but not bad enough to trade place with him.

"Is that guy serious about serving time in jail?" I asked Steve.

"Oh, definitely. He got caught on bank robbery twice. The word has it he did it because his new wife was pregnant with their second child. When he got out of jail, he was so huge from lifting weights, his wife was terrified of him. The kids, too. You may not have noticed that he has a hard time with people telling him 'No' or 'You're fired.' She filed for divorce a week after his release.

"His mother-in-law called the cops when they saw his purple and white van pull up inside the apartment complex one Friday night. His ex-wife wouldn't open the door until she heard the police sirens getting closer. He got so pissed off that night she wouldn't let him visit his babies. Rumor has it he wanted to bring them some stuffed animals, which he no doubt stole.

"He knew it was a violation of his parole to be there that night, so he tried to leave before the cops came into the building. His ex-wife jumped on his back to slow him down. As the cops got out of their cruisers, the only thing they saw was her taking flight out of the second floor hallway window. And him yelling through the broken out window, 'The crazy bitch just jumped!'"

All I could do was shake my head. "So how do you get hired if you have a record? I saw him just walk down the stairs with ten thousand dollars cash he made Barney go to the safe to get."

"When he got out of jail the last time, Barney desperately needed people to work for him. Barney had started his business as a one-man operation, moving refrigerators, sofas and bureaus by himself. His repeat and referral clients quickly wanted him for their entire move.

"So Barney hired Rhino-man with the understanding he was only to receive cash for his hourly work. Rhino-man only collects the money owed to him every three months. He wanted neither his first nor his second ex-wives leaving him with absolutely nothing after he paid them alimony and child support. After he receives his weekly salary from the Mass Bay Transit Authority, he only brings home one hundred dollars a week. He's a local bus driver. Imagine him as your bus driver. He's no Ralph Cramden." Steve finished with a smile.

He motioned for me to climb up into the cab of the truck, where Gordon waited behind the wheel. Positioned between these two older men, I was forced to sit with the stick shift between my legs. I relaxed thinking I would probably have more in common with these coworkers. The plus side was I could have been getting molested if I were working with Rhino-man right now.

We started driving, and no one said a word. First gear was a quick shift to the right and a movement to the nose of the truck. Second gear, however, was a shift that stopped in my groin. I exhaled when the truck moved into third gear. I quickly assessed the numbered gear pattern on the top of the gear shift knob. Fourth gear was aimed at my right testicle I winced as we picked up speed.

Gordon pulled the gear shift back with force. I sucked in my chest, stomach and pushed my booty as deep into the crease of the seat as I could. Steve and Gordon watched my movements out of the corners of their eyes.

Gordon spoke, "So I hear you are this, like, super athlete. You won awards for playing football. How fast are you in the forty-yard dash?"

I told him my last clocked time, "Four point six seconds." My answer was good enough to get a head nod of approval.

Then Steve spoke up. "How do you like sitting in the middle, rookie?"

"I figure one of the three of us has to sit with the stick shift between our legs. Gordon is driving, which narrows the list down to me and you. You need room for your precious front bike tire. I just figure it must be my turn to sit in the middle."

Steve countered, "Every day you work with me will be your day to sit in the middle. We call that seat the 'bitch seat.' It's reserved especially for rookies like you." The gear shaft shifted to sixth. "I'm going to make you my bitch. I want to be the one known for making the football player quit."

With that said, Gordon turned on the radio with the volume turned all the way to full blast. The rock-and-roll guitar blazed from the speakers. I had no affinity for rock and roll. I was an easy-listening, rhythm-and-blues fan. Every Saturday night to early Sunday morning, I stay up listening to P.J. Porter's Mellow Madness broadcast from MIT. I sing slow jams until I go to sleep. Sometimes I wake up in the middle of the night as a classic song is playing. I also enjoy hip hop and jazz music when I'm in the mood. Somehow, in the truck, I was going to have to get used to the yelling, the smashing drums and the loud guitars.

The Beast in me kept whispering to kill them with kindness. The Animal wished for a mosquito to fly in Steve's face so I could justify smacking his dread head out the open window. Better yet, why not just reach across his body and pull the door latch up? I could push him out so he could see how sixth gear felt from a different perspective. The Voice of Reason kept me quiet. The Voice of Reason kept me calm.

Driving down Massachusetts Avenue from Cambridge into the South End of Boston, we turned right onto Tremont Street. We stopped at a big white building on the second block, near the intersection of Camden Street. From the age seven until almost ten I had lived at 106A Camden Street, part of the Lennox housing projects. I could see my old two-level apartment from the truck.

When you're a child you tend to make the best out of whatever situation you are facing. We lived in Lennox because the rent was cheap. My father had graduated from nearby Northeastern University. My parents sacrificed all extra money to send me to parochial school.

Every first Friday of the month Mission Grammar School was only half day, so my three female cousins and I would come back to the apartment. Tess was two grades older than the rest of us, so she was allowed to cook on the stove. She made us fried bologna sandwiches or fried spam sandwiches, or we would eat premixed tuna fish sandwiches. Tess's favorite item to cook was cheese toast. She cooked the toast in the oven on broil until the top of the cheese burned just a little. I never liked eating charcoaled food no matter how much Tess told me the burned food is good for my insides.

When I felt like cooking, it was usually grilled cheese sandwiches. I'd cut from the solid block of government cheese that stood in the refrigerator door, place the uneven slices between the bread, insert the result inside a brown paper bag, and turn a clothing iron to scorch. As far as I knew, that was the only proper way to make a grilled cheese sandwich. My parents had government cheese in the refrigerator but we weren't on welfare. I never quite figured that out.

We did our homework after lunch. Then we would take the twin mattress from my bed and set it at the top of the stairs. All four of us would ride it down the stairs until we crashed into the wall. I believe we were the official kiddie version of crash test dummies.

Although I saw what we did as fun, I knew my family was broke. The gap between being broke and being poor isn't that huge. When you are poor, there is no extra money to be sacrificed for anything but living. We were maybe a paycheck or two away from being poor. Ironically, my parents worked too hard to be able to transition themselves away from the poor state in which they were raised.

You know you are broke when you eat pancakes, eggs and bologna for dinner four out of seven days in a week. The other three days, you are sent over to Grandmama's house on Castle Gate Road because she can feed you a little better. You know you are broke when you go the entire school year with Scotch tape holding your glasses together in three different places. To keep them from breaking more often, my father made me wear an elastic strap around the back of my head to hold the glasses to my face.

I was a kid. I couldn't help breaking my glasses. I was just happy some days to be playing with the other kids without them excluding me. It was hard constantly being reminded I was the ugly duckling with the oversized glasses.

I prayed every night to wake up the next morning and see without things being blurry. I wanted people to judge my worth from my actions rather than how I looked on the outside. Those prayers have gone unanswered since the age of six. But an angel in the form of Grandmama would always appear with new frames for me. She picked up the slack when my parents couldn't. I sometimes think she took it harder than me that I was wearing broken glasses.

One day after Grandmama had brought me a brand new pair of glasses, we were let out of school early on a half day. My cousins and I, along with some other kids, walked down to Dudley Station to catch the bus. I was in the third grade at the time. While we stood waiting for the local bus to go to Tess' house, the bully Reesey, one grade ahead of me, started in.

Reesey licked his index and middle fingers and rubbed them into my glasses. "Kamaul!" he yelled in my face. "I think you need to clean your glasses."

My bodyguards—my three cousins—always jumped to my defense.

"You ain't nothing but a big bully," Tess said. "Why don't you pick on someone your own size?"

Reesey had obtained a laughing audience from the other kids. When I went to wipe my glasses clean, Reesey swiped his hand at my glasses knocking them to the ground. On impact, the new frames smashed in two with the right lens popping out of the frame.

Bird, Aunt Baye's daughter, jumped in Reesey's face first. "My Grandmama just brought him those glasses yesterday, you stupid boy!"

"You better go home and tell your grandma he needs another new pair." Reesey was chuckling along side the rest of the other kids.

Fayfae chimed in "No, your crusty mama is going to pay for my cousin's new glasses because you broke them."

As my three cousins defended me, I felt around the pavement for the pieces. The two broken sections of the frame were held attached to the black elastic strap Daddy made me wear. When I had all the pieces in my hands, bringing the parts to within inches from my face so I could examine them more clearly, I realized that my promise had been broken. I had promised Grandmama the day before that I wouldn't break my glasses anymore—I had given my word. All I ever had was my word, and I didn't keep it.

Not being able to keep my promise or being able to see clearly past my own nose and hearing only the sounds of my cousins fighting my battle, something in me snapped. I knew the moment the family found out I had broken another pair of glasses I was going to be in hot water. I just lost it. This was the first time I let the voices in my head take over.

I can't see much more than a blur, but my hearing is pretty acute. I squinted my eyes as hard as I could without letting them shut, just barely making out the oversized boy wearing the baby blue shirt and tie with the three plaid skirt uniforms surrounding him. I looked through the jarred loose right lens to verify the figures. I stuffed my broken glasses inside my coat pocket, zipped it up, and slid my schoolbag off my back. I ran towards the four figures yelling with the schoolbag in my right hand.

The Beast told me, "We may only get one shot at this, so swing as hard as you can. Then we're going to take off running in the other direction."

I swung with everything I had, knocking Reesey to the ground. The initial swing broke the arm strap to my school bag, which in turn lengthened the range of my weapon. I was swinging my backpack over my head like a modern version of the ancient sling that killed Goliath.

Reesey was knocked off guard by the blow and got up quick. No one else mattered at that moment.

The Animal yelled, "Swing again!"

The next hit caught him again on the back. The books inside my bag carried enough weight to make an impact. Reesey took off running down Washington Street en route to Egleston Station. I wasn't cognizant of the fact that I couldn't see clearly. All I knew was that I was chasing this boy who had broken my glasses down the street. I could run fast enough to keep up. My cousins ran after me because they knew I couldn't see.

The Animal just kept yelling for me to swing. I hit Reesey about thirty times as we ran down the right side of Washington Street. The only reason I stopped running was because we had made it to the intersection of Washington Street and Columbus Avenue-about a mile down the street. Reesey darted across the major intersection, and I couldn't make out anymore blurry figures. My cousins were right on my heels. The second they caught up to me, we all started crying.

My cousins were crying because during the battering foot chase I was almost hit by two cars. I didn't even know it. They had never seen me react that way. I was the docile child. Even though Grandmama always understood, I still cried because I didn't want to tell her yet again that I had broken my promise.

Irony is an unwelcome truth. The park that I ran by as I chased Reesey, I would visit that Christmas morning. That Christmas Eve, while we were over Grandmama's house, our apartment would be robbed for the third time since we lived there. Everything was taken inside the house except for the beds and my school uniform. The only thing my father was able to do to make sure I had a Christmas was to buy a pair of skis before the stores closed. He took me to Washington Park that snowy Christmas morning for four hours because that was all my parents had to give me. I fell in the snow so many times I couldn't wait to get home. That Christmas evening I vowed to never go skiing again.

Hazing at Big Barney's is a ritual introduction to measure the breaking point of the newly hired. Some rookies quit before lunchtime. Some rookies make it to the end of the first day, as was the case for pretty Tommy Blake. Rookie status officially continues to the summer's end. While hazing is a way of life, it can get old if the rookie doesn't break. Most veterans let the rookies with stamina off the hook as soon as they get a fresh fish tugging the line.

Since the crews switched around every day, I underwent a daily interview. Where did I live? Where did I grow up? What degree was I pursuing? Did I have a lady in my life? Why was I carrying a pager? Was I a drug dealer? Was I in a gang? I had to make sure my story was always the same. Since I didn't know nor trust anyone yet, I never told anyone the truth about my world. I was too private a person. My father always taught me, "What happens in this house stays amongst us that live in this house."

I had no problems discussing politics, religion, sports, and world events. I just thought I was hired to do a job. I felt the people working with me couldn't relate to my world. But, I was wrong. Turned out I was the prejudiced one.

I was tested throughout March, April, and May. I was ignored when other more experienced workers had troubles moving pieces in tight places—no one wanted to hear any suggestions from the rookie. I was yelled at frequently—when a tool was left behind, if we left any rubbish at the customer's old or new house, if the truck wasn't swept out at the end of the day. I was yelled at if the truck was not straightened up at the end of a job to match the sketched drawing on the rear wall.

I literally caught a bad break less than a month after I started. I was the fifth man on a two truck job. I was on a "white glove move," which meant they only wanted the best to move a high-end customer. Ted, the company's most experienced leader, was running the job. Ted definitely had a deity complex. He swore he road to work every day in a chariot amid the clouds with his full head of all white hair and white beard. However, I watched him get out of his red little matchbox car every morning.

While we were at the on-load, he pointed, "You, neophyte" (that was me) "wrap these pieces of glass and marble and place them inside of the cardboard bin."

I was wrapping the glass as I had been taught. I admit in the beginning I mummified most of the items with too much tape. I figured more was better, but I was about to learn a lesson. I folded the single pad around the medium piece of marble, then realized I didn't have enough tape left to go around the body once. So I leaned the slab of marble up against the wall while I went to look for a new roll. My shoulders hunched when I heard the thud of the wrapped marbled sliding down the wall and hitting the flat floor behind me.

I got a roll of tape and went back to the marble. I soon discovered the single slab I had leaned against the wall had multiplied once it reached the floor. Damn! I informed moving deity Ted at the first opportunity. He grunted, and informed me the now useless slab of marble was from Tiffany's and was valued at ten thousand dollars. One slab of marble was worth all the money I wanted to earn that summer. Ten thousand for some people is nothing—for others, it's an education. And for all I knew, my education just smashed up with the marble. Would I get fired over this?

After that day, I was no longer "the rookie" or "the neophyte." I was known as "the marble breaker" every time Ted and I crossed paths. I was scared to wrap or carry any form of glass, pictures and especially marble. I had no clue how to tell what was expensive from what was not. Ted and I never worked together again—I was black-listed from all of his jobs.

I'll be honest with you—I hate being yelled at or talked down to. I was forced to get better so I wouldn't be reprimanded. But I believe there are better ways to motivate people than to belittle them.

I was yelled at for not being able to take a door off of its hinges. So I went home and practiced popping pins from the door hinges with a hammer and a flat-head screwdriver. I learned what screw drivers to use if the door were painted over or rusted.

I was yelled at for not moving faster on the stairs. Veterans like Steve the blonde dreadlocks man would run up the stairs behind me, pushing his hands on my back, to force me to move faster. I am not a fan of my space being invaded unless I invite a person inside, and I had yet to do so. In fact, the number one pet peeve I have is someone who I don't particularly care for touching me. I knew that there weren't too many people who worked the trucks who could match foot speed with me. I was built for speed.

Some of the more experienced guys would think of new an ingenious ways to torture the rookies. They would make us carry a bin of pads inside the house only to have a veteran jump out from underneath once it was set down. Some rookies would return from a fourteen-hour day only to find their bikes had been taped to the telephone pole. And when the veterans wanted to torture you in the extreme, they would pick a spot with no air circulation along the route you had to run with the boxes. The man inside the house or the truck packer would pass gas at the place leading up to the dead air spot. I remember getting the sudden urge to vomit when stuck in a gaseous corridor in the first ninety-degree day in late April.

I have been called an old soul throughout my life. Those who know me better refer to me as a mean old man. I'm cool with that. I have maybe been a little too serious but that's my style. I have always found acceptance from those a little older than me. There has always been a better chance to relate musically, spiritually and in general.

Dominic, the Big Barney's dispatcher my first summer, was one such person. He more or less called off the hazing on me—he got the dogs to heel. We chummed around talking about playing basketball at different courts around the area. He had played for a local university before he married and had kids. He convinced me he still had a sweet jump shot when he goes out to the black top.

Dominic pulled me aside one day. He told me he thought I was ready to move up to be the push man (the man inside the house). The push man dictated the pace of the job. I would also be in charge as second man to get the truck ready and stocked depending on what the paperwork called for. For example, if the job included moving a piano, I was to make sure we had the additional supplies of a piano board, a piano block, two power straps, a four-wheel dolly with good wheels, and an adequate supply of Masonite to protect the floors from the weight of the piano on the dolly's wheels.

The paperwork for my first job as second man looked a little peculiar. We actually had two jobs to do. The first job called for three men to shift a baby grand piano from one side of the room to the other. The customer was being charged a two-hour minimum. This was my first time moving a piano. I had seen other experienced coworkers actually do the physical lifting, but this would be my first time to run the show. Movers were always paid a cash bonus for moving heavier items like this.

So that job was rather straightforward. The job that had me puzzled was the second one. Since Dominic was there putting out the paperwork for all of the other crews, I asked him to explain the second job to me.

"Oh, that's the separation job," he said in a matter-of-fact way.

"I don't understand," I said. "Why does she want us to park around the corner three blocks away until exactly nine thirty? Then the paperwork says we are not to wear our green company shirts or drive a green company truck to this job." I was very confused.

"The customer called yesterday to say she is leaving a bad relationship. She wants to be moved out while her boyfriend is at work. We need to move as much as possible. She is hoping that she can get all of her personal belongings out of the house before he comes home. The only problem is he works two blocks from the house, and he comes home for an early lunch. So your crew is going to have to move super fast."

"Dominic, does a job like this seem a little strange to you?" It wasn't adding up to me.

"This whole moving game is strange. You will meet people you wouldn't think existed in your wildest dreams. When you tell people outside this warehouse about the situations you encounter, they will all accuse you of making it up. From the stories you swap back and forth with the other workers, you'll know you are not alone out there."

"Out there, most of the times I feel like I'm alone in here," I said without the slightest hesitation.

"I know in the beginning the way the boys leaned on you was hard. They had to make sure you would be on their side at the end of the day. I personally make sure no one on a crew goes home unless everyone is on the way home. By this time, you have seen at least forty or fifty guys come and go."

I nodded in agreement.

"It's like a handful of wet noodles from a bowl," Dominic continued. "Throw the noodles against the wall and then watch as they all slowly peel off and fall to the ground. The noodles that are still stuck to the wall at the end of the day are the ones with substance. They were meant to outlast those on the floor. But you would never find that out unless you dunked all of the noodles in the same bowl of water the same way."

"Can I be honest with you, Dominic?" I was talking to him but looking down at the paperwork. "I think there are good noodles worth eating even though some don't stick to the wall as long. Everything that falls to the floor is not necessarily trash."

He smiled and shook his head. Apparently, my wisdom didn't apply to movers in his eyes. So we agreed to disagree. It's true that two sets of eyes can see the same sun rise on the horizon, but there will be two different descriptions of the colors and beauty of the sunrise. The commonality is held in the fact that the sun did rise.

It was fifteen minutes until seven. I had the necessary supplies inside the rental truck for the first and second jobs. Looking up at the posted sheet, I saw the name Leroy Butler over mine. I knew a Butler family that lived on the top floor when Grandma lived on Castle Gate Road, but I doubted it was anyone from their family. Then I noticed the red question mark below my name.

"Excuse me, Dominic, who is on my crew today? Well, it's not my crew. But who am I working with today?"

Dominic was smiling. "Sometimes awkward jobs deserve an awkward group to handle them."

I was thinking, *What the hell did that mean?* when I turned around and saw Leroy.

Leroy, standing tall at five feet, four inches, had this little scowl on his face because he knew we had just been talking about him. His overall look with his messy cropped haircut automatically brought a smile to your face. I thought, *Leroy is shorter than Baby Girl.* I was missing her a lot since she was up at Amherst and I was home. It was May, and I knew she'd be home after finals week. It was hard thinking about her as I smiled in the face of this man wearing a black leather fanny pouch around his waist.

Dominic spoke to Leroy. "How was your time off?"

"The trip up to Amsterdam must have been good because I blacked out and can't remember a frigging thing." Leroy seemed irritated as he spoke. "Then I went back to Ireland to visit my mom the last two weeks. I couldn't get out of blasted Cork City fast enough."

Dominic picked up on his irritableness. "What's wrong, Le?"

"This white underwear is sawing up my crack." He was digging in his butt. "Plus I hate coming back to work here. I should have taken five months off instead of just four. Big Barney sucks. Moving people's shite sucks. I hate the color green with a passion. It reminds me of poison ivy then I can't stop itching. I know you're smiling because you are going to hand me a job you knew sucked yesterday but thought it would be funny to give to me today."

"Leroy, this is your second man today, Kamaul." Dominic gave me the introduction with a smile on his face.

Leroy extended his right hand to shake hands.

"No disrespect, Leroy, but you were just digging in the crack of your booty. I'll shake your left hand." I was just being honest.

Leroy was about Dominic's age, which placed them both in their mid-thirties. I wanted to bust out laughing because he was wearing over-sized company issued black shorts with mix-matched socks. He had a calf high sock on his right leg and an ankle sock on his left foot. Not to mention the bright yellow sneakers on his feet. He caught me looking at his get up.

"You think you're better than me? You think because you have muscles that I won't jump all over you like a whirlwind?"

This little bastard was headed toward me when Dominic grabbed him by the arm.

"Let me tell you, the Irish are the Blacks of Europe!" Leroy spat out. "So you might as well start calling me 'brother' right frigging now or I'll unleash a wrath of fury on you, you never dreamed was possible."

Dominic casually held Leroy back by the strap on his fanny pouch.

"Believe me it's not the size of the dog in the fight," Leroy's tirade continued. "It's the size of the fight in the dog."

This miniature jolly green giant kept right on growling at me as Dominic held him back by his fanny pouch leash. I could now see why we needed a specialized leader for this "awkward" team. I wasn't sure if Dominic snapped his fingers or not, but all of a sudden Leroy was out of his hostile trance.

Turning around he asked, "So who is my third man today?"

"Big man" was all Dominic said. It was enough to enlarge Leroy's small pupils.

"Where is he?" Leroy asked, looking around like someone had yelled that the ice cream truck was here.

"He called to say he would meet you at the first job. He wanted to go to the gym this morning." Dominic replied.

I handed over the paperwork to crew chief Leroy. He snatched it away from me and growled. I was following him out the door when I passed deity mover Ted.

Ted said in his monotone: "Good to see you back, Leroy. Sorry to see you're working with the marble breaker. Don't let him carry any fragiles."

Leroy didn't break stride. "He should have broke the marble against the back of your head. He would have knocked your ass right off the top of the golden totem pole where you swear you sit."

When we got in the truck, Leroy took me under his wing. "Don't be afraid to make mistakes out here, man. No one is perfect. If you make a mistake, learn from it. Grow from it in the sense that if the situation ever presents itself again you know exactly what to do. Remember even when you do a job perfectly right, the human nature in other people will always find fault in what they feel you didn't do. If you know you've done your best at the end of the day, no one can take what you did away from you."

With that said, Leroy started up the truck, turned on the radio to Stephanie Mills singing, "What Cha Gonna Do with My Lovin'." He asked me if the song selection was okay. So I told him how I am the biggest Stephanie Mills fan there is.

I saw her in downtown Boston when I was seven years old with my Auntie Baye and her daughter Bird for a Concert on the Common performance. From the moment I heard her sing "I Never Knew Love Like This Before," I was in love. I was in love with the woman, the voice, and the way the song made my heart and body feel so free. I started singing and snapping my fingers. I was feeling the music.

Leroy yelled over my singing, "Who sings this song again?"

Exuberantly, I yelled back, "Stephanie Mills!"

He shot back, "Then let her sing it."

I navigated Leroy to the house in Melrose for the baby grand move. We talked all the way of the thirty-minute drive. It felt good to get schooled by a veteran without him yelling or trying to speak down to you. I know I can comprehend quickly. Talking at me only pisses me off to the point where I don't care to pay attention.

We talked about the marble-breaking incident. We talked about what the boys in the office expected of the newly hired. Leroy warned me to make sure I never used profanity or had discussions about graphic topics while out on the jobs. He explained how we are customer service at its finest. People will pay well to receive the best customer service possible. They don't want you to kiss their backsides, they just want to receive the best professional service available when they're paying their money, period. Leroy kept it as simple as possible. "Just hold all of the swearing and complaining about customers, company and coworkers for inside the truck."

We took the right-hand turn onto Oyster Street, approaching house #36 on the right. I didn't see any cars outside the teal dwelling.

"Leroy, where is our third man? He's not in front of the house. I thought he was going to meet us here?" I worried about moving the piano.

"He's behind us," Leroy said. "He's been following us since Main Street."

The purple and white van pulled up to park in front of the truck. Rhino-man. I swallowed hard. All I could remember was his wild threats while I passed Barney's office on the way to the bathroom.

Leroy jumped out of the truck, yelling, "Big Man!"

"Leroy! How the hell have you been, buddy?" Big Man's raspy voice sounded as though he was in mid-cough when he started to speak, but he wasn't. They embraced with a hug when they were close enough.

I stood off to the side, amazed at how big this man actually was. Since the weather was in the upper seventies, Big Man (as he will now be called in this episode) was wearing a white wife-beater. His muscles were stretching his tank top to the limit.

I wanted to know, but then heard Leroy asking, "How much did you lift in the gym this morning?"

"I maxed out this morning. I bench pressed six plates on both sides. And I squatted ten plates on both sides." Big Man seemed rather disappointed about his workout.

I did the quick math calculation in my head. "That's five hundred and eighty-five pounds on the bench press and nine hundred and forty-five pounds on the squat!" Did I say that out loud? All eyes were on me once I opened my mouth.

Leroy broke the silence. "Big Man, have you met Kamaul yet?"

"No, I think I saw you on the dock a couple of times, but we never met." He held out his hand upon the introduction.

"Big Man, your favorite mover nicknamed him the 'marble breaker.'" Leroy was grinning as the two of us shook hands.

Big Man's eyes opened wide. "I've been looking for someone to team with me to kidnap Barney's little snitching bitch. We can wait until nighttime, throw a bag over his head and get him in my van. I know I can knock him out in one punch. Then let's shave off all of his hair. I figure we can strip him naked, cover him in tar and feathers, then dangle him from the light pole in front of the warehouse. Dudes, let's do it! Hello!"

I could tell he had considered this plan before, probably more than once. He just needed a team to pull it off. I can't lie, I was thinking about it until Leroy spoke up.

"I am not shaving anyone naked. Plus the guy hasn't been with a woman since he was damn near seventeen. He is almost forty years old now, he would probably like it. Come on, boys. Let's go move a piano."

As we stood at the door waiting for it to be answered, Big Man spoke. "Kid, don't believe any of the crap Barney or his group of bitches uses to convince you about guys like me and Leroy. See we, and that includes you, too, do not fit in his mind as the perfect specimen of a mover. Leroy is too short. You are black. And me, I'm just too handsome. He wants everybody to kiss his ass, but we would never do it. I would actually kill him before I kissed him."

I knew at that moment I finally had some allies.

Moving the piano was easier than I could have ever imagined. We all grabbed a corner and baby-step walked it across the living room. Five minutes of work earned us two hours of work time—there was a two-hour minimum for moving a piano. Plus, we received a separate check of one hundred and fifty dollars. Seventy-five dollars was the piano surcharge and the other half was the gratuity. We all made fifty dollars cash and it still wasn't eight o'clock yet.

Since Leroy was broke from his travels he decided to go to the bank and cash the one hundred and fifty dollar check (the customer had made it out to him). I was standing outside the truck talking to my new ally when I heard my pager start beeping (remember this was still 1993). Three in a row was pretty unusual for this time of the morning. I excused myself, interrupting our conversation to see who was calling me.

I reached into the truck to grab my pager which was underneath my green company T-shirt I had taken off. The first number read: 50538-50538-50538. I smiled because I knew this was Nina's call from up in Amherst. I turned the pager upside down so I could read the message the way she meant it. Nina was sending me BESOS-BESOS-BESOS. She always knew how to set the morning off right: kisses, kisses and more kisses.

The second number was coded 194, then a phone number. 194 turned upside down was my code name HGI—"He Got It." Someone was looking for something on the streets. The third phone call was a message left on my voice mail.

Leroy was still in the bank. I didn't see Big Man, so I crossed the street to use the pay phone. I figured I would check my message first before I called back the phone number.

The one who left the message didn't have to say his name. I knew from his Jamaican style of running all his words together it was my boy Walls. Walls had to leave the United States because he had been set up by his lady and he was facing jail time. I had been waiting for the phone call to confirm he was off US soil and back home where he didn't run the risk of doing ten years in jail. Walls was a big brother to me. He was there for me when I lost my eyesight, so I was there for him, without question.

One day when we were working together at the video arcade store a little over a year earlier, I went totally blind. This was at 1001 Games, on Massachusetts Avenue in Cambridge. I was walking to the pizza shop at the corner when I began seeing flashes of light in my peripheral vision. Dizzy, I felt forced to sit on the sidewalk a hundred feet from the arcade door. I just couldn't make it back inside. I had walked the twenty paces from where I sat to the arcade door a thousand times. However, walking without sight suddenly makes the process almost inconceivable. I had no sense of direction.

No matter how much I called out for help, people just kept passing me by. One of the young kids who frequented the arcade must have gone inside to let Walls know what was happening. He sent one of the Dejesus brothers out to look for me and bring me back inside.

I was never so happy to hear a familiar voice in all my years. They brought me inside the cash booth and sat me on the stool. All I could remember was telling Walls to get ahold of my father, the number was in my pager, and he would know what to do. I let him know this wasn't the first time I had lost my vision so he didn't need to panic, when I became completely incoherent and then blacked out.

My vision and consciousness came back at the Cambridge hospital emergency room. I had no clue how I got there. I woke up to find myself on the gurney with a big light in my face. My parents were the first faces I locked my eyes on, and then I saw Walls standing behind them. Once my vision returned, I instantly got the most severe migraine imaginable. The feeling of my head being trapped in the grip of a giant vice was unbearable. I couldn't hold back the yelling—the pain was so intense—as I rolled up into a fetal position.

I was released from the hospital the next day. The doctors wanted to believe I had been using some illegal substance no matter how many times I refuted the accusation. They even gave me a blood test, which came back clean. I stopped into the arcade the following night but Walls wasn't there.

The local weed dealer was there, playing a video game with a large bandage on his left side of his face. Funny thing though, the moment he saw me walk up to the cashier's booth, he left. He and I didn't associate much unless we were gambling on the pool table or playing cards. I respected his hustle, but I didn't have to like it. He sold his stash to everyone, even grammar school kids. Although I didn't like it, the reality was if the kids and adults didn't buy from him they would buy from the next man anyways. There was no stopping a person from getting the fix they craved.

Over the years of gambling in the arcade I had become the person other people like to beat the most. I always accepted every challenge. I lost once in a while but not often. And when I beat you, I made sure everybody knew it. I think most people played me merely to shut me up. But it cost you to try to keep me quiet.

Max, the Korean parking lot attendant, came over to see how I was doing. I let him know about the severe headaches. Then I asked what happened to the weed dealer's face.

Apparently, he had been in the arcade when they walked me inside the day before. About ten people, all the local gamblers, were inside the booth when they could no longer understand any of the words coming out of my mouth. Well, while two people were holding my arms and Walls was on the phone calling my house, a loud smack rang out amid the local gamblers.

Max said when Walls realized that the weed dealer had gleefully smacked my unconscious face, Walls hung up the phone, walked out of the booth and grabbed the empty green beer bottle hidden inside the flower pot. This bottle was soon flying through the air at the weed dealer, where it broke against the side of his head. Walls then made the promise as the dealer ran out bleeding that there was still unfinished business.

A month of dodging me went by before the weed dealer and I settled our business. Walls waited for the weed dealer to come inside the arcade to see his weekend customers. He locked the front glass door and the emergency back door. It's fair to say the Animal in me was let off the leash.

I looked up quick, across the street, to see if Leroy had come out of the bank. Big Man was chugging on a gallon of water. Looking around I still didn't see Leroy. So, I figured I had time to make the call. It was a local number.

"What you want? What you need?" This is the greeting I use to let whoever is on the other end of the phone to know it's me.

"It's the Sergeant C. I want to be like Mike when he was ten, eleven and a real kid at six. I know four people that want to fight like Mike. Two are cussing and two are bitching," said the male voice on the phone.

My response was, "Make sure there are no cows on the dance floor."

Let me explain. Sergeant C is a cop in Cambridge looking for three pairs of the new Air Jordan's in boys size six and adult sizes ten and eleven. The same cop wanted to purchase four "black boxes," or decoding devices, to watch the cable premium channels for free. The black boxes I sold I guaranteed for up to two years. The black boxes were installed with a gold chip so the local cable companies could not fry the circuitry when they sent a surge through the system during the Tyson fight for those receiving the transmission without paying. He needed two for Cambridge, hence the word *cussing*, and two for Boston (*bitching*), since they are serviced by two different companies. The cows referred to the payment being cash on delivery with no one else around. That transaction netted me six hundred dollars. Not bad for a five minute conversation.

I crossed the street as Leroy was climbing into the truck. Big Man told Leroy my girlfriend had been paging me.

"How does your girlfriend like the hours you work so far, Kamaul?" Leroy asked.

"She has no complaints because she's up at Amherst. She'll be back tomorrow night."

They both simultaneously began laughing.

"What's so funny?" I wanted to be included on the joke.

"See, we have both been through our women complaining about the hours we work. I can't find a relationship that can withstand the off season let alone a summer in this intense line of work. You and your lady won't make it to the end of the summer for sure." Leroy was shaking his head laughing.

Big Man chimed in. "Your work hours will be fine Monday though Thursday because she's working, too. That first Friday night date that you miss all hell's gonna break loose. The first thing she'll say is, 'No one moves at ten o'clock at night!' She'll call you a liar. She'll think you aren't even at work because the company phones go right to the answering machine. When you get home, she'll tell you how you're neglecting her and now she wants a divorce. Then the next thing you know you are paying alimony and child support." He gave a guttural laugh. "Oh, wait a minute that's me."

I wanted to say Nina wasn't like that, but I already knew she was crazy. I only had a couple of days to figure out how I was going to battle my woman in addition to staying energized for this line of work.

Big Man broke my train of thought with his raspy voice, "Remember first and foremost, all women are crazy. You can't change that. That's why I'm happily divorced." With that said, we drove around the corner to the second job.

A quick spring shower fell on the way to the second job. You could see about ten dried spots on the wet ground from people who had probably just been picked up by a bus. Nine thirty on the nose, Leroy parked the truck in front of the house on Putnam Street. Big Man parked his mobile second home down the street from our unmarked truck at a meter. He planned to watch his van and the meter from where we were working.

The lady customer came running outside once she heard the truck. She was at the front gate waving us to hurry up. When she removed the extra dark sunglasses, I couldn't tell if her eyes were so puffy from crying or as a result of a domestic dispute. Since there was no bruising, I figured the prior.

"Please hurry up. Charles usually comes back home for lunch around eleven thirty, and I would like to be far away from here by then," Patsy said as she briskly walked into the house.

I had never seen a house in which absolutely everything was all white before. Way white. The rugs, the leather sofa, the curtains, the television stand and television casing—all we saw was white. I personally felt as though I should take off my shoes while she showed us around. Time however was of the essence.

"Please take as much as you can so we can get out of here. Don't worry about wrapping the furniture in blankets, we just don't have time because I want to be gone before he comes home. Charles is a madman. While you guys get started I'm going to get my car around the corner to load up my clothes. Guys, here is an extra fifty dollars for each of you, now please hurry." She handed Leroy the cash and went out the front door wearing her pink sweat suit.

Since money speaks louder than words, we were in a full go mode. Leroy packed the truck. I was in the middle, leaving Big Man inside. Patsy returned a couple of minutes later driving her tan station wagon. She parked directly behind the truck, and moved as fast as we did loading up her car with clothes, lamps and dishes. It struck me as funny that we were moving all of this white furniture into a white moving truck.

I was handing Leroy the white upholstered dining room chairs when I heard Patsy let out a scream and take off, half running and half limping in the direction of Big Man's van. However, once she reached the corner she took the left, putting her out of sight. Running after her was a middle-aged man wearing a white linen suit, white sandals and a straw hat. He also turned the corner.

Leroy and I were looking at each other bewildered when three cop cruisers rolled up, one in front of the moving truck and one in back of the station wagon. The third followed Patsy and the man in the white linen suit.

An officer yelled, "Put your hands where we can see them," while unsnapping his holstered weapon.

Leroy threw his hands in the air quick. I hate to admit this, but this wasn't my first or even my second time having this phrase directed at me on the streets of Boston. I have never been arrested, but I know the procedure. So while Leroy stood there with his hands held high, I took the next step and placed both palms against the wall and spread my legs apart.

"Who do you work for?" the officer in the truck grilled Leroy.

"Big Barney's Moving company, sir." I could hear Leroy's voice shaking.

"We received a call for a possible breaking and entering at this address. A neighbor saw the ex-fiancé of Mr. Jones hanging around the last couple of days. Do you have a work order to be here today? I need to see both of your identifications."

Leroy gave the officer the paperwork and his driver's license from his fanny pouch.

The other officer standing behind me was waiting for my information, but I had a little problem. Like I said before, since I know the drill it was just a matter of calling out my movements aloud. I'm not stupid. I know better than to make any sudden movements, unless I'm trying to make the eleven o'clock news as statistic of the police accidentally using excessive force, once again.

"Sir, I would like to retrieve my wallet. It is in the second pair of shorts closest to my body underneath my sweatpants." I knew he didn't want to be the one reaching into my underpants to get my identification.

"You boys can relax for a minute while we verify your information," the lead officer said.

Leroy and I both stood at the back of the truck while the two officers who had gone inside the house radioed back the house was empty. Leroy and I glanced at each other and smiled as we saw the white reverse tail lights of the purple and white van come on. The van pulled off, taking the right hand turn at the far end of the street.

The head officer was back. "Your information checks out, except there was a third mover with you today. Where is he?"

Leroy spoke up, "He went home on an emergency right after we got here today. His wife is pregnant, she paged him. Tomorrow was supposed to be her due date but she was having contractions, so he went to meet her at the hospital."

The officer asked, "Which hospital?"

"I believe he has gone to meet his wife at Massachusetts General Hospital, sir." Leroy never hesitated for a second. He and Big Man had played this game before.

The answer was good enough to satisfy the officer. But they were still trying to figure out what was going on at this house.

I whispered over to Leroy, "Are these the type of jobs Dominic usually sticks you with?"

He rolled his eyes and said, "Wait until we really get into the summer. You haven't seen anything yet. I told you this job sucks."

We had to move all the stuff back into the house. Good thing we had her credit card information at the office so we could get paid. Moving is like that. Any job we have can get strange that way. With all the inventory sheets we fill out, it's the comments section on the form that really tells us when something's a bit off. We usually never hear the ending of these little moving dramas. And that's okay—as long as we get paid.

CURIOSITY KILLED THE KAT…

Eager to know
Eager to observe
Eager to learn
Eager to play.
The rules are unspoken
Yet, simple enough to comprehend.

Are you sure you want to know me?
In order to understand my tendencies
You need to step outside with me.
I don't use the door
I use the window to come and go.
Oh yes, I use the ledge.
I only know how to walk on the edge.
Still curious?

You can't observe me from inside there,
And most people like to call me scary.
I like to talk while I walk
Since it's nighttime
You will need to let your eyes adjust
Take an extra minute
You don't want to take a wrong step
We are nine floors off the ground.

I'm no different
From the average finicky cat.
All factors in my life
Must remain constant.
I like to be fed at the same time every day
I like to run around frantic

LOOK WHAT I FOUND UNDERNEATH THE BED...

Especially when everyone is asleep
But most of the time I just want to relax.

Follow me around this corner
You can't be afraid to live
I live to learn
More importantly,
I have learned to live.
This walk is part of a journey
I wouldn't suggest you walk in my shoes
I don't wear any.

A sudden wind gust blows
Kat off the ledge on the corner's turn
He meows as gravity brings him down.
It was curiosity that killed the Kat.
It was satisfaction that brought him back.
Now he has seven lives left.

The first Monday morning in June, a few months into my working with Barney's, the weather forecast called for overcast skies. I threw on my blue windbreaker jacket and my matching blue and white Yankees baseball cap. I rode the ten speed bike to Barney's in my to-date best time of five minutes. I hate being cold, but I can't stand being wet.

The daily schedule was pinned to the cork board. I wasn't scheduled to work with a crew this morning—I would be working by myself delivering empty boxes for packing. Box deliveries were good for me since it was raining and I'd spend most of my time behind the wheel. That day, I had ten different deliveries throughout Massachusetts. Since this was my fourth time doing the deliveries, I knew there was no reason to rush.

After a year of working at various sites on security, I knew how to get around the state pretty well. I didn't have a problem reading the map book. I rode in an automatic transmission fourteen-foot truck, which was not that much different than driving an SUV. I had a radio, so I could sing to whatever I was listening to as loud as I dared.

The only problem I had was driving in the summer heat after lunch. I was fine from seven in the morning until noon. But after I eat lunch, you might as well give me a blanket and a pillow and let me take my green T-shirt, socks and shoes off, too. It's naptime. This eating-itis is expected and respected after meals like Thanksgiving dinner. However, there's nothing worse than the sandman blowing his magic particles in your face creating that unshakable haze when you are on the highway driving sixty-five miles per hour.

I've had cars honking at me to stay in my lane. I caught myself having to jam on the brakes on more than two occasions because I was within inches of hitting the car in front of me. Once, truckers kept honking their horns at me and pointing. I couldn't quite understand what the heck they were trying to say until a car pulled up next to me and the passenger mouthed the back of my truck was open.

When I pulled over to check, sure enough, the back of the truck was wide open and all of the remaining boxes were hanging on the edge. I didn't know how many had fallen out, but during the final delivery I was nine boxes short. The sad part is I always keep five extra of each size box on the truck just in case. I guessed the boxes were scattered on I-95 North. I watched the news that night to see if any flying boxes had caused any accidents, but thankfully there weren't any.

Before I began driving my own truck, I hadn't been aware of my after-lunch nap habit. The crew chief on the other trucks always drove, and the second man usually navigated him to the offload site. Being a newbie, I would usually fall asleep trying to avoid the rock and roll on the radio. I always awoke refreshed and ready to offload the second half of the job.

The third time I delivered boxes, the urge to sleep was so strong that I pulled into the parking lot at a local strip mall. It was siesta time for me. I was out for at least an hour, and woke up fully invigorated. I still finished the deliveries in the allotted time. So I concluded I could hurry along the morning deliveries, eat lunch, and get a power nap to avoid causing an accident at the wheel. I was good to go.

This being my fourth box delivery, I had my system down pat. It was a cake walk for me now. The deliveries up in the northern part of the state were done first. It would be more efficient to leave the local deliveries until after my siesta so I wouldn't get caught in any traffic. That day's afternoon nap would be that much more enjoyable since rain was pounding the windshield. I'm not saying this was my reason for pulling off to a side street, but it gave me more than enough justification to rest my eyes for a spell.

I awoke to the sun rays beating down on the cab of the truck. *Note to self*, I thought, *next time leave the windows partially rolled down so you don't cook in this makeshift oven.* If there were a cooking thermometer set, it would have rung some time ago. Since the afternoon air had turned humid, I rolled down both windows. It was mid-afternoon and all the deliveries had been done except for the last two—one stop in Arlington and another on the way back to the warehouse.

I jumped off Rt. 2 in Arlington. It was just after two thirty when I made the left onto Park Street, which would lead to the next drop off on Linden Street. When you are driving, the only thing you tend to pay close attention to are the other cars either beside you or moving toward you. Parked cars are stationary, so you rarely have to watch out for them. So when I heard the tremendous crunch while driving along singing, I was taken aback for a minute.

I looked into both side mirrors to make sure I hadn't hit anyone. Nope, no human or animal bodies on the ground. I pulled over to try and figure out where the crunch had originated. I was confident I had gotten enough rest during my afternoon nap, so sleep deprivation wasn't a factor.

On the driver's side of the truck, I noticed chips of wood covering the ground. A silver-haired white woman in a pink house coat and slippers ran out her front door. The front half of her head was filled with pink rollers.

"Earthquake!" she shouted. "We are in the middle of an earthquake! The entire house is shaking!"

That's when I saw the huge tree limb on the ground. I'm not talking about a branch. I'm talking about half the tree. A branch would have been like the tip of a fingernail. This tree limb started at the right elbow and now the entire arm was on the ground. Damn!

The silver-haired fox started pointing at the truck with one hand and covering her mouth with the other. She never even looked at me. Now I was scared to look in the direction that she believed caused the earthquake. It hadn't occurred to me that maybe I had caused the "Big Bang" theory with the truck this afternoon.

I had to force my eyes to look in the same direction as the earthquake chaser's glare. The top passenger-side corner of the fourteen-foot truck had caught on the elbow of the tree and ripped it right off, while tearing into the truck itself for about four feet. It looked really bad. When I opened up the back of the truck, it became apparent to me it was ten times worse. The roof of the truck had begun to cave inward. I could stuff my entire body into the hole and I wouldn't be a sufficient plug for the damaged hole. I had turned the miniature truck into a hardtop convertible.

I called Dominic at the first payphone I passed. He advised me to finish the deliveries first, then bring the truck back. I don't even remember finishing the last two deliveries. I already had the nickname "the marble breaker." What nickname would this earn me? And I'd probably get it right before they fired me. I had never been fired before. I steeled myself for a grim afternoon.

I pulled into the yard at the warehouse just after three o'clock. The other miniature box delivery truck was already back and pulled into the loading bay. Why did this have to happen to me? Why couldn't it have happened to the other delivery truck instead?

Dominic was sitting at the dispatch desk when I walked into the main office.

"Are you all right?" he asked.

"Yeah, I'm okay. I just can't believe I hit a tree. I never even knew the truck was getting close. But it was obviously my fault."

"Don't beat yourself up too much. It happens to the best of them some days. You need to go see Stanley James because he'll need you to fill out an accident report." I did appreciate the fact Dominic never yelled. It took me back to another comforting voice.

I was sitting on my Nana's lap eating clementines, her wearing her navy blue house coat with the white lace trim around the neck. Our arrangement for this pastime was simple. Nana would peel the miniature oranges, and I would eat. She loved to watch my face pucker as I bit into the tangy fruit. Nana had a neighbor from the Caribbean who always made sure there was a bag for us to enjoy whenever I came over to stay a night.

Earth, Wind and Fire were on the radio singing that afternoon. They had just begun singing the song "Reasons," when Nana began talking to me. Nana never talked during "Reasons" because it was her song, except for today.

She smiled as my mouth puckered. She kissed me on the side of my big afro and hugged me tight. I loved to feel her warm hug.

"Baby, you will have a tough road to travel because your daddy and all my other five kids had a tough road to travel. Try not to become too upset with him. I know he will do his best but he has that attitude that makes him so stubborn sometimes. But he means well.

"Your mother is a good woman. I'll admit I gave her a hard time when I heard she was pregnant. I thought she was trying to trap my baby. I didn't accept her until I saw your face. I saw that same face when I gave birth twenty-one years before. I knew you were my son's boy from the second I looked into your eyes. I walked over and apologized to your mother. No matter how grown your children become they'll always be the babies you gave life.

"I will always be with you, baby, even when you can't see me anymore. I'm going to be close by whenever you need me. Whatever obstacles you encounter on your journey, baby, please remember to keep on smiling. Don't let anyone take your beauty away from you."

Nana sang along with Philip Bailey the remainder of the song to me in my ear. I laughed because she gave me the giggles whenever she whispered in my ear.

That was the last time I ate clementines. It would also be the last time I would sit on Nana's lap. My Nana departed this earth when I was six years old. But whenever I hear the song "Reasons" I get to go back and sit on her lap one last time as my mouth automatically puckers from the taste of the miniature tangerines.

People live life theoretically through planning. "I'll do A if B happens. But if C and D become a factor, then XYZ." It's the random events from E through W that we can never predict. What do you do when the other innumerable iterations of misfortune rear their ugly heads?

In hindsight, we always see 20/20. That's when most of us think, *I could have done this, I should have done that, I would have done the other thing if I had had a moment more.* But when alternatives present themselves, all the original theories get thrown out the window. We rely on our instincts. The most powerful piece on the chess board can be the pawn if it is nurtured properly.

I heard once, "Live for today but prepare for tomorrow. Just in case you're blessed enough to witness your tomorrow." Sometimes we forget that tomorrow has never been promised to us.

I had seen Stanley walking around the warehouse most mornings doing his regular truck inspections. He was one of the men in the office who stood over six feet, five inches tall. The rumor mill had it that Stanley was a minority owner in the moving company. So he was always there to make sure things ran smoothly, especially the trucks.

Stanley was at his desk waiting for me when I approached. He motioned for me to take a seat.

"I need you to fill out exactly what happened. This form is for insurance purposes." Stanley was straightforward.

"I just want to apologize for causing the damage. I totally didn't factor in the tree." I was hoping my apology would be enough to salvage my job.

"Don't worry about it. When it rains it pours, then it starts to rain all over again. The total truck damage for today is now at around twenty thousand dollars."

I was so dumb-founded I stopped filling out the accident report. "Are you saying I just caused twenty thousand dollars in damage?" I knew I was getting fired for sure. I'd caused damage worth twice as much as the money I was trying to earn.

But Stanley said, "No, your damage is only half the total. The other box truck's corner was knocked off as well. It came into the warehouse as you were calling in your accident to Dominic. Now we have to get two trucks repaired at the height of our season."

Stanley James caught me smiling, and he didn't appreciate it.

"Please do not sit in my face and smile when you have caused this much in damage," he said sharply. "You have ruined a truck. You have also broken a ten thousand dollar piece of marble, which we are currently purchasing. So please, do not smile in my face. Just fill out the accident report and go."

I don't think I ever wrote so fast. Dominic stopped me as I walked back past his desk.

"I'm putting you on a long day tomorrow, so get a good night of sleep tonight." This was Dominic's way of easing my fears of being fired.

I just gave him a head nod to confirm what he said. Unlocking my father's bike, I realized my margin for error was narrowing rather rapidly. The need to step up my game was key if I were going to make it to the end of the summer.

As I rode the bike past the box truck, I couldn't believe the damage. Then I cycled past the other box truck and realized I wasn't the only one today. I smiled again, once I was out of eyesight. I had lived another day.

Calling the boating line each night fills your thoughts with curiosity about the following day. Who am I going to be working with tomorrow? How bad will the job be? How many hours will I work? Am I going to be working with the names mentioned before my name and after my name? Wait a minute—am I sure I heard my name called? Let me call back to make sure.

Since I first teamed with Leroy, we probably worked together every Tuesday and Wednesday. It was good having the consistency to develop the chemistry with one specific person. We talked. We would argue inside the truck. We also developed a playful banter in front of the customers. Sometimes customers would think we were fighting, but they couldn't help but laugh along with us. When it was time to work, we complemented each other very well. We almost made it look like a dance, the way we moved furniture together. I knew what he wanted to do. He anticipated my movements, we moved effortlessly in sync.

Leroy helped me find the fun in a job that was tougher than anything I had ever done before. The thought of work being fun was blasphemy to many other crew chiefs. Even the luxury of smiling was bad. So unless I was working with Leroy or a handful of other crew chiefs who were cool, I didn't speak much and I definitely didn't smile.

As far as excellence in dispatching, Dominic was the top. Then again what did I know—I had never worked with a dispatcher before Barney's. But I thought Dominic was good because out of the seventy workers we had during my first summer, I generally teamed with the same people once or twice a month. The constant rotation gave you a chance to work with people you liked and appreciated sweating with side by side. Then there were the guys who made work a living hell, which fit right in with the summer heat. Only working with them twice out of a possible twenty-four times a month was definitely a plus.

At 6:30am the next day, Hans, the German crew chief, prepped the two trucks we were going to need for the day. Hans never said much of anything to anyone. When he did speak, it was in short sentence commands. He in turn expected immediate obedience. He made sure he was in on the lifting of all of the valuable pieces. He did his job and did it well. Hans was one of those guys who always received the most difficult jobs. If you saw your name underneath his, it meant you were not going home early at all.

Hans's crew for the day included A.J. Sullivan, Steve the blonde dreadlocks, Beeman and me. I officially wasn't the rookie on this job since Beeman started working at Barney's a month after me. He was a couple of years older than me, having attended and graduated up at UMass Amherst. We never crossed paths when I was up there, but we both knew of all the hot spots. The only problem I foresaw with Beeman was the fact he took every job-related disagreement personally.

I had worked another job with Beeman about a month prior. We carried a dresser up the stairs into the daughter's room. The mother made the decision she would rather have the dresser placed into the basement. Once we reached the basement, the mother realized the basement might be too damp for the wood dresser so she asked us to bring it up to the attic for certain.

On the way upstairs, Beeman whispered to me, "You know the only reason she's making us carry this dresser all around the house is because she hates me. I can tell by the way she looks at me. It's the way she talks to me."

"But hasn't she been talking to the both of us, Beeman?" I never heard her address him personally.

"I know what the problem is. Someone must have told her I was Jewish. She shows the entire telltale signs of an anti-Semite."

Beeman could find an anti-Semite anywhere he looked. He has even accused me of being a hater of his race on several occasions.

A.J. Sullivan was quite down to earth. He liked to play practical jokes all day long because he was the butt of most of them himself. A.J. is a handsome man, standing an easy six feet, two inches, with a solid build, brunette naturally wavy hair and deep blue eyes. But when A.J. opens his mouth to smile, the individual looking at him usually goes from a smile to a rapid look of disgust. A.J.'s front tooth is jaggedly chipped and his four upper teeth and two on the bottom row are discolored due to rotting. Yet he loves to smile.

The rumor mill has it A.J. is from South Carolina. The Sullivan clan, a well-to-do socialite Southern family, was said to have sent A.J. up North for his schooling. A.J. is the middle child of five siblings. All of his other siblings have returned home after their degrees as doctors, as a lawyer, and as an architect.

I would never ask A.J. if he finished his degree at Harvard University. He seemed to avoid any references toward college and his family life. A.J. drove a little red hatchback. Sometimes A.J. walked to work from his temporary housing at the YMCA. Those were the days he looked as though he were trying to walk off his hangover.

The four out of five members of Hans's crew were there on time. Beeman was notorious for showing up five minutes late. Hans was not a fan of starting the day off his mental schedule. The pissed look in his eyes meant he would be talking to Beeman on the ride over.

Since Hans had the four of us ready, he decided to give us an overview of what to expect for the day.

"A.J. and I packed the house yesterday. Other than a couple of boxes that need to get closed up, the three-level brownstone is all set to go," the German said.

A.J. chimed in his southern drawl. "Fellows, I'm warning you right now, do not go into the third floor kitchen. No matter how much the customer baits you into the kitchen, do not go inside. Hans made me pack the kitchen yesterday, so I'm warning you from personal experience." A.J. was smiling, displaying his jagged front tooth, because he and Hans knew something we didn't.

"So what's inside the kitchen?" Steve asked. "Now you're informing us not to look because you really want us to go into the third-floor kitchen." Dread man was a psychology major, but we could all tell that A.J. had seen something in the kitchen that they hadn't then packed up. He purposely left it. Why?

Hans added, "Our customer Mr. Derrick Harris is an openly gay man. I saw a police uniform in his closet, but I'm not positive about what he does for work. He is a nice enough middle-aged man who likes to flirt a lot. He will definitely make the entire day interesting." Hans and A.J. smiled as they waited for our reaction.

I didn't have any reaction since at the young age of twenty, I had never yet interacted with an out-of-the-closet homosexual. I had questions about some of the guys on the high school football team when they would slap you on the butt absolutely every time they passed by you. Or the teammates who liked to leave their hand on your bottom while they spoke to you. Those were the same guys who would stay in the locker room talking after practice while the rest of the team took showers. After a while, I stopped taking showers after practice and just waited until I got home.

Beeman pulled into the parking lot as Hans was finishing up his overview on Mr. Harris. It was five minutes past seven. Steve pulled off his biking pants, leaving only his Spandex biker shorts. He also changed out of his green T-shirt, putting on a company-issued tank top instead. He let his dread locks loose from the hat that usually adorned his crown and zipped up his bag. He grabbed his front tire of his bike, stood erect and declared, "Now I'm ready."

"What for?" Beeman asked as he approached.

"Our customer today is a flirtatious white gay man. I want to give him something to look at while we're moving him today." Steve was dead serious.

"Are you saying by making yourself look more provocative to our gay customer, you are expecting to earn a better gratuity?" I was trying to clarify and justify the message he was sending.

Steve answered back, "That's exactly what I'm saying. Mr. Harris is a man just like us. We men are visual creatures who, if we appreciate what we see, will pay accordingly."

"That is a whole wheelbarrow's worth of bullshit!" A.J. was no longer smiling. "You might not even be Mr. Harris's type. Meanwhile you are willing to show this customer the outline of your penis and your butt by wearing your hooker/biker shorts because you believe you have a better chance for a tip. Plus you add in your tank top so he can have a better view of your upper torso as well. At what point do you cross the line? At what stage should your outfit be deemed unprofessional? Personally I don't think you look cute at all wearing your little tight Super Mover costume. Hans, please give him a green cape to throw over his back so he completes his ensemble."

"You say it as if I'm standing here naked," Steve complained. "My outfit is no more unprofessional than if I were wearing long pants like Kamaul, who never wears shorts. Yet he has on a tank top underneath his company shirt every day. The moment he starts to get sweaty his tank top will be exposing his muscular upper body. Or is his body merely more accepting because he fills out the tank top better than I do? And if for a split second you think yes, than I refer back to what I said about us men being visual creatures.

"For example, every morning our trucks are parked at either the Brazilian bakery on Cambridge Street or at the MIT convenience store. This simply because all of the women who work in these establishments show their ample cleavage first thing in the morning. It doesn't matter if it is raining, if it is snowing or if it is hot as hell outside. At seven o'clock, you are guaranteed a breast shot every time one of the girls reaches down into the front display cabinet to get a muffin. And we all know the muffins are not that good."

Hans had heard enough. "Let's go move Mr. Derrick Harris. I get the strong impression he will be right there waiting for us. Beeman, you ride with me—I need to talk with you on the ride over. A.J., you can drive the second truck with Kamaul and the sultry mover wearing the biker shorts. We have a long day ahead of us, gentlemen."

A.J and Steve played the radio game on the way. The game begins by pressing the scan button on the radio. The first person to name the song and the artist is given a point, but you have to name both. If your opponent challenges your claim for title or artist, the radio must remain on that station until the DJ confirms the song title and artist. Two additional points are given to whoever wins the challenge. The game is played until someone reaches ten points first. The game is deemed incomplete if you reach the job site and no one has reached ten.

I never play this game. There is only one station that plays hip hop, one station that plays jazz and two stations that plays pop music. Meanwhile there are eight rock-and-roll stations. I don't like to gamble when the odds are that far out of reach. No sucker betting for me.

Steve actually played in a band. The score was eight to five when A.J. realized we were close to the on-load site so he called a challenge on a song. The song had just begun so there was no way there would be enough time for the DJ to confirm the song title and artist. A.J. strategically dodged a bullet. The loser was supposed to pay for lunch.

We parked both trucks in the reserved parking spots Mr. Harris obtained from the city for the day. We stood on the steps of the brownstone, sweating even at seven thirty in the morning.

Hans pressed the doorbell at the top of the stairs. I stood behind A.J. on the steep front stairs. Beeman stood across from me pouting. I couldn't tell if he had the sour puss face on because he had just been chewed out or because if he looked up he would be staring into the crack of Steve's biker shorts.

"What's wrong, Beeman?" I asked. The customer still hadn't answered the door. I moved closer to hear his answer but made sure I didn't lift my head.

"Hans wants to run his crew every day like it's a concentration camp. You can't be late five minutes. You can't eat lunch until he's ready to eat. Every time you turn around to take quick water breaks, he's there cracking the whip with his sarcastic tongue lashing. I told him on the drive over here that I am tired of his anti-Semitism." Beeman was still looking down so not to make eye contact with Hans.

Everyone seemed to be engrossed in their own private conversations. Finally, on the fourth ring, the door swung open. Derrick Harris was standing in the doorway with a white cordless phone in hand. He was also in the middle of a conversation, all smiles.

The phone wasn't the first thing the five of us standing on the stairs noticed. Mr. Harris wore a white dress shirt with rolled up sleeves, unbuttoned to expose his blond chest hairs. He must have run down the stairs in haste because he forgot his socks and shoes. In fact, the only clothes on Derrick Harris's person were the white dress shirt and the mighty tight white briefs he used to cover his genitalia.

We were all standing quiet from shock as Derrick stood in front of us finishing his phone conversation. "I am going to have to let you go, Love. I have five handsome movers in front of me. I am not wearing pants. ...Yes, I'm serious, if I turn around right now all of Boston can see my supple ass. ...So what if they've seen my ass in the past—the movers haven't seen my ass before. Well, at least not until they follow me up the stairs anyways."

Derrick appeared to be blushing a bit. He probably had a mental image of us following him up the stairs.

"Love, I told you I have to go and get this move started. This handsome German in front of me is no doubt charging while he's standing here and I'm talking to you. ...Okay, okay, I'll describe the movers briefly and then I must go.

"First to lead today's parade is our nice hunk of German cake. He has sweet calf that I would die to lick frosting off." Derrick waved Hans up the stairs and moved on to A.J. "Next on our desert cart is the delectable Savanna Trifle. He is absolutely adorable as long as he keeps his mouth shut. Or even better if he's talking to you from behind. You know what I mean, Love?"

Steve was next. We were anxious to hear the impression his sumptuous work attire would get. Hans and A.J. even paused at the top of the stairs to listen.

Derrick paused and savored. "Um, Love, I just had a flashback to the Reggae Fest '91 in Toronto. Do you remember Troy? Well imagine him White with blond dreadlocks. I might have to test out the negative to this photo to see if it develops like the original." As Steve walked up the stairs, he gave a little extra hip shift to his walk. I wondered how bad he wanted that tip. Or was it even about the tip anymore?

Beeman and I were left on the outside staircase. I wasn't happy about being critiqued. But, it all seemed to be in good fun so I smiled as I advanced. I wanted to get my evaluation over with.

"Love," Derrick cooed. "I feel like I'm in the ice cream parlor with all these flavors. You know how I like to top my sundae off with extra caramel sauce. Well, if caramel was a man he would be standing in front of me right now. Love, he has muscles, dimples and a cleft in his chin. Wait a minute, do you know who he looks like? I'm going to let it be a surprise for you later. But I'll give you a hint—he's one of our top ten favorites."

As I walked up the stairs past Derrick Harris, I didn't necessarily want to know who their top ten favorites were. I could feel a set of eyes burning a hole into my booty. I was so focused on trying to get up the stairs without tripping I totally missed the opportunity to hear Beeman's evaluation. I just hoped Derrick gave Beeman a favorable review, so this wildly gay man would not be accused of being an anti-Semite.

Given that Hans and A.J. had packed up the house the day before, the job went along smoothly. Derrick found a suitable pair of shorts to wear after we started the job. The shock factor of him in his underwear became old rather quick.

Steve was the first of the uninitiated to be lured into the kitchen on the third floor. I figured something was up when he just kept saying, "Bypass" as he walked down to the truck, the universal term for "just keep walking." He looked totally disgusted. Standing at the top of the stairs I could see the smile on A.J.'s face stretching so wide I saw he had even more discolored teeth than I knew. Steve wouldn't say what he saw. Hans laughed hard at him when he reached the truck.

The next trip to the truck, I overheard Steve mention "Yardstick." When he saw me coming, he shut up. I knew Beeman and I were some way, somehow, going to be forced to find out what was in the kitchen. I was tempted to walk upstairs to just get it over with, and then again I thought maybe it was in my best interests if I didn't.

It took us five and a half hours to load the two trucks. So far it was a ninety-nine degree morning, and the sun was showing no signs of letting up at all. I had changed into my second green T-shirt for the day. It was definitely going to be a four-shirt day.

Hans sent Beeman and me into the brownstone to gather the remaining supplies. Beeman started on the first floor. I worked the third floor for a final walkthrough before we officially closed up the truck.

Walking through the third floor I poked my head inside each room to make sure it was empty. I closed the door to each room to remind myself I had checked those rooms. Soon, I found Derrick Harris was sitting in the kitchen staring at the wall.

"Excuse me, Mr. Harris, but I believe everything is out of the house at this point. The only items in question that I can see are the chair and folding table where you're sitting."

Derrick seemed to be half listening. He came back to earth for a second to give me an answer. "I told Hans I was going to leave the table and chair here. But I guess since the entire house is clear you might as well take the chair and the table, too."

Derrick stood up away from the table as I folded in its legs. I was facing him when he said pointedly, "I'm trying to decide if I should take the picture on the wall behind you or should I leave this treasure behind for the new buyer?"

I turned my head and then jumped back so fast I lost my footing and fell to my right knee. It was too late. The image of the picture was already seared into my mind. I grabbed the table and the chair and went downstairs.

I passed Beeman on the second floor and knew I had to share the wealth. He saw my hands were full and asked if there were anything left upstairs. I let him know that Derrick had one last picture he wanted to bring that was still upstairs. I waited, rooted to the spot, as I heard Beeman ask Derrick where the remaining picture was. Beeman then let out a yelp. It confirmed I had seen what I thought I saw.

"Yardstick," the framed poster in the kitchen, was a lovely collage of naked men. Each man was in a different pose displaying an enormous erection. No matter how much I shook my head I can't get the image to go away. When I reached the rest of my coworkers outside, I just mumbled the phrase "Yardstick." Everyone busted out laughing.

The summer heat is definitely my favorite time of the year. Most people toss and turn all night due to the humidity in New England. I have never had an air conditioner so I guess I never missed it. I have no problems waking up at the crack of dawn. I guess I'm just grateful to be able say my thanks every morning at having the opportunity to witness another day.

On hot days like that when I was a kid, we usually spent the time under water. The summer of 1979 on Castle Gate Road, one of the older kids would grab a big wrench and pry open the fire hydrant. We all waited as the brown water cleared to a free flowing pressurized fountain. All of the kids put on their brown or clear jelly shoes or a pair of old sneakers.

The boys ran around bare-chested while the girls put on their bathing suit tops.

The older men took the opportunity to give their cars a thorough washing, and then standing back drinking beers wrapped in brown paper bags. The older women like my grandmother were not leaving their perches in the windows no matter how hot it got out there. They just enjoyed watching everyone else having fun. These older women would dare the boys and young men to drench the women and men getting off the bus coming home from work. People would try to outrun the crowd, but they never could.

I always thought the adults enjoyed being forcibly dragged though the water as much as the kids did. Even after someone well-dressed was caught trying to make it home from work, a board or can was strategically placed at the hydrant to create a cascading semicircle waterfall that everyone ran under. The well-dressed person was only angry temporarily—just until they made it to their apartment to change. Then they would be outside yelling, daring the crowd to get the next person off the bus on Blue Hill Avenue.

The fun never lasted forever. The bright red fire truck would make its way onto the street to turn off the water. And just like clockwork the sound of the ice cream truck came right behind, bringing treats to keep the people on the block cool even if it were only until the summer's heat dried everyone's clothes and skin.

The rainbow in the middle of the street kept my attention. I sat on a car on the shaded side of the street. I always waited to see if the rainbow would last as long as the line of people waiting for ice cream. I knew Grandma had given money to buy me ice cream to my Uncle Deek (only five years older than me), so I waited. I had been trampled once and my glasses were broken, so I wasn't allowed to get in line anymore. I just watched the rainbow—the remnant of urban people, playing urban games, having urban fun.

The rainbow I was looking down at now was the remnant of the half gallon of warm water I poured over my head. I had bought the jug of water early that morning. One hundred and four degrees at almost five o'clock was just about unbearable. I dowsed myself with water because that was the closest I was going to get to a pool this evening. I wiped my body dry with the first of the sweaty shirts I had changed out of that morning.

Derrick Harris and his crew of five friends showed their approval of my changing my shirt with their applause. They were on the roof deck of his new four-level brownstone, sipping frozen cocktails out of their lime green frosted martini glasses. I couldn't help but think these men were viewing us, the movers, as possible appetizers to accompany their drinks. With all the giggling and pointing, I knew we were on today's menu.

I guessed between the frozen drinks, extra short shorts and tight tank tops, Derrick's crew was bearing up under the weather rather well. They hollered for me to take more off, especially my nylon sweatpants. I gained my first insight into exactly what women go through when walking past a construction site. No matter how hard I tried to pretend the cat calls weren't for me, I couldn't help but see the jealous look in Steve's eyes because none were being directed to him.

Steve was welcome to the attention I received, especially the calls for me to remove my pants. That definitely wasn't going to happen. It isn't that I'm ashamed of taking my clothes off. At one point, my mother had even suggested as my body developed to a hardened muscular form that I should consider becoming a male exotic dancer. Since I had a chocolate brown Stetson hat, we developed the ongoing joke of me performing under the stagename of the "Caramel Cowboy." Although my mother always had both a full-time job and a part-time job, she was always asking me, "Can you loan your mother twenty until next month?" She was always thinking of ways I could make a quick buck.

But I had my own reasons for keeping my clothes on. You see, I have what my peers refer to as chicken legs. No matter how much I work on my calves, they will not grow. I knew there was profit to be had in shaking my money maker, and I do like to dance. I could see myself getting into a dance routine hard. I don't need a gold pole to break it down. I would get so into my dance routine, eclipsing every other dancer in the room, until I would tug off my breakaway pants. My fantasy would end there, when I imagined the cheering coming to an end. I would see a line of women walking up to the stage in a line to take their dollars back for a refund. I always wear long pants because I have no desire to expose my insecurity.

One more truck to off-load, then we could go home. Nina had paged me six times by this point. She had gotten off work at the bank about an hour before and she was waiting for me. I didn't see any pay phones around so Nina would just have to wait some more. But I couldn't vouch for what her mood would be when I finally called.

Derrick Harris was good about supplying us with enough cold water and Gatorade to last the day. He even put out bags of pretzels and energy bars for us. The truth of the matter is I believe the sun had sucked the energy out of everyone before lunch time. The problem that I have working in that kind of heat is I can't eat heavy foods. I can taste my lunch with each trip up the stairs. So, I tend to stay closer to water-based fruits and salads. Plus, I had to fight my body against the urge to take an afternoon nap—there just wasn't any time to spare.

When Hans is the crew chief, lunch is always quick. Sometimes he even tries to convince you that stopping for lunch isn't worth it. But that day, Hans was outvoted, so we went to Charlie's Sandwich Shop on Columbus Avenue in the South End. Charlie's is one of those spots you should definitely visit if you're in the neighborhood, but don't go out of your way to get there if you're not on either Columbus Ave or Tremont Street. Charlie's stops serving food around two o'clock. That day, Charlie's was the perfect lunch place because it was only two blocks from Derrick Harris's new home.

I forced myself to eat the special of meatloaf, potatoes and vegetables. Hans informed us before lunch that most of the heavier items—the armoire, the triple dresser, the sleep sofa, the mattress, the box spring and the giant headboard and footboard—were going up to the fourth level. These bigger furniture items wouldn't fit up the stairs, so they had to be hand hoisted. I knew I would need my strength for later in the evening. Thank goodness Hans was smart enough to wait until the sun started to set before we tried to pull these items up the front of the building to the roof deck.

We started hoisting a little before seven o'clock. Hans placed everyone into position after he rigged the nylon straps around each piece. Beeman and Steve were on the sidewalk manning the tow lines, which are used to pull and hold the items away from the building on their way up. Otherwise, the gravitational swing of the item would tend to smash it through a window.

Hans placed me in between himself and A.J. up on the roof. Hans figured my smaller height would throw us off balance if I weren't in the middle. The three of us would do most of the lifting.

Hans was anal retentive about hoisting, which I respected. He used the box spring and mattress as the test runs so we all were in sync. The footboard and headboard were hoisted next with the same level of success.

Derrick's three friends also actually played significant roles. Each stood behind one of us, to pull away the slack of the nylon straps so it didn't become entangled around our feet and legs.

Derrick and his friend referred to as "Love" were down on the ground level with the crowd that had gathered. We had unquestionably become quite a side show. Love had out the camcorder video, taping the hoists. Derrick was outside meeting his new neighbors and the people in the crowd. We had delivered the Titanic of ice breakers for Derrick. I could tell he was going to relish every second of his new popularity. I couldn't blame him. He was already paying for the outdoor festivities—he might as well make the most out of it.

The dresser, the sleep sofa and the armoire were next. I wondered why Hans had not alternated the lighter furniture with the heavier pieces, which would have given our arms an opportunity to rest. But, I figured Hans knew exactly what he was doing.

We were all sweating pretty heavily. Between the humidity and nylon becoming extremely slick to the hands, the dresser barely made it up. The crowd was applauding from the building across the street and down below, but I had reservations. I was sweating too heavily to get a grip anymore. The sleep sofa was surely going to be heavier than the dresser. I figured I had better speak up.

Hans leaned over the cast iron deck railing, watching as Steve and Beeman secured the tow lines below. I nodded to get Hans' attention, then spoke only so he could hear.

"I was having a difficult time bringing up that dresser. It's too humid out here for me to maintain a grip on the nylon straps."

He could hear the uncertainty in my voice, but was reassuring. "That's why I placed you in the middle of us. Even if the strap slips out of your hands temporarily, Derrick's friend is behind you. He will be holding onto your slack long enough for you to recover. You can do this."

What Hans said made sense. I just kept having a mental image of the strap slipping out of my hands and pulling one of the others over the railing to the waiting crowd. However, Hans believed in me so I kept my mouth shut. I simply readied myself.

A sleep sofa is not too heavy when two people are carrying it. They can distribute the sofa's weight equally between them. However, when trying to hoist it straight up, you need to factor in the laws of gravity. Hence, multiplying the weight times four flights. The fact that you have a third person also pulling up the weight is cancelled out by the humidity and hot weather. What you have left over is an inescapable conclusion of impossibility.

I've had a love/hate relationship with sleep sofas for years. Our family condo only had two bedrooms. When my parents bought the condo, they allotted one for them and one for my sister, who is eight years younger than me. They figured I was going to be leaving for college in four years anyway, so I was given the sleep sofa. For four years. We also agreed that since I have always maintained a job, my weekly rent would be fifty dollars. Once I came back home to go to college my weekly rent increased to sixty-five dollars. I didn't complain about having to sleep in the living room because the floor model television was there. I have always been a television junkie-that may be why my vision is so bad.

Prior to the condo, we lived at 425 Cardinal Medeiros Avenue in East Cambridge. We'd moved there when I was twelve. Cambridge was a very diverse community. Our street block was entirely Portuguese. We lived directly across from a huge white Portuguese church. Our new apartment was also two blocks away from the Roosevelt Tower Housing Development. I met some local boys on the basketball court behind the Harrington School and soon became part of their crew. We played basketball from sun up to well past sun down every day.

My parents, sister and I lived in a three-room apartment with accordion doors separating each room. Sleeping quarters were tight. If I laid on my stomach on the red carpeted floor in the middle room, stretching out my arms and legs, my body could actually touch all three rooms. There were only two bedrooms. I had to share a bed with my little sister, who is eight years younger than me.

I clearly understood that my parents provided us with what we needed. The wanting to have such things as my own room, let alone my own bed, was irrelevant. My parents sacrificed for the both of us, my sister and me, to attend parochial school. So, I rarely asked my parents for anything. I didn't want them to think I was a burden or was ungrateful for what we had. I relished in my role as the first-born child.

I became a security blanket for my sister most nights. I knew it was a huge relief for my baby sister to have her pillow and me lying in the bed next to her at night. Because our apartment was directly behind a bakery, the two-story building was inundated with roaches and rats. As soon as the lights went out, the rats began to run through the walls and the apartment ceiling like it was recess time. My sister spent just about every night huddled up underneath me as her wide eyes followed the movements of the scampering rats back and forth inside of the drop ceiling. When the rats ran through the walls right next to the bed it always felt like they were going to burst through the walls and run across the bed, but they never did.

Whenever my sister had to go to the bathroom during the night, I went ahead of her to clear the way. I had to walk through my parent's room to reach the kitchen, which also held the bathroom. Turning on the kitchen lights during the night became a game to me. I picked up my mother's slippers on the way into the kitchen and readied myself before I turned on the light. I was a ninja/mercenary against an army of cockroaches for at least twenty seconds with both my mother's slippers in hand whenever I turned on the kitchen light at night.

I motioned for my sister to go to the bathroom after my twenty-second battle was finished. I cleaned up while she used the bathroom. My nightly average body count was twenty-six roaches. It's funny, no matter how much I washed the dishes, swept the floors and put out the trash, every night the number of roaches never seemed to diminish.

In our bedroom, my sister listened as the rats continuously played tag over our heads. Eventually she would fall asleep in my arms but it wasn't from counting sheep. My job was to make sure my sister slept even if it meant I was up all night listening to the rats play musical chairs.

My parents finally bought the two-bedroom condominium in Cambridge before my freshman year of high school. The condominium definitely had more square footage than the apartment, plus there were no rats in the basement-level space. The rationale behind purchasing a two-bedroom was simple. I was leaving for college in less than four years, so I didn't need a room of my own. I had made my way into a publicly private high school. My parents no longer had to pay for my education. My father felt this was the opportunity to take the money they had become conditioned to spending and save it. Therefore, no bedroom for me. A pullout sleeper sofa would suffice until I left for college. I took this in stride.

However, I did get upset when my grandmother, her niece and her niece's daughter dropped by one day. They had been at the mall clothes shopping, and on the way home my cousin had to go to the bathroom.

They figured since our house was close by, they would stop off and say, "Hi."

My grandmother and her niece were already sitting on the sofa talking to my mom and me when my cousin returned from the bathroom. My cousin is what my family refers to as "big boned." If you ask me, I say she is what she is, and there is no need to sugar coat it. My cousin is obese. She walked around the coffee table to plop down on the last empty cushion on the tan sleep sofa with the pink flowers. I can raise my right hand now to testify I have never heard metal wrench around in such a manner. Less than a split second later, all three of them fell the remaining six inches to the floor.

My mother and I quickly helped everyone up. Embarrassed, my cousin left with Grandmama and niece. I waited for the car to drive away before taking a crowbar to pry the metal loose. The frame was so distorted I would no longer be able to sleep in the bed the conventional way, that is, from head to toe. I now would have to sleep across the middle, sinking down like a hammock. Of course, my parents expected me to keep paying them rent of sixty–five dollars a week. It was crazy. I couldn't even watch the TV to go to sleep anymore.

As the sleep sofa at Derrick's reached the level of the third floor window, A.J.'s strap slipped from his hands. A.J.'s system included pulling his strap up left hand over right hand and then looping the strap around his right forearm. The sofa jerked him toward the railing. Derrick's friend holding the slack caught A.J.'s arm. Hans and I could both see the fear in A.J.'s eyes as he was being pulled to the edge of the roof deck.

Hans yelled, "Steve!"

Steve must have started to bolt up the stairs the moment he saw A.J.'s side of the sofa slip. The crowd below gasped. Beeman managed to hold the sofa away from the third floor windows so there wasn't any crashing. I knew Steve was fast from all the times he had chased me up the stairs. I was hoping his sprint training would pay dividends tonight. By now, A.J was holding onto the railing so as not to get pulled over. The looped strap being pulled in both directions cut into A.J.'s arm.

Hans and I braced on our straps against the railing. We both lay with our backs flat against the deck's floor, our feet pushing against the cast iron railing to keep the sofa from moving. This also helped to maintain our leverage. But my hands were slipping—my palms were too sweaty. I closed my eyes to focus on not letting the sofa's weight pull the strap from my hands.

I could hear Steve's feet running towards A.J. on my left side. He leaned over the railing and grabbed enough of the strap to allow A.J. the chance to get his arm free.

"My strap is slipping!" was the only thing I could yell out.

A.J. came to my rescue since Steve had secured the left side. As soon as I got the chance, I wiped my hands to secure Hans's side. Once we were all back in a standing position, we quickly pulled the sofa up. Hans's hands were free. So he talked the three of us through it until he had both of his free hands on the straps securing the sofa to our pull straps.

Once again the crowd cheered and applauded as we lifted the sofa onto the other side of the deck's railing. We all fell to the deck from the exhaustion. The sweat was dripping from my chin as I bent over with my hands on my knees.

"Those are my movers!" cried Derrick. "Big Barney's Moving Company is the best!" Derrick and Love had become the biggest cheerleaders on Dartmouth Street.

Then I heard Hans say, "Rest up quick. We still have one more piece to hoist. The day is not over until everything is up. So let's finish up strong."

Hans made the necessary adjustments for the armoire. Instead of using three people to hoist the oversized clothing cabinet, Hans placed Steve upstairs making it four. This distribution of weight made the lifting easier among the four of us. The armoire came up smoothly.

Standing on that roof deck looking at the crowd below, I felt good. I realized I had just overcome a fear of heights that I had never shared with anyone before. Just like my skinny legs, there had been no need to let anyone know this little insecurity either. Yet, never in my life before today would I have ever even considered standing this close to the edge with a bunch of guys I barely knew.

The thought of being exhausted was being overshadowed by an exciting feeling of accomplishment. I made it through that day. It was the first day since being hired that I felt as though I were part of the team. We all needed each other to get through that tough day. No one ever gave up. No one was left without a role to play. And no one man was greater than the team.

In an emergency, I have always measured the people within my inner circle on their loyalty. I don't call just anyone a friend. A true friend is someone I never need to ask for anything twice. The people closest to me know I live for the promises I make. My promises are better than my money. Therefore, I don't make many promises. I never want to leave any outstanding debts.

At the arcade where I worked since sophomore year in high school, I learned more about loyalty. The mid-afternoon sun beat through the floor-to-ceiling glass windows. The air conditioner cranked out on high. It was always either on high or off—there was no in-between. I personally hated the air conditioner being on because it inflamed my sinuses. There's nothing worse than trying to breathe in the summer with a stuffy nose. I spent most of the work days walking outside and watching the inside of the arcade through the windows.

It was at the arcade that I met Walls. Walls was the manager of the arcade and we had become goods friends. He made sure after my freshman year up at the UMass Amherst that I had a job to come back to if I needed it. Walls always looked out for me.

About two months after I lost my vision, Walls and I found ourselves working together again. I had promised myself I was going to relax more, and I had been given medication for the migraine headaches. But I'm not a fan of medication since it doesn't allow me to feel free. The orange bottle of pills found a permanent home in the top drawer next to my sweat socks.

Walls and I stood on opposite sides of the glass display counter. It stood about three and a half feet high, with five levels of glass shelves holding the arcade's toy prizes. I worked on the interior of the booth, attending to customers who wanted to redeem their skee-ball tickets. Walls counted the tickets and watched the floor to make sure all was well.

The coolness in the air told you the fall season was approaching. Walls's powder blue linen shirt and pants draped over his wiry frame. He had every color linen pants and shirt imaginable. Walls stood six feet, one inches tall, with a close haircut that was like five o'clock shadow on his head.

Funny thing about Walls, as skinny as he was he only liked women who outweighed him three times over. All of his women were very pretty in the face. When it came to their bodies, Walls looked well beyond the surface. He used to tell me in his Jamaican accent, "Look mon, me want a woman tat I know will create a challenge for me to swoop up off da ground when I make love to she. When me on top kissing she, me neva want me feet to come close to touching da floor. When me hold her round body tight in da air, me want to show she, I am not afraid of all of her natural beauty. It is she, who should be afraid of me." Walls and I talked about everything. He was twelve years older than me.

Everyone in the arcade was too preoccupied playing their video games to pay any attention to me and Walls. Plus, trying to decipher our conversation over the loud simultaneous noises from the seventy-two video games was impossible. We both fixed our eyes in the direction of the customers. We never made eye contact when talking seriously in public.

"What's up mon? Ya seem not da same since you come back home," Walls said.

There was no need for me to lie to Walls, we didn't play that game. "I'm straight. I'm just dealing with a couple things on my mind."

"Ya been looking like someone stole ya bloody spirit, mon."

I hadn't told many people about what happened at school, but I knew I could trust Walls. "I feel like my heart, my soul and my mind have been extricated from my body, Walls. Part of me died up in Western Mass. I went through a lot of things those nine months, partner."

"Mon, is der anyting ya need to get off ya chest?" I could tell he was genuinely concerned. He'd been my friend for more than six years.

"Not yet. My dreams don't allow me to sleep most nights. I'm learning to cope though." Up at UMass, a little bit of everything had escalated out of control. That story will come another day.

"Tell me tis, mon? Did ya bring back home da machete me gave ya?"

"Of course, I brought it back home."

"Did ya use the machete when ya were up der at UMass, mon?"

"I had no choice, Walls. I did what I had to do in order to make it back home."

"Ya getting a chance to live ya tomorrow today boy. Let what happened yesterday remain in da past. If ya don't, believe me, it will eat ya life away. Don't let da dead feeling ya dealing wit consume ya. Some of da most agile cats neva make it back to deir feet after falling from da edge, mon." Walls knew me well. Sometimes he knew me better than anyone else.

"Walls, believe me, I'm fighting ghosts without faces every night. I am searching for a reason to see my tomorrow. I just keep coming up empty though. Lately I been hoping I don't get a chance to see another sun rise."

I could feel Walls's eyes looking at me. We didn't get a chance to finish the conversation because little Roland was walking towards us. We had nicknamed him Donut. He wasn't fat. Roland's mouth always looked so dry, like he just finished eating powdered donuts. The irony was, his mother worked at the drugstore next door part-time. It turned out she also worked with my grandmother's sister during the week. Roland's mother never gave him any lip moisturizer. Walls always joked about buying a bottle of lotion to keep inside the arcade. Walls wanted to make it a prerequisite for Roland to put on lotion before he would be allowed to play any video games.

"What's up, young blood? What are you doing in here on a Saturday afternoon? You usually come in on Sunday." I shook Roland's hand and smiled because I could see Walls out of the corner of my eye shaking his head. I knew he was looking at Roland's powdered mouth, ashy hands, cinnamon covered kneecaps and his crusty forehead.

"My mom went next door to pick up her check. I told her I wanted to come in and say hi."

Walls chimed in, "If ya muda went in to get her pay, ya should run to ask she if ya house needs lotion too. Maybe ya all run out. If ya are, today would be a good day to buy some."

The observation flew right over the ten-year-old's head. I caught a glimpse of his mother waving for Roland to come outside. "I think your mom is ready to go. I'll see you tomorrow, right?"

"Yeah, I'll ask my mom if I can stay until her lunch break tomorrow. Then she can take me home." Roland was always such a happy kid.

I waved bye to Roland and his mother as they walked away from the window.

Walls made the sound of sucking his teeth. It was his way of displaying his disgust. It was automatically followed by him swearing in Jamaican. "That *bumbo rassclaat* Corey stealing tickets again." We could both see through the corner mirror the rear of the arcade where the skee-ball game was. Corey spent most of the day watching everyone else play. He gave advice on how to beat each level of each game. He knew better than everyone else how to play each game, yet he never had more than a dollar to play.

Corey utilized his dollar waiting for me and Walls to become distracted so he could play skee-ball and throw all of the nine balls into the one hundred point cylinder. We knew that when we weren't looking, he would climb up the front of the machine to score more points or to steal tickets. One time we caught him with his head trapped in the net. Why didn't we ban him from the arcade? Actually, we kept anyone around who made the day go faster. He was part of the atmosphere. Nine hundred points gave fifty tickets. Corey always came up to the booth carrying two hundred tickets. He used all of his tickets to get candy.

One day Corey came up to the glass counter dragging behind him more than three thousand green tickets. From the moment he placed all of his tickets up on the counter, I could see Walls' eyes rolling. Corey started listing absolutely everything he planned to redeem his tickets to get. After he got picky, saying he only wanted candies that had red wrappers, Walls kicked him out of the arcade for a week for stealing tickets.

Today, though, we could both see Corey with his head stuck in the netting of the game. Walls motioned that he was going to walk around the front to catch him. I knew he wanted me to walk around the back so he couldn't escape.

I decided not to walk through the booth door because the door always made a loud squeaking sound. Walls used the squeaking as his silent alarm so to speak. I wanted to catch Corey in the act. It was always more fun catching him with his hand inside of the cookie jar, that moment of surprise and shock is priceless. So, I thought it would be quicker if I hopped over the glass display counter. I did this all the time, effortlessly. Walls started down the three steps that led to the front of the arcade. He turned around for me to move into position.

I placed both hands on the steel frame that encapsulated the display counter and hopped into the air, propelling my body over the counter to the other side. As my feet started to vault over my right boot hit the top of the counter, stopping my momentum in mid air. My backside crashed through the top of the display case.

Falling downwards, I instinctively caught both my arms and feet on the outside of the steel frame. A quick moment had passed before everyone inside the arcade realized I was in trouble. I was in a sea of sharp teeth, with the glass pushed down by my body but wanting to snap back up. The glass countertop had been built to prohibit the top from breaking easily. I looked as though I was being swallowed up by the display case.

I could feel the skin being sliced away on my left inner bicep and a sharp pain on my left side. I was glad I had decided to wear jeans that day. The glass top was cutting my pants to shreds around my legs.

"Nobody touches me!" I saw a couple of adults who were in the arcade with their kids motioning to try and help me out. Walls quickly moved everyone back.

"Mon, ya bleeding pretty bad on ya left arm." Walls seemed as though he didn't know what to say.

"Walls, look underneath me. How many feet are there to the bottom of this case?" I needed to assess my situation.

"Ya have tree feet to the bottom. Ya have five glass shelves underneath ya body, mon."

I knew I had fallen into the middle of the three display cabinets. If I fell inside to the bottom, my body weight would more than likely force the cabinets at my head and feet to collapse as well.

I heard a small kid say among the group, "Daddy, is that man going to die when all of that glass cuts him up?"

Something inside of me yelled out, "We are not dying like this, not today!" I looked at Walls, "Back everyone up. I got to get out of this."

"How do ya want me to help ya? Me can grab ya arms or something." Walls was ready to assist.

I knew if anybody touched me and I slipped out of their hands, I would be cut to shreds. "You can't. I need to save myself."

With that said, I grabbed the sides of the display counter. My left hand was covered in blood. I lifted my body weight into the air. It was like doing a lower dip press in the gym. I pushed my body weight out of the temporary glass coffin.

I was standing up looking back at the mess I made of the display counter. A split second later my wounds began to throb. The cut on my left arm was definitely nasty. The blood was pouring down into my palm. However, the sharp pain in my side was a thousand times worse. I looked down to my side to see a seven inch piece of glass protruding from my rib cage. Walls was looking at the glass, too.

I grit my teeth. "I need you to pull the glass out of my side, Walls."

"Me not pulling it out. Me can cause ya more damage to ya by pulling da damn glass out. We're two minutes from da hospital. Let da doctors pull it out."

"Walls, I would never ask you to do anything unless it was important. Don't send me out of these doors with glass hanging out the side of my body. I'm already cut up. If I could pull it straight out of my own body, you know I would. But right now I can't because my left arm is too cut up. I only have the energy to ask you one more time. Please pull this glass out of my body. You will, if you are my friend."

I turned my head as Walls took hold of the jagged edges to extract the glass from my side. When he finished, I walked out the rear emergency door of the arcade. I jumped into the passenger seat of the white Cadillac. Walls came running out with a pocket full of money. He took all of the money out of the cash drawer before he handed over a twenty dollar bill to Corey to mind the arcade until he returned. Even though we both liked Corey, we knew Corey would rob the arcade blind the moment we were out of sight.

I received twenty-one stitches to close the wound on my inner bicep area. Ten stitches were used to close up the wound on my left torso. The doctor said I was a millimeter away from severing a major artery and a centimeter away from puncturing my kidney.

When I went to sleep later that night, I found myself waking up in a cold sweat. The pain from the lacerations were intense. I was cut up pretty bad. The cold sweat that wouldn't allow me to sleep were the product of what happened up at UMass Amherst. I was still getting over it. Bloody situations from the arcade would bring it all back again.

QUIET CONFIDENCE

What attracts a man
To a beautiful woman?
Most men would say
A gorgeous face.
The average man would say
A head-turning figure.
I say it's the woman who displays
Quiet Confidence.

Confident that her appearance
Is pleasurable to those
Who happen to take a second glance in her direction.
Men hoping,
Trying to make enough eye contact,
So maybe, they can approach
This lady of shear loveliness.
But to no avail,
She never turns.
Their eyes never meet.
She's quiet.
She is intimidating.

He has failed to realize
There was much more to this woman
Than a visually intoxicating persona.
She is a complicated character with
Simple needs and realistic desires.
Needs that she hopes will be
Fulfilled by her man.
And if not her man, she's willing to wait
For the perfect man, a fantasy man.

Who is this fantasy man?
What separates him from every other man?

Well, he too is confident.
Not arrogant nor conceited but confident.
He is more interested in getting to know
And better understand the woman
He's hoping to spend time adoring.
He wants more than a pretty face.
He wants a companion.
He wants a friend.
He wants to grow, fulfilling their desires together.
He knows what pleases her and he does them all.
She sits quietly,
Attempting to picture his face.
But in her dreams, he's much more than a face
He's a feeling.
A sensual feeling.
So she's willing to patiently wait.
Confident of their inevitable meeting.

Big Barney's used individual calendars to create the team schedule. We would mark an "X" over the day on our calendar that we needed off. For any day not marked, it was assumed we could work. I decided the day after I turned the small box truck into a convertible I would work as much as possible. Knowing I couldn't afford anymore mishaps, I set my mind on making all the money I could until I got canned. So I always handed back my calendar with no marks at all, with my name written clearly at the top (in my signature blue ink, but that's another story).

The second-to-last Saturday in August was the only day I crossed off my work calendar that whole summer. It was my only mandatory day off—too much time and preparation had gone into making the Third Annual Family Reunion Cookout possible. I was looking forward to it, but still had some grueling weeks ahead of me first.

The first and last weeks of the month are the busiest in the moving industry. Most customers are closing on their homes or moving into new ones around this time. Customers are also switching apartments as their old leases end. This means most of us are working an upward average some where between 60 up to as high as 80 hours in a six-day work week. I worked so much I couldn't even make it to the bank to deposit my checks. After six weeks of this, I began to sign them over to my father to deposit.

My father opened my first bank account when I was too young to remember. He always maintained that I should have access to my money. He referred to money accessible between the hours of nine to five as the "bankable money." What was in your wallet was "chump change."

Then I had my stash. My stash was the profit I made from bringing different sellers and buyers together without them ever meeting. The funds earned from being the middle man, loaning money at fifty cents on a dollar, collecting money for different associates, gambling, selling different products and services all added up. I kept most of the money I earned from extra activities—all the business obtained via my pager—in the broken dishwasher in our kitchen. No one inside the family or out ever thought of looking for anything in the dishwasher. This was my private storage spot since my exclusive household chore had been washing dishes since I was tall enough to reach the kitchen sink.

There are so many days in our lives when it seems we are walking around aimlessly in the darkest of rooms. We constantly bump into everything only to hear something shatter before we get a chance to save the object we just blindly destroyed. Then one pivotal day out of the blue, someone miraculously turns on the overhead light. In the light, everything suddenly makes sense. This unveiling of knowledge from someone wiser has frequently helped to make difficult situations comprehensible to me. Their overhead light gave me knowledge. That knowledge in turn earned me respect.

Back inside the warehouse, someone thumb tacked to the cork board over the daily work list the phrase, "No one should want to go home until the last truck is on the way back." Everyone figured this came from Barney, in an attempt to enhance solidarity among the men. I planned to take full advantage of any opportunity to work that came my way.

As the summer kicked into full swing, so did the work intensity. The company damn near doubled in size. We went from forty men when I started to close to eighty by mid-June. I was glad I had started back in March. It would have been too chaotic trying to adjust to the work load in the middle of the hottest season.

Ninety percent of our work force was either new college graduates or current college students. Twenty or so workers returned after their spring semester finals were over from the surrounding universities—Harvard, Boston University, Northeastern and Boston College. The other twenty or so Irish lads were here on JI visas, which allowed foreign students to come to the US to work over their breaks.

Barney regularly sponsored students from the universities in Ireland to come to the US and work for the summer. It was his way of giving young men from his homeland a chance to see America. This was good for Barney, too, because it guaranteed the company cheaper labor for three months of his busiest season. Once the students reached America on the JI visas, they were relegated to work only for Barney and the moving company until they returned home in mid-September.

The Irish lads brought a new flavor to the buffet table of characters. All the rookies naturally stuck out like baby deer caught in a truck's headlights. They made me vividly remember how wide my eyes had been back in March. The boyish good looks of the Irish rookies showed their naiveté;

their fashion sense had clearly not be influenced by America. The Irish men I had met so far, Fast Eddie and Leroy, were already Americanized with their Nike sneakers, tube sweat socks, loose fitting shorts (although Leroy clung to his black leather fanny pack as his fashion accessory).

The students on the JI visas all wore Barney's company issued green T-shirts. Just below the seam at the bottom of their T-shirt, you could see a small strip of their white shorts with the green trim. If it wasn't for the fact that some of the JI rookies had their shirts tucked into their shorts, I might have thought they were planning to work solely in the long T-shirts, mistaking them for short skirts or even kilts, like their Scottish brethren. Where I grew up, those tiny shorts are classified as "booty chokers" or "nut huggers." No self-respecting guy would wear them. Yet there they were, on the Irish. The shorts could easily have been a throwback to any one of the Celtics first sixteen championship teams, apropos for the Irish namesake team. Red Auerbach would have been proud to light up a cigar just seeing how much his era was still influencing my generation. I couldn't help but to visualize him puffing away, grinning at how the old uniforms were being used in this present-day draft.

Glancing down the row of melanin-less legs that first day, there was no doubt in my mind that these rookies were going to get sunburned. Not one of these guys wore sweat socks. They had on the black silky dress socks we Americans wear to church on Sunday mornings. The Irish work ensemble was complete with the brightest, most colorful pair of no-name sneakers imaginable. These were the kind of sneakers sold at the supermarket in the same aisle with Fourth of July decorations, multicolored beach balls, and white Styrofoam coolers.

The warehouse dock in mid-June was reminiscent of a pickup game of basketball. The JI rookies stood in a line with their backs against the wooden storage vaults, the same way I had on my first day. Each of the twenty crew chiefs were obligated to take out at least one new JI rookie and get them up to speed. No one knew the kids' names on that first day—there were too many new guys for Dominic to keep track, so he didn't even try. The chiefs who came in earliest had the first pick.

Hans, as always the first chief at work, took a close look at his choices. He knew his work day would be intense, so he took the most lean, athletic young man in the bunch. But this didn't guarantee anything. It was a crap shoot.

Being one of the first regulars at work that morning, I assumed I was working with Leroy. Leroy always showed up right on time—no earlier, no later. Since I was early, I had the chance to watch twenty minutes of this year's moving draft.

Gordon and Steve chose the plumpest young man in the group. The two had spent more than ten minutes on the side giggling, trying to rationalize the perfect team pick. Steve was salivating at this opportunity to break a new rookie. Although the season was far too early, Steve's evil grin told me he had chosen the best Thanksgiving turkey available. The fresh, portly young man would not have a chance with that day's weather reaching an expected high of ninety-three degrees. Their job was moving a law professor with an estimated one hundred and sixty book boxes from a fourth floor to a third floor. This husky young man would be Steve and Gordon's kicking stick until he collapsed. This was how they chose their pick.

Leroy didn't have the lead on today's move. Six men were selected to our crew, and Leroy was second. I was in the number five slot. The crew chief that day was a man who would easily have been mistaken for a lumberjack if he were wearing the red plaid jacket with the matching hat. His full grown scruffy beard was so thick that when he finished eating a sesame seed bagel, it looked like he had beard dandruff.

Standing around six feet, seven inches tall, Mr. Lawrence Matthews wore his New England Patriots football hat to cover his receded hairline. If he had been an oak tree, he would have been the sturdiest in the forest. When he smiles, eight teeth show on top. The rest of his uppers are missing. He is the only mover I have never seen in a bad mood, ever.

Mr. Matthews read our job's paperwork off to the side by himself. It called for a white glove crew, the top personnel available. A white glove crew knows exactly what needs to be accomplished without questions. We were moving one of the most renowned neurosurgeons in Boston. Daniel, the dwarf who conducted my hiring interview back in March, was also on the warehouse floor. He was Barney's head estimator/salesperson. He hand-picked Mr. Matthews for this job because the moving deity Ted was scheduled to impress another high end customer.

Daniel's tan slacks matched his tan necktie. He finished his ensemble with a classic white shirt and white sports jacket. Daniel huddled together with Mr. Matthews, Jacob, Brian and me to give us the lowdown.

He was excited. "This is a major job that we have to do well. This neurosurgeon from Mass General Hospital is one the five best neurosurgeons in America. I didn't get a chance to go by his home to do an onsite estimate due to his busy work schedule, but he says he has a lot of classic art work. Dr. James Spriggs, Sr., has taken out insurance on his belongings in the amount of three million dollars. If we do well with this job, we can pick up more jobs from other doctors. This is an angle we have been looking to explore for some time now."

"Do more doctors mean higher pay increases for us? Or do more doctors mean more money for Uncle Barney?" Leroy walked up, showing his tendency to make his presence known as he approached the five-man huddle.

Leroy always seemed to talk down to Daniel, both literally and figuratively, since Daniel was one of the few people Leroy was taller than. It was hard trying to decipher who had the larger Napoleonic complex. We were all working in the land of the giants.

Brian chimed in. "Daniel, Barney's working us like dogs. He has taken on more work so far this summer than ever before. Why is Barney working us like mules?" I hadn't noticed Brian's Caribbean accent until now.

"Barney's chasing after *Boston Magazine*'s 'Best of Boston' honors for this year," Daniel explained, filling us in on the front office's business objective. "We are in the top five in the running right now for the magazine's Top Movers in Boston Award. We just have to finish strong this summer until the results are announced in August. If we win the award, it should send Labor Day weekend rates through the roof." Daniel was excited as he explained.

"So Barney's plan is to work us like dogs so he can win an award?" Jacob mimicked Brian's accent.

Jacob and Brian are friendly enough co-workers, so Brian didn't take Jacob doing a bad Caribbean accent personally. Jacob was a recent graduate from UMass Amherst. His family owned greenhouses in the northern region of Massachusetts. Moving was Jacob's way of escaping the family business after graduation.

"That's fair to say," Daniel answered.

Leroy was the first in the huddle to catch Daniel's upward glance to the only window overlooking the warehouse. "Caesar is in the high tower, gentlemen," he warned.

Everyone's head turned to witness Barney in the window giving Dominic the head nod.

"Caesar must have words for his minions," Jacob said. "Will Caesar actually address us himself or will he utilize one of his henchmen already in the trenches with the peasants?" Jacob dropped the Caribbean accent to speak only to the huddle. Everyone looked sidelong at Daniel, waiting for him to speak.

The warehouse was full to capacity with movers. Hans, Steve, Ted and their crews were all in attendance. The head nod from Dominic must have been to let Barney know everyone had been accounted for.

Barney slid the window open, exposing a small stack of index cards in his right hand. Barney is a large man with a presence. Unfortunately, he is soft spoken. Barney would be granted job security in any position at a local museum or as a very tall librarian. This is probably why Barney decided to speak from "on high." The acoustics are incredible, especially if everyone else was being quiet. From that position in the window, it almost appeared as though Barney were speaking in a tunnel. With the wall of the bay doors on the left and the stacked rows of wooden storage vaults on the right, the eighty-plus workers stood at the middle of the tunnel to hear Caesar speak.

"Guys, I'm not going to take up to much of your time this morning. I know most of you already have full work days in front of you. Let me start by thanking all of you for your hard work and the valued customer care you give each one of our customers. I pride this company on hard, honest workers who are willing to give the best customer service available."

On cue, the door at Barney's left squeaked open. Someone should have sprayed oil on those hinges months ago. From our standpoint in the tunnel, we couldn't see who was in the doorway, but whoever it was made Barney's face flush crimson red. I had thought everyone was accounted for until I heard the familiar guttural voice.

"Hello, Big Bird! Who are you talking to? More importantly, where is my money?" Rhino-man was in attendance.

Everyone cheered up instantly. We couldn't help it. We didn't need to see the man—the voice was more than sufficient.

"Hi," Barney said, "I am trying to conduct a meeting right now. Can we take care of your matter after the meeting?" Barney tried to maintain his composure.

"What fucking meeting? Are you bullshitting me? Don't make me come up there!" Rhino-man issued the kind of promise Barney hated the most.

"If you come inside, you will surely see everyone else is in attendance. I want the men to be in sync with the goals of the company. This way we all, office and work staff, have a clear definitive direction for the course of the company." Barney's cracking voice echoed through the tunnel with the pride of a parent for the maturing adolescent.

"Screw you! You have five minutes to finish up. I want my money." The door slammed with a thunderous roar that echoed through the tunnel of listeners.

It was obvious from Barney's face that Rhino-man was the most agonizing thumbtack Barney had stepped on years ago. A manageable twinge in the beginning, Rhino-man had evolved into a pain worthy of a walking stick.

The smirks on the veterans' faces made it difficult to keep a straight face. We laughed to ourselves because Rhino-man had stolen Barney's moment yet again. It wasn't that Rhino-man was purposely trying to let all the air out of the Barney's party balloons. Rhino-man just had a way of making sure all the balloons Barney inflated had pictures of Rhino-man with his pants down making his butt smile. In less than one minute, Rhino-man's presence deflated Barney's morale and horrified the brand new Irish workers. The rest of the men silently cheered for the true slayer of giant men. Rhino-man just didn't care.

Barney's looked like he'd had his lunchbox taken away from him. He now had less than five minutes before the slayer would be back to collect his milk money. Barney elected to abandon the notes on his index cards. He was running short on time.

"Men, I apologize for the interruption. But I would like to return to the topic at hand so everyone can get started on the work day.

"We as a collective company are pursuing the award of being the top moving company, according to *Boston Magazine*. We are now one of the top three moving companies in the running. We are encouraging the office staff to contract each and every job when customers call. Let me clarify. The office can book the work, but we need you men to get the jobs done. We are receiving a lot of calls for late day jobs and even Sunday work. I need to know by a show of hands everyone who is willing to meet the challenge in the pursuit of being named the 'Best of Boston.'"

Hands quickly began to levitate toward the ceiling, but they were mostly from the newer employees. The veterans kept their hands by their waists. Working longer days to earn some magazine award was not quite the right incentive to get the veterans to work harder during the summer.

Leroy tapped me on the arm right before he blurted out, "So, are we receiving pay increases during this pay check or are we waiting until the next paycheck for helping *your* company compete for an award? There are only three experienced employees with their hands raised. In order to compete, I'm pretty sure you need your top movers readily available. All of us veterans have already taken note of the influx of work compared to last year. By law we truly only have to work one job per day that is consistent with a full shift. If we were unionized, we would receive our hour break per day plus a fifteen minute break per hour. We cannot be intimidated to work a second or an extra third moving job that exceeds the eight-hour day shift according to the Commonwealth of Massachusetts.

"So once again, we, your veteran moving staff, would like to have the question answered. Will we be receiving pay increases? Once the money is no longer an issue, we can all collectively pursue the challenge."

Everyone cheered. Leroy was good at getting everyone to place their cards on the table. The sentiments of the men were clearly heard. We all knew exactly what Barney was chasing—a legacy. Most of us students would be happy enough just to have ample work on a daily basis to make extra money.

Barney nodded. "You are absolutely right, Leroy. It is obvious you are not speaking solely for yourself. You are representing the men. Everyone's pay increases were given before this meeting. Therefore, this week's paychecks will reflect the changes. I am happy we can all work together at trying to become the best moving company in Boston, and hopefully all of Massachusetts thereafter." Barney's face was glowing.

Caesar was on high once again. He had tossed to the peasants a few gold coins. He stood proudly in the open window, overlooking the empire he had created. But just as Caesar began to address the crowd once more, the sliding window door began to close forcefully. We watched as Rhino-man escorted Barney in the direction of his office. Barney's five minutes had elapsed.

Leroy nudged my arm for me to bend down to his height. He didn't want anyone to overhear his thoughts.

"Never forget," he said, "the squeaky wheel is always the first to get oiled."

Our crew for that day was six men and two trucks. Mr. Matthews chose Liam, a young man from Cork City, as our sixth man. Liam was without a doubt the wiriest young man in the bunch. The green company shirt hung on his shoulders like a circus tent. Good thing there was a slight breeze outside to inflate his shirt. But if the overcast morning skies were to turn to rain, and if Liam were to get soaked, I think he would barely weigh one hundred and ten pounds. It is fair to say Liam would have gone last in that morning's draft had it not been for Mr. Matthews.

When we arrived at the neurosurgeon's building, the elegant doorman showed us where to park our trucks. The efficient concierge called our customer to inform him we were on the residential site.

Dr. James Spriggs, Sr., lived in a loft apartment at the Charlestown Navy Yard luxury condominium complex. This much information I gathered from the conversation as the elevator operator carried us to the sixth floor in the service elevator. That day just seemed like one of those days you shouldn't let get too far ahead of yourself or you are going to miss out. Since my vision is not that great, I figured I should try keeping my eyes opened wide and blinking less than usual. There was this intangible vibe in the air.

It was a good thing our job was so close, just across the Gilmore Bridge connecting Somerville to Charlestown. It was also a good thing Rhino-man had showed up to shorten that morning's company meeting. Leroy said the last time Barney had a meeting, it lasted nearly an hour. An hour filled with empty promises and pointless ideas on how to make the company run smoother. Leroy surmised the previous meeting had been an hour-long opportunity for Barney to hear how well his voice resonated along the tunnel of workers. He was convinced Barney truly enjoyed what he heard—himself.

Loft door 609 was answered by a distinguished looking gentleman. The salt-and-pepper full head of hair and matching beard lead me to believe the good Dr. Spriggs was in his late forties or early fifties. His wire-rimmed glasses made him look more like a college professor than a doctor. This was the very first neurosurgeon I had ever met. Titles have never meant much to me when it comes to meeting people.

My father always said, "A man is a man. He should be respected for being a man first. Every man opens his eyes when he wakes up and closes those same eyes when it's time to sleep. Everyone sits down on the toilet. We all leave behind an unripe scent. It doesn't matter how many matches you strike. It doesn't matter how many candles you light. You can spray the whole can of aerosol. You can hope you don't need to use all three at the same time. But the result is inevitable."

My father felt that any man who goes out of his way to inform you of his title, whether he is a lawyer, a boss, a police officer, a pastor or even a father, is using that title as a forbidding outstretched arm to distance himself from the next man. He is hiding behind his title. Respect the man who respects you for being a man.

"Who do you think you are?" he'd ask me.

"I am Kamaul David." I always held my head high making sure I locked eyes with the questioner.

"And who is Kamaul David?"

"I am a young man who is work in progress." I loved to try to zing my father.

"Wrong! The answer to the question, 'Who is Kamaul David?' should only be answered internally. The answer will change countless times before you are truly satisfied with the answer. But no one else needs to know who you feel you truly are. Do you feel you can only be explained by a title? You were raised to be much more than a one-word title. Your destiny will be the result of your collective actions over your lifetime. To use a title simply limits you to that one action.

"Most people can never answer the question, 'Who do you think you are?' People usually reply with a puzzled look, followed by, 'What do you mean?' That's because most people will never know who they truly are. Their journey will never take them down the path where they can explore the answer. Kamaul, no matter how far you travel in this life, never pretend, forget nor deny from where you come."

My father's words played in my head like one of his forty-five records. Daddy would place the needle on an album right after he came home on Friday evenings. The ritual of playing his records ended the work week, whether it was a good week or not. I always considered my father to be my first teacher—and my best teacher, and my favorite teacher.

Dr. Spriggs shook everyone's hand upon introduction.

"Before I take you fine gentlemen inside to show you around," he began, "I first want you all to understand that I am rarely here. I am a workaholic. I have not had an opportunity to prepare for this move today. Nor will I have the luxury to see this day through. I was paged moments ago by the hospital. I need to leave within the next ten minutes. One of my assistants will be here within a couple of hours to assist you if you have any questions."

Mr. Matthews took control. "Dr. Spriggs, since your time is restricted, why don't we go inside so you can show us all around? This would be the most efficient means of optimizing your remaining nine minutes. I am sure you have more pressing matters that require your attention."

"Perfect!" he exclaimed. "I placed a load of dirty dishes inside the dishwasher. The dishes should be near the completion of the drying cycle. But absolutely everything is going that isn't bolted down." With that being said, the six of us followed Dr. Spriggs into his abode.

Other than the kitchen off to the right, the rest of the loft was completely visible when we stepped in. Four columns spread throughout the room, keeping the ceiling from crashing down on us. We got our first glimpse of close to twelve hundred square feet of space, cluttered with stuff.

Without walls breaking up the view, it seemed like there was an endless amount of freestanding clutter. If someone told me a hurricane traveled up the east coast during the midnight hours and only tortured this one apartment, I might have believed it. If someone told me the local trash truck backed up and dumped everything on apartment number 609, again, I might have thought it was possible. It was a fifty-fifty toss up on whether the papers on the floor were useful to Dr. Spriggs or whether it was all trash. Every square foot of floor space was covered.

I leaned back to whisper to Leroy, "If it were January and I were blindfolded, I would think we were walking in a snow drift."

"No, instead it's June. It's hot as hell out there. In five more minutes my job description will change from mover to waste management employee of the month," Leroy answered back with a smile.

Overhearing us, Brian chimed muttered, "Imagine you were the patient of this guy. Would you let him surgically operate on you if you saw his apartment first?"

Mr. Matthews noticed the three of us floating behind everyone else. He knew what we were probably talking about. Mr. Matthews' baritone voice rang out, "Listen up! We are running short on the good doctor's time. I don't want any mistakes because something was not heard. Continue, Dr. Spriggs."

"Thank you, Mr. Matthews. As I was saying, the most important items in this loft are the artwork hanging on the walls. The artwork is priceless to me because it is all that I have left after a fire that took my worldly possessions away."

The twenty pieces of art each had a spotlight shining bright on it. The natural brick wall of the loft was the perfect backdrop to enhance each piece. Everyone's eyes locked on one original oil painting. It was more than a painting. It clearly had a story behind it.

"It's the colors that catch your eyes first," Dr. Spriggs said, sadly. "My wife Hilda worked tirelessly on the garden in the front of our house. She planted perennials, annuals, rose bushes, and every plant, shrub and tree that surrounded our two acre home. Hilda loved Massachusetts because the seasonal changes always gave her something to look forward to.

"That monstrosity of a house was my dream, my goal. I wanted everyone to see the fruit of my hard labor. Hilda believed the flowers from Mother Earth were the perfect complement to the home I wanted built.

"After the exterior of the house was complete, we traveled searching for original pieces of art that made us feel good on first sight. Hilda believed the interior of the home is parallel to an individual's soul. We worked hard together nurturing, building, fusing, complementing one another's souls. We traveled the globe in search of harmony. We purchased nineteen pieces that made us feel special when we looked at them.

"I went away lecturing for two weeks. The day before I was scheduled to return, I received a phone call. The authorities notified me that there had been a fire in my home. Everything was destroyed. Everything was lost, including my Hilda.

"Three months after I buried Hilda, I received another call. A private investigator asked me if I would be willing to meet with him. He had been contracted to find and return items to me from a third party. The investigator met me at a warehouse in South Boston.

"The investigator took me to a restoration artist. I entered the facility to see all nineteen pieces I had purchased with Hilda, resting on easels.

My emotions overwhelmed me instantly as I stood in the artist's studio crying. The artist informed me that he had been hired by my wife to make new frames for each piece of art in our collection. Each frame had to complement one another leading up to her gift to me for our twentieth anniversary—a portrait of us looking so happy standing in front of that big home.

"I didn't remember ever posing for any pictures in front of the house. All I knew was three months before the investigator contacted me I had lost it all. The only pictures I had were in the photo album in my mind. This artist gave me my Hilda back. Those nineteen pictures tell the story of two nurturing souls, so much in love. That one picture tells the story of a love and a life I will never know again. But I'm all right, because my Hilda is back with me."

The six of us walked out the front door to the service elevator. I wasn't the only person with a sudden case of the sniffles. I used the knuckle of my index finger to wipe away a few tears. Mr. Matthews was the last person to step onto the somber elevator.

The doors to the elevator closed. We were descending when Mr. Matthews spoke without looking at anyone.

"I come to work every day to help people. I will never tell you I love this work. You will never hear me say I hate this work either. You will always hear me say I respect what we do every day. I respect you gentlemen for helping me to assist other people every day. Some people are in need of more help than others. Let us do our job right this one time and take home the knowledge that we helped someone that had to leave us to lend his expertise to help someone else."

"It seems as is everybody has a story to tell." Those words were uttered from the newest member of our team. Liam seemed to be catching on quick.

Daddy used to ask me, as early as I can remember, at least twice a week, "Son what do you want to be when you grow up?"

I would shrug my shoulders and answer honestly, "I don't know, Daddy. What do you think I should be?" I never answered by saying a doctor, a lawyer or anything like that. With all the books and catalogs he received from NASA, I knew exactly what Daddy wanted me to be. He never answered me back though. So we played this game for years.

One day I remember Daddy asking the same question. "Kamaul, what do you want to be when you grow up?"

For some reason I looked back up at him through my taped up glasses and said, "I want to be a garbage collector."

The puzzled look was followed by a smile. "Why do you want to be a garbage collector son?"

I just shrugged and said, "Why not, Daddy?"

My father placed his large hands on my head and said, "Well, you be whatever your heart tells you to be. But first you go to college and graduate. And if you still feel that you want to be a garbage man, then you should be the best garbage man you can be."

"How am I supposed to decipher the clean clothes from the dirty clothes from the trash among the clothes?" I pulled on a clean pair of Latex gloves from underneath the bathroom sink. My question was to no one in general.

"Do what I've been doing," Jacob replied anyway. "Throw everything in a box and just give the approximate location where it was." Jacob was packing the area around the desk. His words were a bit muffled due to the blue surgical mask he found and now wore over his nose and mouth. He also had on Latex gloves to try to keep the dust from the books from starting up his allergies. There were many, many books. And, there were as many loose papers scattered on the floor as there were in the binders on the bookshelves.

"You should probably make up two separate boxes," Leroy suggested helpfully. "Then after you sniff the armpits and examine the shirt collars for sweat stains, it will make your decision clearer which of the two appropriate boxes the clothes belong." Leroy laughed because he was packing the kitchen and at least all the dirty dishes had been cleaned in the dishwasher. The rest of us were not so lucky.

"Hey, Kamaul, I don't think the doctor was too concerned if his clothes were clean or not," Brian said. "Did you see before he left to go to the hospital how Dr. Nasty grabbed the nearest shirt on the floor next to his foot? I don't know if you guys were watching but the shirt he grabbed had a huge coffee stain on the back. Dr. Nasty looked at it as if it were no big deal." Brian packed away the electronics in the sitting area. We could all tell by his disgusted look that he was not in the mood to touch too much dirt.

Packing boxes is such a monotonous task. First, you tape up the bottom of the box with three strips of tape across the seams. Then, you fill the box until it appears to be overflowing. After forcing the flaps closed, you tape up the top of the box with three more strips of tape across the seams to ensure the box is closed. Finally, you should write on the top as well as the side the general area where the contents of the box had been. The more experienced the packer, the faster the boxes seem to accumulate.

It was a little after eleven o'clock in the morning before we even knew it. There was so much packing to be done. Everyone just seemed lost in completing their part of the overall task of packing. Dr. Spriggs's bed rested in the middle of the loft apartment. Mr. Matthews carefully tended to the artwork. We all watched each other's progress from where we worked. There was just no reason to comment. No one wanted to slow down the momentum. More importantly, we were getting close to lunch time. I was definitely hungry. It is always the call of the crew chief to decide when we all go to lunch.

"Leroy, what are you grazing on in the kitchen?" I was just placing the third strip of tape over the seam of another completed box when I noticed Leroy sneak his hand into a clear plastic bag. From my angle it was hard to tell what he was stuffing his face with but it was obviously good.

"Mind your own business. You don't see me watching you working in your area. Kamaul, develop tunnel vision and focus on your task at hand."

"How can you eat anything in this apartment when this place is so dirty?" Jacob yelled from over in the office area. He wanted to contribute to break up the packing monotony.

"What do you mean how can he? Leroy is always eating," I said. "Leroy only wears the leather fanny pouch around his waste to hold his stomach in place. Have you ever witnessed Leroy taking his sweat soaked T-shirt off at the end of a job? Leroy doesn't have a six pack—he carries around a mini keg all day long. He's lucky this is the 1990s and not the Prohibition years. Leroy may have been accidentally batted in the belly by the police thinking he was trying to smuggle alcohol under his shirt." I have been picking at Leroy's miniature keg belly ever since I first saw Leroy expose his frame when removing a wet T-shirt.

The laughter filled the open room fast. All eyes were on Leroy as he shoveled another handful of sustenance into his frowning mouth while showing me the middle finger of his free hand.

Mr. Matthews addressed Leroy, "Share what ever it is you're eating with the rest of our dysfunctional family."

Leroy purposely walked by me to share the half-eaten bag of pretzels with Mr. Matthews first. He mouthed a couple of three and four letter profane curse words in my direction as he passed me. It was fine with me—I didn't take it personally.

Everyone grabbed a handful of pretzels except Brian. Brian waved Leroy away as he approached the living room area and kept muttering phrases about calling the local television station on Dr. Nasty. Some investigative reporter could do a behind-the-scenes piece on how doctors live away from the hospital. Brian thought Geraldo Riviera would be the best journalist to expose the truths of the "Dirty Doctors." By the time Leroy reached me, there was nothing more than salt and pretzel granules in the bottom corner of the bag.

"I think I saw a pack of rice cakes in the cupboard if you're hungry. Rice cakes go well with you guys with six packs. Pretzels are best served with a keg." Leroy patted his hair-covered fleshy barrel affectionately.

The next two minutes passed with Leroy standing in the kitchen, hiding behind a fort of packed boxes, tossing miniature white rice Frisbees in my direction. I had just finished taping up my last box when I felt something land on the top of my head. Five voices suddenly burst into a cheer. I reached up to remove the rice cake from the top of my head. Turning my body around towards the direction of Leroy's fort, I locked eyes with him, took the rice cake from my hand and promptly ate it. I never realized rice cakes were so damn good. But everything is good when you're starving.

"Mr. Matthews, I'm done packing up the bedroom area." I used my tongue to search my mouth for remnants of rice cake. From what I could see, everyone was just about finished packing.

"We're going to take lunch in forty-five minutes, so either break down the bed or wrap the furniture in pads." Mr. Matthews was working on his last framed piece of art.

I opted for the bed. The toolbox was in the hallway just outside the apartment door with our other supplies. Grabbed a rice cake off the floor on my way, I whipped the small diskette in Leroy's direction. Leroy let out a yelp as the white flying saucer smacked the back of his neck.

It took me all of ten seconds to retrieve the toolbox. Carrying around the toolbox gave me purpose. I enjoy taking furniture apart so I know then how to reconfigure it at the new location. I admit I'm not the fastest with a socket wrench. But I love to disassemble and reassemble anything.

"Oh, God! Who gave Turtle the toolbox?" Jacob always got frustrated with me whenever we worked together. He even hid the tools from me on one job when I wanted to disassemble a table. Jacob didn't find it funny when I instead used the edge of a dime as a replacement for a flathead screwdriver. I learned that from MacGuyver.

"The bed is in my area," I retorted. "You just heard Mr. Matthews tell me to break down the bed or wrap furniture. I choose to break down the bed. I'm just following my instructions." I hated been called Turtle. Since I was a rookie, nicknames from the veterans are a given. This one really irritated me, though, because I was pushing myself to be faster. It was just taking time.

"I'll take the bed apart so it doesn't take all day. It irks me to even listen to Turtle with the toolbox." Jacob headed around the obstacle course of boxes towards the bed.

"Jacob, are you done with the office?" Leroy asked.

"No. I'm almost done."

"So then, why are you concerned with the bedroom? Everyone spends way too much time watching what the next person is doing instead of fulfilling their individual roles." Leroy was right.

"I refuse to watch Turtle either disassemble nor reassemble anything while I'm working today." Jacob was closing the gap between us.

"Did I do something to piss you off at me?" I spoke coolly, matter-of-factly. "Because you do realize you are about to step on my toes."

"You pissed me off by picking up the toolbox. You suck with the toolbox. You are horrible, Turtle!" Jacob was raising his voice. "And when I step on your toes you will know it."

What I did next could only have come from the fight in me. I learned it from the best.

A few years after getting glasses at the age of seven, I had to stick close to my Uncle Deek. He was my mother's youngest sibling of Grandmama's four children. The formality of using the names Auntie Baye and Uncle Deek when I addressed them in conversation wasn't forced on me by my mother and grandmother, as it was for my father's brothers and sisters. I was taught to be respectful, but in this case it wasn't forced. Deek was more of a big brother than an uncle. Since Deek was five years older than me, I was his responsibility when we were outside.

I remember entering Grandmama's first floor apartment one summer day while Deek was eating French fries.

"K.D.," he asked, "what are you doing back inside? I thought you were playing kickball in the alley." We played kickball every day in the alley way between Building Six and Building Ten on Castle Gate Road.

Uncle Deek never wanted anybody to ask for or touch his fries when he was eating. Once Auntie Baye took a couple of fries while Deek went to the bathroom. When he came back to the table, he noticed the fries missing right away. He automatically grabbed in turn into the palm of his hand the faces of me, Bird, and my cousin Scoop to smell our breath. When we appeared clean of the fry theft, he naturally took off after his older sister Baye.

Auntie Baye had a head start. She was already turning the corner onto Blue Hill Ave. when Uncle Deek ran out the apartment building door. Deek gave chase, only to realize upon reaching the street corner that Auntie Baye was waving goodbye to him from the back window of a local bus. So disgusted was he when he returned to the kitchen table, that he threw away his entire plate of fries. He posted himself on the front stoop to wait for her return. He waited until twelve o'clock midnight, when Grandmama finally made him come inside. Auntie Baye stayed away for two days waiting for the hothead to calm down.

After getting my glasses, I became used to getting picked on. When it became too much, then I told Deek. "Deek, Angelo punched me. Then he took my turn to kick the ball. He said if I came in and told you he took my turn, he would kick my ball on the rooftop."

"K.D., people will always mistreat you if you never stand up for yourself. Sometimes, if someone mistreats you, you have to turn around and get them back right away. If you don't, they will only continue. If they throw a rock at you, you have to turn around and hit them back, but with a brick. That way they will think twice before picking up a rock to throw in your direction. I know you don't like to hit people because you're scared they might break your glasses. But the next time someone hits you, trust me, hit them back with all your might."

"Can you go get my kickball?"

"No, I'm eating."

"Can I have some of your french fries?"

"No, go play kickball or bring your ball inside."

So I went back outside. I waited for my turn again. Everyone quickly dispersed when a summer shower fell. I seized the opportunity to grab my ball and wait inside the hallway of Building Ten for the rain to stop. Angelo lived on the top floor, so he ran into the same building.

"Give me the ball so I can bounce it!" Angelo demanded.

There were four other kids standing in the hallway including my cousin Scoop. Since Scoop lived upstairs on the second floor, we were pretty much always together. Before I had a chance to reply, Angelo swung a blow to my left shoulder. Scoop was the same age as Angelo, two years my senior. It would have been nice if Scoop would have stood up for me, but he was pretending to be captivated by one of the many stains on the hallway ceiling.

It was safe to say Scoop didn't see me get punched. The scaredy cat was too afraid he was going to get punched next, which usually happened anyway. Scoop and I never shirked when it was time to fist fight each other. Deek and Meso, our other cousin who lived just around the corner, coaxed Scoop and me into 95% of our fights. Since I was smaller than Scoop, Deek and Meso coached me on how to win most of our fights. They would yell out for me to bite Scoop whenever Scoop was getting the best of me by putting me in a headlock. Since I'm a good study, I followed my instructions until my combatant would begin to cry and run upstairs.

One time Scoop and I were fighting and Deek handed me an orange. Meso told me to throw it. I threw the orange without hesitation and hit the bull's eye. The orange smacked Scoop dead in his left eye. He ran upstairs crying and later that night came down with a black eye. Scoop's mother chased Deek and her nephew Meso for two blocks until she caught them both and beat the mess out of them.

Fighting outside the safety net of the family circle was completely different. Seeing my cousin still studying the ceiling, I forcibly extended my right arm back in the direction of my slightly older assailant, Angelo.

The shot that I retaliated with hit Angelo in the dead center of his chest and he gasped. "Why you hit me so hard, K.D.? I just wanted to bounce your ball." He was rubbing his chest area where I struck him.

I made up a new rule. "Every time you hit me, I'm going to hit you back from now on." I said as I snatched my ball back.

And that did it. From that day forward, Angelo became a good friend of mine. If you looked up, you would see us jumping from one rooftop to the one next door. We would go to Franklin Park golf course to play along with the other neighborhood kids. Angelo taught me how to caddie and shag balls to earn some extra summer candy money. When the other neighborhood kids wanted to fight or pick at me, Angelo was the first to stand at my side. We fought and played side by side until we got older and grew apart.

The fighter came out in dealing with Jacob.

"Actually, Jacob, I may not. I started wearing steel toe boots long before working here."

"Turtle, look down. You have Nikes on your feet. You only wear Air Jordan or Nike every day, everybody knows that about you. Do you even think before you open your mouth?" Jacob shook his head in the most belittling way.

The toolbox sat on top of one of the closed boxes I had packed. Jacob brushed passed me and pulled the mattress off the frame, standing it up against one of the room's support columns. He turned around quick to do the same to the box spring. He had a determined look. I knew I was standing on the tracks with a bigger train approaching fast.

Now the box spring was with the mattress against the column. I hadn't moved, except now I had the toolbox in my hands. Jacob had awakened both the Animal and the Beast the moment he brushed passed me.

"Give me the toolbox!" Jacob demanded.

"I'm definitely going to give you the toolbox without a shadow of doubt," I agreed. "Before I give what you have coming to you, can I ask you a couple of questions?"

"Yeah, go ahead." Jacob's eyes were fixed on the toolbox.

I bent down, placing the toolbox on the floor underneath my left foot. Never losing eye contact, I stood up showing Jacob both of my hands were free. I felt the group of ten eyes watching me. My adrenaline was charged.

"Have you ever held a baseball bat in your hands before?" I started. "Silly question—of course you have. However, I bet you don't know the measured length of your hand grip when you're holding a baseball bat while staring at the opposing pitcher, right before he throws the ball across home plate."

"I don't have time for this stupid question. We're moving furniture, idiot." Jacob bent down motioning towards the toolbox.

"Do not! Do not take your eyes off me." Jacob abruptly stood erect in response to my tone. I continued, "I'm trying to play fair here. I'm going to give you what you deserve after I ask you my last three questions." The Beast wasn't finished yet.

"Guys, you should stop before this gets serious." Some voice with a Caribbean accent was speaking, somewhere in the room. But my tunnel vision was focused on the individual in front of me. We had escalated past serious when the first question was asked.

Jacob's eyes were locked onto mine. "No, I don't know the measurement of my hand around a fucking baseball bat. I do wish I had a baseball bat right now. Do you know your hand measurement, Turtle?" Jacob had fire in his tone.

I answered with a satisfied smile. "I actually do know the measurement." I flashed the palm of my hands open to show Jacob before I placed my hands around my invisible baseball bat I held to the slight right just below my chin. With cupped knuckled hands stacked upon one another, I said, "My hands are a little large. Stacked together they measure just about eight and a half inches when my adrenaline is peaking."

"You have two more questions?" Jacob's patience was wearing thin.

"Have you ever heard me use the term 'two hands and a little bit' before this very moment?"

"No, Turtle. I don't give a shit about two hands and a little bit. You have one question left, Turtle." A smirk was forming in the creases of Jacob's face.

"My name is Kamaul. My last question is simple. Every morning you are dropped off by a curly brunette driving a red Honda Accord with a New York license plate. She stands about five feet, six inches tall. She's not hot but she puts you in mind of the cute girl next door. Her ass is a little flat, but she has the perkiest C-cup breasts. Damn near look augmented."

The smirk had vanished from Jacob's face. Rage was starting to replace the initial disbelief in his eyes. I could hear the crew inside the apartment moving in closer.

Continuing in the same nonchalant tone, I said, "Kelly works Tuesday through Saturday nights closing down Red Bone's B.B.Q. joint in Davis Square Somerville." Sadly, I shook my head. "Kelly's been so depressed lately. She graduated from UMass at Amherst three years ago. Moved down here to Boston to be with you, and you still haven't proposed. Kelly's been doing a lot of crying and even more drinking after she drops you off at work in the morning." It's amazing how speaking in a soft monotone voice captures the attention of an audience. "Oh yeah, my last question. Did you know Kelly used to play against my co-ed softball team back in 1991 when I was up at Amherst? Kelly actually gave me the nickname 'two hands and a little bit.' Kelly's a damn good pitcher."

The Beast in me began to smile a devilish grin. I took two steps backwards relinquishing my foothold on the toolbox. I never let my eye contact with Jacob lapse for a second. But Jacob had lost control of the situation. His mind was racing with questions intermingled with rage. Jacob picked up the toolbox, seething.

As Jacob turned his back to walk around the bed, Leroy asked the question on all five of their minds. "What does 'two hands and a little bit' mean, Kamaul?"

Keeping my eyes fixed on Jacob, I answered, "There has never been a reason to explain this to another man. The full effect lies in the seeing, not in the telling. But because you asked me, Leroy, and you will never visually witness it, let me explain." The Animal picked up where the Beast left off.

"The baseball bat is actually a metaphor." I placed my hands back around my own personal invisible "baseball bat." My stacked hands slowly began to descend from chest height to the area approximately three inches below my navel.

"When it's time to play, I like to show off my bat by placing both hands around it. Even still, there is always a little bit more bat left uncovered. The more excited I become, the more of an adrenaline rush I get, the more a little bit expands to a little bit more. Hence the nickname, 'two hands and a little bit.'"

The plastic toolbox fell to the wooden floor like a bad habit. Jacob came charging fast around the bed frame. "I'm going to beat that metaphor out of you!" he shouted.

My four co-workers stood their ground between Jacob and me. Leroy had the biggest grin on his face. I guess he enjoyed my answer.

"Enough is enough gentlemen. Let's go to lunch." Mr. Matthews stopped Jacob's struggling to reach me with a single extended hand. This was an easy task for the limb of such a great oak tree.

"We are not done here yet, you fucking Turtle!"

"I told you already, Jacob, I always wear my boots. And my name is Kamaul."

Fuming, Jacob left through the apartment door with his face red hot. Brian and Liam trailed Jacob, attempting to calm him down. The apartment door closed behind the three of them.

"Did you shag his bird? Did you give her that two bits and a hand job thing you said?" Leroy was grinning from ear to ear.

"It doesn't matter. Right now all Jacob knows is that he wants to try to hurt me bad. The only thing I can do is defend myself. So when we get outside, let whatever is meant to happen follow."

"I told you, Lawrence," Leroy crowed. "I told you my boy was something. He was definitely a little too graphic on the overall raunchy scale. But I told you he can withstand the heat." Leroy was shaking his index finger in my direction.

"Here Leroy, take this and buy you three guys lunch on me. Make sure Jacob is calm before he comes back up here. Make sure he fully comprehends the importance of completing this job in a professional way upon your return from lunch." Mr. Matthews handed Leroy a twenty dollar bill.

"Are you coming?" Leroy had a hand on the doorknob.

"No, I want to talk to Kamaul for a minute. We'll do lunch up here."

The apartment door latch clicked when Leroy left. The room was silent as Mr. Matthews and I stood with five feet of full boxes between us.

"Kamaul," he began, "You are an antagonist! You found an interesting way to remain relaxed while you were pushing Jacobs's buttons. But I think it was the cocky, arrogant smile you gave Jacob that pushed him over the top." Mr. Matthews's brief character analysis hit the mark.

"It's a defense mechanism, Mr. Matthews," I explained. "I've been playing the dozens, trading insults, since I was seven years old. I spent most of my youth being verbally and physically assaulted by the same people who were supposed to be on my team. Now, I play by my own rules of the game. I find it humorous to verbally assault an opponent to the point where they want to beat me up. You can't grow up where I have without knowing a good defense sets up your offense."

"What happens if Jacob punches you in the mouth the minute you mention Kelly's name?" asked Mr. Matthews.

"Well, if Jacob does actually throw a punch at me first, then I would be in the right to officially whoop his ass without hesitation. Jacob was the one becoming more disrespectful the closer he got to me. The main game from the moment Daniel gave us the work order this morning was to remain professional. Jacob wasn't being professional. And, Mr. Matthews, no disrespect to you as the crew chief, but you had a moment or two where you should have sent him back to packing his area but you neglected to do so. Why?"

"You're absolutely right. Under most circumstances I would have stopped Jacob the moment he left his area. I wanted to see how you responded under adverse conditions. It was my opportunity to see if you would keep your head. Most people love to dish out a barrage of insults, but they usually can't accept it when they are the ones being pummeled. I wanted to see if Leroy was correct in giving you the praise he has about you being a good guy." Mr. Matthew's smile was reminiscent of a teacher giving back a corrected test paper with a good grade.

Yet standing there, I just didn't feel like I passed any test. "See, Mr. Matthews, I'm black—you're not. You have no clue how it feels to have to assimilate. Every day I show up to work, I have to assimilate. I wear the same green work shirt that everyone else wears every day, yet I'm viewed as threatening because I work out and I'm a little more muscular than the man standing next to me. I have to deal not only with my coworkers but also customer insecurities. I usually remain quiet so everyone around me can feel more at ease. I'm not a difficult person to understand. I am a complex individual with simple goals. All I want to do is earn enough money to pay for my college education on my own.

"Every day I push myself to be known as the hard-working coworker. I get a chance to relax, to be myself when I finally take off the vomit green shirt and ride away at the end of the day. Removing that shirt means removing my mindset from another day of assimilating. My coworkers don't want to know who Kamaul is. My coworkers ask me questions to see how well Kamaul fits into the stereotype they already have for a young black male from Cambridge. But the truth of the matter, Mr. Matthews is I'm not from Cambridge. My building blocks were formed in Grove Hall, Dorchester. Those are two totally different sides of the bridge. Survival on either side of the bridge has been instilled in me.

"The other tough part, Mr. Matthews, is, if I would have started a shoving match after Jacob had brushed past me, I would have been the one reprimanded. If I hit Jacob first, I'm the one viewed as the angry, black, uncontrollable mover. I run the possibility of being viewed as the malignant cancer. We both know a malignant cell must be removed.

"A rookie assaults a proven veteran while on an important job. The office and Barney would probably know what happened out here long before we got back to the warehouse. No matter what, I wouldn't be in a position to win today. Nor am I in a position to win now. This is one of the main reasons I tend to just keep to myself while at work, Mr. Matthews."

He listened respectfully, but all he said was, "Kamaul, why do you keep calling me 'Mr. Matthews'? Lawrence is my first name. You can call me Lawrence like every one else."

I shook my head. "I call you 'Mr. Matthews' out of respect. I was taught to address my elders by their surname to show respect for them. For many of my parents' friends, I have never uttered their first names nor would I feel comfortable doing so. It just sounds comfortable to me to call you 'Mr. Matthews' since this is the first time we have worked together."

"I can understand that," he replied. "However, your feelings as to why you need to keep to yourself may be more of a problem. When you're moving, you are part of a team. There are those in the company who could be your friends if you allow them into your world."

My head again shook "no." "Number one, I have no friends. There are a couple of guys that I'm cool with like Leroy and Rhino-man. We all show an overall respect for each other. All of my life I have wanted to be friends with the people around me. The reality is, everybody I meet will either like me or not like me. It's just personal preference.

"I don't need to be liked on a personal level to do my job. I would rather those working alongside me simply respect my work than like me personally. For example, I had thought Jacob and I worked well together before today. But today showed me how much stored up anger Jacob has toward me. I'm not a mind reader so I'm shocked to discover this. Jacob could have pulled me to the side on any number of occasions to tell me what I do that bothers him. Yet he waits until today to show me up in front of all you guys.

"So, I have no choice but to view working here from a business stand-point if I'm going to make enough money to pay for my education. Now I have a new unresolved issue to deal with, called Jacob."

"If I were you I wouldn't worry too much about Jacob. He comes from a family of florists. What is he going to do, assault you by giving you a bunch of weeds?" Mr. Matthews began to laugh. He left at that point to go downstairs to the deli shop. He treated me to lunch, too.

The game inside the game is always interesting. Who is the puppet? Who is the puppet master? Does the puppet master actually have dangling strings connected to his limbs? If so, who is controlling him? Most people when they get in the position of authority use their power frivolously.

Guys on the trucks love to play catch up with their friends when they finally get the opportunity to work together. They don't care who is listening when they begin to vent. These men gossip way more than most women I know. For that reason alone, I keep my personal business out of the mouth of others. But it hasn't stopped me from listening when my co-workers like Jacob complain about their troubles at home. I like to observe with my ears for some future date. That's why others have given me the nickname, "The File Keeper." I had never "played baseball" with Kelly. I just made it all seem probable.

I had asked for a turkey and cheese sandwich with everything on it. I started to wonder if I were actually going to eat the sandwich because I wasn't feeling too trustful of Mr. Matthews either for the role he had played as puppet master between Jacob and me. But the growling in the pit of my empty belly told me what I would do.

I decided to keep myself busy until the food got there. I opened up the toolbox and grabbed the socket set of wrenches, finding the correct metric fit to loosen the bolts on the bed. First, I needed to unscrew the quarter inch plywood board laying across the length of the bed frame. The board was being used as extra support on top of the three cross slats. Unscrewing the twenty-three-inch drywall screws gave me some time to reminisce.

My sophomore year at Boston Latin School (1988—1989) saw the construction of the new gymnasium. Due to the construction, the sopho-more class was sent across the street to Massachusetts College of Arts on Huntington Ave. for classes. Since we were the eldest class over at the new facility, we automatically became celebrities. We didn't have to look up to the juniors and seniors because we rarely saw them.

Even after being let back on the team by Coach Ramsey, I ended up getting kicked off along with eleven others before the season's last game because of failing grades. Eight of these students were members of my hanging crew, my home boys. We were a brotherhood, a support system. We bonded over fighting to survive at Boston Latin.

We knew we had the aptitude to be there among the rest of the brightest students Boston had to offer. Pride stood in the way of using the tutors the school provided for free. None of us got the help we so desperately needed. It just wasn't cool to need a tutor. I can say now, we were fools.

My classes consisted of Latin, Spanish, English (of course), and for some inexplicable reason I elected to take Ancient Greek as well. Math, computers, physics, health science, economics, gym, and history rounded off the rest of my curriculum. It was fair to say that if you did not spend at a minimum of three hours each night on homework, you were going to flunk out.

During football season however, I was lucky enough to finish my assignments for the following day. It was to no surprise that my first term grades were the first six letters of the alphabet except the letter E, with the fourth and sixth letters getting some special repetition.

Those entering Boston Latin can be accepted in either the seventh or ninth grades. I came for ninth grade. Two of my closest friends, Sparrow and Fellis, had been attending since seventh grade. They had been tight since the two of them decided to repeat the seventh grade together three years before I met them.

Fellis had been failing from the beginning of seventh grade. Even though Sparrow was passing all of his classes with no problems, he decided to fail them all too so Fellis wouldn't be by himself the following school year. Ever since I met Sparrow and Fellis, they have been as thick as thieves.

Sparrow's birth name is Trevor Redenbacher. I asked but he claims he's not related to the famous popcorn family. His family is from the island of Montserrat.

Now, in tenth grade, the eight members of our sophomore class hung out every day after practice trading insults at Al's Pizza Shop. The joke fest didn't officially begin until everyone had at least their first slice of pizza on the table.

Trevor fired first. "K, you'd think you would be a little bit faster with your legs having so very little meat in the calf area. Every time I look at your legs during practice, I just get an immediate taste for chicken. I just want to run into the pizza shop and tell Al to fry me up an order of chicken wings." The good-natured laughter from the crowd was a sign of a sure hit.

"Trevor, I have to admit you are a speedy boy out on the field. But answer me one question, why is your nose so damn flat?"

Since Trevor had his mouth full from his single bite of food, I continued my attack.

"Is your nose aerodynamic? Your nostrils must have some wind efficient qualities allowing you to move faster."

"K, the girls think this nose is sexy. At least that's what your little groupie Miss Preston was saying to me on the phone last night." Trevor kissed both of his index fingers, tapping his nose before firing both barrels of his finger pistols in my direction. He naturally started to high-five the members of the crew.

"Oh, wow!" The other fellows yelled out and grimacing, signifying it was time for the gloves to be taken off. If we had been on the football field a yellow flag would have been tossed into the air.

There were a couple of girls that were linked to me as friends. Miss Kathleen Preston was the only girl in our class whose name actually made it inside the pizza shop after the school bell rang at the end of the day. You had to be a special girl to be mentioned in Al's Pizza Shop.

Everyone respected Miss Preston because she dressed and carried herself with class and not at all like a sixteen-year-old. The jealous girls referred to her as the well-dressed ant—skinny and dark skinned. The fellows referred to her as a fudgesicle—Kathleen was definitely cool enough to hang with any crowd. How could you resist the temptation of a frozen dark chocolate treat? All the fellows knew she was a catch. So far, I had been the one lucky enough to get her attention.

When class was boring as all hell, the one thing you could do to look busy to the teacher was writing notes. I would write notes in my study class to pass to various people in between classes. Sometimes I would come back to my locker to find a few notes stuffed inside my locker. But all the notes in the world meant nothing unless I received at least one from Kathleen Preston. We wrote each other a couple times a day.

One day in Greek class, a substitute teacher maintained that the New Kids on the Block was the best singing group to emerge from Boston. Kathleen and I both jumped on the teacher and the rest of the class in disagreement. I had personally attended the same parochial school with the youngest member of the New Kids. I was happy for his success, but his singing couldn't compare with Ralph Tresvant, the lead singer for New Edition. Even if Ralph had a cold and Ricky Bell had to take over, New Edition would vocally be stronger. And don't even talk with me about the dance routines.

Kathleen and I held our ground on the agreement that the singing group New Edition was the most talented group to come out of Boston. This cemented our friendship. Then after class, I debated with her over whether New Edition was a better group with Bobby Brown or without him. Our passionate debates crossed many spirited topics, but always evolved back to a discussion of classic rhythm-and-blues ballads.

The note bait I used to keep her attention was a game where we both wrote down the first verse to a classic R&B song. A note might go like this:

Why do I keep my mind
On you all the time,
And I don't even know you?

Why do I feel this way?
Thinking about you every day,
And I don't even know you?

Take me in your arms
Thrill me with all of your charm.

The recipient of the note had to figure out the song's title and artist before the end of the day. Kathleen was good. She would usually write back in response that the group Bloodstone recorded the song "Natural High." Some days she even named the year the song was recorded. She was always right.

So, it was safe to say the two of us spent a lot of time together becoming closer. Since Miss Preston and Trevor were good friends, she confided to him her feelings for me.

So now at the pizza shop, Trevor left me no choice. The words automatically passed my lips: "Yo Mama! After yo mama saw yo face at birth she must have tried to smother yo ugly ass to death. Yo mama must wear glasses too, because she picked up an encyclopedia instead of a pillow and flattened your nose to hell. Now your nose looks like a god-damn arrow. You shouldn't be known as Trevor anymore, you speedy, arrow-nosed bastard. We should all call you 'Sparrow' to remind you of the attempted murder your mother tried to commit. Looking in the mirror every day must surely be an unpleasant reminder." So the nickname stuck. Even Al, the owner of the pizza shop, started calling Trevor "Sparrow."

Fellis wanted a nickname so bad after that, he would purposely try to play the dozens, trading insults with us everywhere we went—in class, at lunch, in the hallways. Fellis was born on the island of Cape Verde, off the coast of Africa, the oldest child of five siblings. I never felt comfortable making fun of Fellis outside of the eight of us on the football team. Fellis' complexion is beige but covered with dark brown freckles. Every time I saw Fellis, I would picture him pouncing out of a tree like a leopard. When I said that joke one day, Fellis' facial expression fell hard and fast. It reminded me of how I used to look when I wore my thick glasses. So I made the mental note to never verbally attack Fellis in that way again. You never apologize when you play the dozens. But when you can tell you hit too hard, you just don't do it again.

Getting kicked off the football team sucked, but there were eight members of our crew in the same predicament. We should have walked into the tutor's office, but we didn't. Instead, we all went over to Al's Pizza Shop to figure it out. Sparrow and Fellis said they knew how to get us out of the dilemma. Since they had been in this situation before, we played follow the leader. It was really more like the blind leading the blind.

While huddled at three pushed-together tables, we watched Sparrow and Fellis go to work. We all watched in amazement as they changed their D's and F's to B's. First, they blotted the report cards with the tips of fresh erasers and the altered the results. Within minutes we all had new report cards. Taking the advice of teammates who had also failed wasn't the most ingenious idea, but I needed to buy some time. I just needed the Band-Aid to stay on long enough to keep me out of summer school.

The altered report card went over well with the folks. I also knew that my father, being who he was, would be at this school within the next month to follow up with my teachers at the next parent/teachers meeting. So I buckled down and studied. But I still didn't get a tutor. There were so many days I sat in my classes lost. It felt impossible to grasp all of the knowledge I was being force fed. The only class I understood from the very beginning was, of all things, Greek. It was easy because Kathleen and Fellis were in the class. The three of us studied together vigorously. Greek was the only class in which I received a legitimate A.

I read as much as six hours a night trying to catch up, and it was stressing me out. I tried hard, although I felt I was getting my behind handed to me. Latin and Spanish were the subjects I just couldn't grasp. I got to the point that whenever I was called on by the teacher to participate, I would breakout in an instantaneous sweat.

Self-doubt was creeping up on me. I figured I was getting close to becoming that statistic from the first day of orientation. I remembered the smiles on the Asian students' faces when they saw me sitting to their left or right. There was no doubt in their smirk who was going to be the one who didn't make it to graduation. Two weeks after the football season ended so abruptly, two members from my football crew transferred to less stressful high schools.

My teacher for my Latin class wore eyeglasses, a white shirt, a black tie and trousers and resembled Master Yoda from Star Wars. He had given us a book to read for a major test coming up after Thanksgiving vacation. I was horrible at Latin. I had to force myself to memorize the conjugation of verb tenses in this dead language.

Wednesday night before Thanksgiving, my mother and sister were over my Grandmama's house getting ready. My father was out and about visiting friends. I was home alone. I took the book we'd been given to the bathroom to start on the hopeless task of reading yet another Latin book I was sure I wouldn't understand. I thumbed the book open. I didn't even know the title because the book had a brown paper cover on it. This was the school system's way of preserving books for future usage.

I flipped to the back to see how many pages I was supposed to read. I would have fainted after seeing the number six hundred if I had not already been sitting down. I had never read more than a three-hundred page novel before. This was going to be the equivalent of reading two books. One of the book's previous owners had artistically reconfigured the name "Homer" to leap from the opening title page. *The Iliad* was soon to follow.

Was I in for a surprise. I had never encountered a book so alive. The poetic verses translated into English were so intense, as I read the words I could actually envision the battle scenes in my mind. It was like a movie being played on the screen of my mind's eye. I couldn't put the book down. Four hours after I had sat down, my legs fell asleep. I found myself falling down onto the cold ceramic floor when I tried to leave the bathroom.

Over the course of the next couple of days, I awoke and fell asleep with *The Iliad* in my hands. The best spot was lying on the bathroom floor. I didn't have my own room since I slept on the sofa. My mother couldn't understand why I went in the bathroom for hours to read. Her sewing machine sat on the end of kitchen table next to the bathroom door.

"Kamaul, are you still in the bathroom?"

"Yes."

"Did you fall asleep?"

"No."

"Have you been touching yourself in there for the last two hours?"

"No. I'm reading."

"Have you been reading about ways of touching yourself for the last two hours?"

"No. I'm reading *The Iliad*."

"Does that book have pictures of naked women in it?"

"No."

"You know that you can talk to me if you are having problems exploring your body?"

That did it. "Maaaaaaa! Leave me alone! Even if I were in here doing what you think I'm doing; why would I want to carry on a conversation with you during it?"

Her laughter on the other side of the door confirmed our little dialog was over. She always knew what to say to me to get me to smile. She always says I take life too seriously.

Later:

"Kaaamaaaullll?"

"What, Ma?"

"Do you think you can loan me twenty dollars for sewing material when you come out of the bathroom? I'll pay you back in two weeks."

"Will you stop talking to me until Sunday evening? I need to get ready for an exam."

"Sunday evening is a long time to go without speaking to my firstborn. But I can make that sacrifice for forty dollars worth of sewing fabric."

"It's a deal! Now stop talking to me, please."

Pause.

"Kaaamaaaulllll?"

"What now, Ma?"

"Can I ask one last question before Sunday evening gets here?"

"What?"

"Can I have my money before the fabric store closes tonight?"

I could hear her hands clapping for joy as I slid the two twenty dollar bills underneath the closed bathroom door. Then she said, "I can stop talking to you for a couple of extra days if you slide me an extra twenty."

The Iliad changed my life at Boston Latin. This one book helped me to understand the beauty of a story told through words. It made me realize that each person who sits down to write sees these visions in their heads before they attempt to relay them to the reader. I never appreciated the likes of William Shakespeare, James Baldwin, John Updike and Richard Wright until after I read *The Iliad*. I became receptive then to the visions of other authors.

I didn't ace the exam, but I did very well. The follow-up book was *The Odyssey*. I actually began reading it before the teacher assigned it. My grades in Spanish turned around for the better as well. I was able to understand, translate, read and write in Spanish. I was just reluctant to try to speak the language in conversation. I never wanted to sound as if I were stupid.

I still ended up in summer school but only because of trigonometry and pre-calculus. Math was the only class I couldn't catch up in by the end of the school year on my own.

Summer school of 1989 was set to last for five weeks, starting the Monday after the Fourth of July weekend. At the end of five weeks, you either received a passing or a failing grade for the summer. There were only two ways of failing summer school. The first way was to go to class and sit there for two hours each day and do absolutely nothing. The second way was to not show up at all. If you missed more than three classes in the five week stretch, you automatically failed the class. The good part was I didn't have to travel far. Summer school was held across Louis Pasteur Avenue from Boston Latin, at Boston English High School.

The students attending summer session came from schools throughout Massachusetts. Most of the inner city high schools were well represented. The students that were bussed out to the suburban school districts during the year were also in attendance. Blacks, Whites, Asians, Hispanics and all other ethnicities were well represented.

Everybody attending summer school was on their last attempt to pass failed classes for the year. No one wanted to repeat the subject they had spent all year trying to pass. Summer school actually became part of the usual curriculum for some students. It was a place to hang out until school started after Labor Day. Most teens I knew either worked or went to summer school. I had to do both, plus my summer book reports had to be complete before the summer ended if I wanted to play football going into my third year. There were no options left for me.

Summer school classes were held at either 8am and 10:30am. Each session lasted two hours with a thirty-minute break between them. My trigonometry class started at ten thirty. At least I had company. Sparrow and Fellis were right there with me, taking their own slew of classes.

Fellis had physics with Sparrow at ten thirty. Sparrow was also taking Latin at eight o'clock. He had sacrificed himself for a woman. Once again, he had purposely failed another class—the only class he had received an A in when we were kicked off the football team—to spend an extra five weeks with a young lady I nicknamed "Poison." He figured it would further strengthen their bond if they spent all their available time together.

"Poison" came from a song by a New Edition spin off group called Bell, Biv and Devoe, also known as B.B.D. The hook to the song is, "Never trust a big butt and a smile. That girl is poison. She's dangerous." Sparrow was naturally hooked by the young lady's pretty smile, big cow eyes and brown sugar complexion. However, every time she turned to leave him to go to her next class, Sparrow became entranced by the departing view. Some days Fellis and I had to literally carry him to his next class. There was no antidote for the poison that ran through his veins.

It was Tuesday, ten o'clock, the third week into summer school. Fellis and I sat on the short concrete stoop outside the school when Sparrow joined us. Fellis happened to be gasping for air, laughing so hard.

"What's so funny, Fellis?" Sparrow grumbled. He wasn't his usual happy, chipper self that morning.

"K was telling me about what happened to him last night." Fellis was barely able to get the sentence out of mouth without choking.

"Okay, what happened last night?" asked Sparrow. I could tell he was pre-occupied. The glaze in Sparrow's eyes made him look as though he was looking through Fellis and me.

"Sparrow, where's Poison?" I asked instead.

"Good question. She told me on the stairs she saw a girlfriend go into the bathroom. So she told me to meet her outside. She said she would find me. So I guess she'll find me before we leave for our next class. So tell me what happened last night?" Since Sparrow got that saga off of his chest, he seemed more interested in important stuff once again.

Fellis busted out laughing at the mere mention of the two words "last night."

"You know I'm trying to get these seven book reports done," I started. "I only have two weeks left to give them to my father so he'll give me permission to play football. I figure two reports left, one per week. I can do this with no problem.

"Well, Tasha Simms calls me the other night and asks me how I was doing with my reports. We chat for a while. She makes mention that I can come over to her house and I can take a look at one of her reports if I want. I didn't have to work yesterday so I go over there about three in the afternoon."

Sparrow threw his hands up in the air. "Wait a minute! Where is Kathleen?"

I looked over at Fellis, who automatically stopped laughing. "I don't know," I said significantly. "We seemed to have lost contact this whole summer."

"My bad, K." Fellis' chin fell to his chest. He still felt guilty.

We had gone to the semi-formal dance together in the spring. I escorted Kathleen, and Fellis took a date. Sparrow didn't go, so Fellis and I went in the same white Rolls Royce limousine my father let me rent to chauffeur us to the dance. Well, at the end of a nice night, Fellis begged for me to take him home last. I agreed.

We reached Kathleen's house. The driver helped us out, and I walked Kathleen up to her front door. I had been waiting to give Kathleen a kiss from the moment I met her. Every hurried note, every spirited talk, every passing glance had evolved to this defining moment on her front stairs.

We were hugging, saying our goodbyes. Then the moment came when we ran out of words to say. In that moment of silence both of our heads tilted to opposite sides as we moved to close the distance between us. My eyes were closed as my head was slowly moving forward.

I heard Fellis yell out. "Kathleen! Kathleen! Don't forget to study for the Greek final exam next week. It's going to be a killer!"

I opened my eyes and turned around. Fellis quickly pulled his head back inside the limousine's open window. I turned back around to catch the disappointed look in Kathleen's eyes. Kathleen squeezed my hand and went inside her house. She and I never talked about that night again. The energy was never the same between us.

"My bad, K." Fellis had been saying the same line since I plunked back down next to him in the white Rolls Royce.

"It's cool, Fellis. I'm just never double dating with your ass ever again." We all started laughing.

"Wait a minute! Wait a minute! So, you hit Tasha Simms?" "Hit" was our equivalent of having sex. Sparrow's eyes were ready to pop out of his head. Fellis started laughing again.

"No, I did not hit Tasha Simms. Let me finish telling you what happened. So I go into her house. She tells me to follow her up to her bedroom. Tasha's reports are in her bedroom."

"K, you don't have to lie. I can look at you and tell you hit Tasha."

"Shut up and listen. When Tasha and I get to the top of the stairs, I see her dad in his home office right next to Tasha's bedroom. I'm thinking nothing of it because you know her dad used to play ball for Boston Latin's Wolf Pack back in his day. He knows about the book reports and the tough curriculum, but he urges me to stay with it. The number one goal is to graduate despite all of the obstacles. He tells me he's going to be looking for my name in the sports section of the *Boston Herald* on Sundays.

"Tasha excuses us. She tells her father we are going to her room to work on the book reports. We walk into her bedroom, and she closes the door behind me. I can hear her father on a conference call, so I can understand the reason she closed the door.

"Tasha pulls out her eight reports and passes them over to me."

"Why did she do eight reports?" Momentarily distracted by someone who would do extra work, Sparrow had the same confused look on his face that I had the night before. Fellis was still laughing.

"That's exactly what I said," I replied. "Well, I sat at the foot of the bed looking through Tasha's reports. Tasha made herself comfortable lying up at the head of the bed on the pillows as I read. I heard her say, 'You can have one of those reports if you want. I don't need all eight of them.'

"John Updike's *Rabbit Redux* was one of her reports. The paperback book was stuck in the back pocket of my jeans as I sat on Tasha's bed. I could save myself a week of reading and writing. I naturally looked up to the head of the bed smiling from ear to ear. That's when I noticed that four buttons of Tasha's blouse were undone.

"So I said to her, 'You do realize your dad is in the room right next door?' But I couldn't stop smiling.

"'I know,' she said. 'But he would never enter my room without knocking.'

"'You do realize the door is unlocked?' I was shaking my head in disbelief.

"'My dad likes you, he would never dream of interrupting.'

"'So what do I have to do to get the John Updike report?'"

Fellis fell off of the concrete stoop onto the ground, laughing. I continued with the tale.

"Tasha exposed the unbuttoned area. The pink bra she was wearing had a front clasp to it. Three seconds was all it took to view Tasha's exposed breast. I was starting to sweat knowing Tasha's father was in the room next door. Or was it the summer heat? I wasn't quite sure.

"Tasha must have been hot too. She leaned forward, throwing her blouse off to the side and she removed her short cotton socks with the fringes on the edges. You know how I like pretty feet. So when Tasha removed her socks I naturally looked down. Her feet were to my liking except for the scar on her left foot next to her pinky toe.

"'How did you get the scar on your foot? Was it a bicycling accident or something?'

"Tasha answered me without hesitation. 'No. When I was born, I was born with eleven fingers and eleven toes. My parents had the doctors remove the extra finger and the extra toe when I was a couple of months old.'"

"So what did you do?" Sparrow just looked confused.

"I can't even lie," I admitted. "I was already feeling uncomfortable. Her dad was in the next room. The door was unlocked. She had an extra finger. She had an extra toe. But I had two perky nipples in front of my face. So I proceeded forward.

"I was slowly moving both my hands up her stomach to her rib cage. Her skin was smooth. Tasha had her eyes closed as my hands made their way around her breasts. I heard her whisper, 'Kiss my nipples.' You know me. I ain't a punk. You don't have to ask me twice about kissing some titties.

"But you know how I'm really nearsighted. Even with my contact lenses, my eyesight is pretty bad. I had my mouth open. I was within inches of feasting on Tasha's nipples, when I became paralyzed by what I saw. The area around Tasha's nipples was covered by hair. There were curly hairs in the middle of her chest as well. Tasha had more chest hair then I did.

"She asked, 'What are you waiting for?'

"I was glad Tasha had her eyes closed. As I moved closer to her chest, my shoulder blades started to wrench together. My mouth was open and I was starting to get the dry heaves. The hamburger I ate before I left the house was starting to travel backwards. I just knew I was going to vomit all over Tasha's chest if my mouth made contact."

"'I have to go to work!' I told her suddenly. 'Oh damn, I told Walls from work I would cover for him today. Tasha, I got to leave.' I could taste the stomach acid in my mouth mixed with mustard, relish and ketchup.

"I didn't wait for Tasha to throw on her blouse. All I can remember was yelling goodbye to her father before I made my way down the stairs. I was lucky that the bus was coming down the street when I got to the corner. I got on the bus. I waved goodbye to Tasha. I vowed to never get caught alone in her presence ever again.

"The screwed up part is, although I never kissed Tasha and I never even put my lips on her, she will not stop chasing me. She seems to be more turned on by my illusiveness."

Sparrow and Fellis were holding one another up from falling down because they were laughing so hard.

"What, what, what happened to the book report?" Sparrow was bare-ly able to get his question out of his mouth.

I pulled the John Updike book from my rear jeans pocket. "Now I know why Rabbit keeps on running. Life is too unpredictable."

We were howling with laughter when I saw the lovely Poison standing behind Sparrow with a girlfriend and some guys.

"What's so funny?" Poison asked with a smile, even though she knew we would never tell her.

"Nothing, we were just over here telling football stories." I was talk-ing to Poison but looking at the three guys following her. All three were soon-to-be seniors and established varsity players. We knew each another from the football team. Sparrow, Fellis and I were hoping to take their positions when the season started. But, we needed to pass summer school first.

Fellis and Sparrow shook hands with the three guys, Dean, Marcus and Sal. I just gave a head nod and I didn't say anything. All three were ogling Poison's backside. Her red summer shorts couldn't contain all of her natural assets. The three predators waited for their opportunity to catch what ever happened to tumble out. If nothing fell out, they would be content just watching and waiting.

"Sparrow," Poison said, " Tanya and I are going over to the school with Dean, Marcus, Sal and Winston while you are going to be in class. They are going over to workout, so we will be across the street when you're done." Poison batted her big thick eyelashes.

Sparrow stood there in silence, thinking. Just then, Tanya walked up with the aforementioned Winston. Winston was expected to get recruited by Brown University on a football scholarship this upcoming year. He was the talk of the school, an exceptional running back. Tanya was notorious for her friendships with all the upper classmen. She had friends on the football, basketball and track teams. Her shorts had just a shade less mate-rial in them than Poison's. It seemed as though both of the girls relished the attention they received.

Tanya spoke, "You know we are all friends here, Sparrow. Plus these guys are going to be your teammates this year anyways. My girl and I are going to be spending the time making up cheers for all of you guys for September."

"Yeah, you don't have to worry, Trevor," Dean offered. "I'll watch your girl for the next two hours. I'll make sure she is right here when you get done with your physics class at twelve thirty. You don't have to worry. I'll watch your back, brother." Dean put his hand out to shake Sparrow's hand.

I laughed to myself.

"What's so funny?" Sparrow seemed to be a little tense.

"Sparrow," I said, eyeing Dean, "you know I'm no good at reading girls, that's a given. But, you just shook hands with a dude who told you twice not to worry. Let me put it to you this way. If Dean's watching your back, tell me this, who's watching Dean?" I was still chuckling.

"Trevor doesn't have to concern himself about me," Dean said. "I've known him from Latin class three years ago. Trevor needs to concern himself with passing summer school."

"Fellis, what name do you call the man standing at your side—the same person you have talked to in person and on the phone just about three hundred and sixty five days since the first time you were in the seventh grade together?" I asked.

"That's Sparrow."

"Sparrow, Dean just called you Trevor twice. Twice he said you didn't have to worry about him watching your sweetheart. The last thing I'm going to say is, watch out for the wolves wearing sheep's clothing."

The thunderous slap to the back of my neck took us all by surprise. I saw Sparrow and Fellis jump forward when they heard the sound of flesh on flesh contact.

"Why don't you shut up and mind your business?" The assailant continued walking pass me. He began shaking hands with the other four fellows standing behind Poison.

"Who told you to put your hands on me?" My eyes locked on my assailant, my neck feeling like it was on fire. I wanted to rub the fiery sensation but elected not to do so because everyone was watching me. The dark brown figure was still shaking hands with Winston, laughing.

Le Baron had just graduated from Latin School. He was the only person in his graduating class who had enlisted in the armed services. He wanted to go fight for his country. Everyone else was going on to college. Le Baron stood a little over six feet tall. He had a decent build for an eighteen-year-old. Sparrow, Fellis and I were all sixteen.

The three of us had seen Le Baron's face enough to know who he was. He was dating a girl in our class so he was always over at the sub-division building. Sparrow and Fellis knew him well enough to speak when they saw him. I didn't know anything about him. I never even spoke to him until this moment.

"I was just saying what's up," he said to me by way of explanation for the slap. "You don't have to act like a little bitch." Le Baron had no problems looking down at me since I am only five feet nine inches tall.

"I'm only telling you one time. Never put your hands on me again. You don't know me that well."

"You keep on crying, I'm gonna slap your ass for real. Then I'm going to take your Air Jordans."

The other five guys laughed. Le Baron was feeling happy about his comedic debut.

"You should just go ahead, slap him again," Le Baron's pudgy friend said. "Slap the taste out of his mouth for talking shit to you."

"I should whoop your little ass and make you walk home barefooted." Le Baron's chest was starting to swell with confidence.

"Yeah, Le Baron, listen to your man," I said levelly. "Come whoop my ass. This time let me see you slap me though. Don't wait until my back is turned. Be a man about it. Don't punk up."

People can smell a fight brewing. There was already a crowd surrounding us. When you have all the spotlights on you there are two choices to make. You can get cold feet and leave the stage. Or you can steal the moment and cash it in for all that it is worth. I personally like to run my mouth. It's show time!

"Le Baron, you leave for the Marines in a couple of days, right? Here's what I will do for you. While you are gone I'm going to take care of that pretty little Puerto Rican girlfriend you have. I don't want you to worry about a thing. She's slightly bow legged but she has nice calves and legs. She looks like she manicures her hands and feet every day. I have never seen her one day with chipped fingernails polish. I like when a young woman takes care of herself. What's her name? Oh, how could I ever forget? That's right, I didn't! Her name is Nina."

As the crowd erupted into frenzy I saw the anger in Le Baron's face. His boys were starting to close the gap. Sparrow and Fellis flanked me on either side. Five on three weren't that bad of odds. Nine on three was the worse case scenario if Poison's wolves decided to join the attack. I was ready to battle.

"Uwwwup! Uwwwup!" I heard a familiar sound off to my right.

"Uwwwup! Uwwwup!" The second time confirmed what I thought I heard the first time.

There are certain sounds that are unmistakable to my ears. I can tell Stephanie Mills singing any one of her songs by the first three notes. I know the sound of my father whistling amid a crowd of people singing. I know the sound of my mother's four-inch heels clicking as she walks through the corridor of any office building during lunch hour. I know the sound of my Grandmama's brown Monte Carlo before it even makes the turn onto my street. And without a doubt I know the sound of role call from a childhood warrior.

Since I don't see all that well, Uncle Deek made up that sound so I would know he was close by. The other kids on the street learned the sound from Deek. It became a neighborhood call.

It wasn't until I saw the extended left hand reaching for the sky configured into the letter C that I naturally took my left hand C and interlocked it with my right hand's backwards C, to form the letter G. My old friends from Castle Gate Road were up here. More importantly, Angelo was here.

These hand signs were our way of finding each other when we were up at the Franklin Park golf course. It didn't matter if we were playing or caddying, I could tell exactly where Angelo was if we were in a crowd.

Now, it was a sight from heaven to see the crew of five slicing through the crowd, cutting off the forward progress of Le Baron and his boys. I saw the shell-toed Adidas and the blue and silver Georgetown University hats and shirts coming towards me. The Georgetown Hoyas were the street kids on the college basketball scene. In order to beat Georgetown on the court, you had to play a perfect game mentally and physically. The Hoyas were inner city celebrities to urban youth, led by a coach who wore a white towel on his shoulder and pushed his young players to be the best. Angelo had a white towel over his left shoulder. Georgetown paraphernalia, which was very big at the time, came emblazoned with a big "G" right on front. You could even get them at Jordan Marsh. Angelo and I slapped right hands so hard it sounded as if someone lit a firecracker. Then we embraced.

"K.D., I thought that looked like you in the middle of the circle," he said. "Your cousin Boot told me you were up here in summer school. Boot knows everybody's 411. She caught me up on everybody's business. She told me you have been running with a crew over in Cambridge. You'll running by the name R.V.T., Roosevelt Towers huh? That's over in East Cambridge, huh? Heard your boys been making a little name for yourselves."

"Yeah, Boot knows she needs a job working for a Grove Hall news station." I was all smiles, seeing how the years had matured Angelo's face. Yet Angelo still looked the same, outside of him standing well over six feet now.

"You look different without your glasses, K.D. Look at you out here doing it up old school style, huh? You still out here ready to throw those hands around? You lucky I showed up right on time as usual to save your ass." Angelo laughed.

"What are we waiting for, Le Baron? Who are these dudes?" blurted Le Baron's pudgy friend.

"Castle Gate, Mother Fucker! If you don't know, you better ask somebody!" JoJo, another of Angelo's crew, was always short tempered, even when we were kids.

The street name had become synonymous with bloodshed. Most people who lived in the area were very hard working people raising their families. The childhood friends I had spent the summer days with, playing four-of-squares, kickball, golf, dodge ball, basketball, touch football and riding bikes, had found a new focus—hustling. The profitable way of life for those who lived on the Castle Gate Road, Blue Hill Avenue, Washington Street and Normandy Street block was interwoven with the distribution of narcotics as well as other street hustles. Angelo and the other guys who lived on the block had transcended from off the block selling weed to selling at some of the colleges and universities in the area. They were independent contractors. There was a demand for everything they could supply. They knew if they didn't supply the market than the next man hungry enough would.

"K, you know Castle Gate?" Fellis asked from my left.

"I grew up with all these dudes. We are family."

"Who is he, Angelo?" I knew Pork Chop from Building Fourteen.

"You know, K.D." Angelo said with a smile.

Even though I recognized everyone, it was obvious no one recognized me without my glasses.

"That's little Deek. Look at the chocolate stain on the right corner of his mouth." It wasn't until the other four looked closer, seeing my birth mark on the right corner of my upper lip that my identity was confirmed.

They all used to sit around saying my birth mark reminded them of a chocolate chip cookie.

"Oh snap, this is little Deek—I haven't seen you forever—You don't come around the Gate that much anymore." The five of them were talking at once as we all slapped hands, pulling one another in close for a masculine hug and back slap. This is the embrace of many men. It is the sign of respect, and in memory of all the fun times we had as kids.

"Damn, this is little Deek. Look at you, all grown up. Who you got beef with up here? You got issues with these five heads or all nine?" Pork Chop inquired.

"I got beef with that six foot sucker." I pointed at Le Baron.

"I was just playing with you, dude," Le Baron said quickly. "I was saying 'what's up' because we all go to the same school and everything. It all just got out of hand. I just want to apologize for allowing things to get out of hand. It was my fault, K." The sweat poured from Le Barons forehead. It had already soaked his grey T-shirt through.

"Angelo, let me shoot him anyways. Deek will appreciate it knowing I shot this dude for his nephew." JoJo lifted up his shirt showing the handle of his black nine millimeter. The tight circle expanded backwards by three steps but no one left.

"It's up to K.D." Angelo smiled.

I shook my head. "No, JoJo. Uncle Sam already owns his punk's ass. I want him alive. I want him to come back from basic training knowing I'm watching him. I want him to come back and see me with his girl. I will keep this promise to you, Le Baron—I will certainly make sure I take good care of Nina."

"Are you all right?" Angelo asked me then.

"Yeah, I'm straight."

"We have to go. We need to take care of some other business up here."

"You need me to run with you?"

"No. Stay up here and finish school. I'm not going to deal with your Uncle Deek later on because he heard you were running with us. You know he never wants to see your hands dirty with our shit. You know how to find me if you need me." Angelo slipped the knife into my right hand when we shook hands again. I knew the knife was for my protection since they were leaving me. I slapped hands with all the neighborhood kids. As fast as they entered the circle, they quickly vanished.

I went on to my trigonometry class. Less than five minutes after the teacher took attendance, someone pull the fire alarm. Everyone filed into the stairwells. I saw Sparrow and Fellis on the fourth floor. We were all walking down the stairs together when we heard the six gunshots rocket through the air. The echoing in the hallways was deafening. We all knew who pulled the trigger. I caught myself wondering if Le Baron knew how close he had just come to never making it to basic training.

Once we got outside, I looked at both Fellis and Sparrow soberly. "The rules to the game are changing," I said. "We're too smart to be here. We can't ever come back here again. We have to make sure this is our last time at summer school. This school year coming up has to be our time."

Summer school was turning out to be for kids who had allowed themselves to fail. But I wasn't going to let us get into the habit of failure. School is school, and street is street. It was time to separate them out.

We all agreed—school was school, and street was street.

Indian summer is the best description for the Friday night of the long Columbus Day Weekend, 1989. The bus ride up to Acton-Boxboro High School game was a little more than an hour. Since we were the only city team in the Dual County League, all of our away games were more than an hour away by bus. Acton-Boxboro was thought to be one of the best teams, not only in the Dual County League but in the entire Commonwealth of Massachusetts. Most of the talent on the suburban teams were products of the inner city. The talent was bussed out of the city to gain a "post high school experience." It was tough to realize that true undeveloped talent couldn't be cultivated in our own backyard.

This would be my first varsity game in a primetime setting. Unfortunately, this would be our only varsity game of the football season underneath the bright lights. The bus was silent as everyone got focused.

Tiny Baby, our offensive lineman, sat next to me. I could hear Public Enemy's front man Chuck D. hyping him up through his oversized headphones. Hearing Chuck D. yell "Fight the power" was the only confirmation Tiny Baby needed to smash an opposing player in the mouth. Tiny liked to pretend he was Nat Turner when we stepped out on the football field. Football was the only constructive way Tiny Baby could act out and release his bottled up aggression against society without being arrested.

Of course, Tiny Baby was anything but small. He was six feet, five inches tall, weighing close to three hundred pounds. If you judged only by his size, you might be intimidated. But just about everyone relaxed once Tiny turned around with his babyish face. Tiny couldn't even grow a mustache. But he was a mountain of a man once he put on his uniform.

Sitting across the aisle from us were Toby-Jean and Chico. We gave Toby-Jean the nickname Jizz out of necessity. Ever since freshman year, Toby-Jean was always getting picked on. A day did not pass in the classroom without at least two members of our crew simultaneously chanting "Kunta, Kunta Kinte," whenever the teacher called his name. Toby-Jean had never even watched *Roots* before he met us. As we all began to mature, Toby-Jean adopted the reputation as the only Haitian of the crew. There were many days when Toby-Jean's school attire reflected his island culture. Sometimes his multicolored bright shirts didn't even come close to matching his just as multicolored pants.

Toby-Jean wore a different Kangol cap for every day of the week. Some hats were made of fur. Some hats had brims. Some were bucket style. Toby-Jean wore his caps when he sold girly magazines to those willing to buy them. Because Toby-Jean looked like a thirty-year-old and had a fake I.D., he purchased a lot of items that most teenagers couldn't buy. Toby-Jean was what I considered a lazy hustler, and eventually he became known as Jizz. He was a habitual liar. He and I spent most of our time together arguing about his telling lies.

Chico and I had history before Boston Latin School. We had been classmates since the first grade at Mission Grammar School and had played Little League baseball on Mission Hill. We both played for the Yankees. Four years had passed before I had seen Chico again in high school.

Sparrow and Fellis sat in seat in front of me. Fellis never wanted to get hit for fear of getting hurt, so Sparrow kept up a smooth flow of affirmation concerning the fact that Tiny Baby would always be there on offense and would never let him get hurt. But Fellis still always sounded like he was on the verge of having an anxiety attack. As usual, Sparrow was there to calm Fellis down.

The six of us were the only members from our clique left to play football. Everyone else decided to use their time to get ready for the SAT exam. This was understandable. We all understood that Boston Latin School was our springboard to get us to the next level of learning. Three of the crew decided to play basketball, with a season that started well after the SAT. However, tonight every member of our crew, as well as most of the student body, was coming to the Friday night game.

Five of my crew were starters on varsity. Fellis led the entire league, earning the most touchdowns, eight, after three games. Tiny figured Fellis ran so fast because he was too afraid to get hurt. If Fellis ran into the end zone before anyone tackled him, he would be all right. This convinced Fellis to take Winston's starting running back position. Winston, the highly recruited running back, became Fellis' blocker.

The rest of the crew earned our starting positions on defense because we played fast and we played hungry. Chico was a hard hitter as an outside linebacker. Jizz was a defensive tackle until he fractured his arm. He had gotten hurt during practice and had just been given clearance to play tonight, so he wouldn't start. Sparrow was the smallest on the defensive line. He was only five foot, eight inches tall but there was no way anyone could measure the heart he played with as defensive end. He utilized his speed to get past the bigger linemen, and led the league in sacks. My position was the easiest—the safety, the last line of defense. I only know how to play football one way. I leave everything I have on the field. I bring the intensity.

"What you writing?" Tiny was looking over my shoulder.

"I'm actually rereading a copy of a note. I gave this note to Kathleen Preston on Thursday during class and she didn't come into school today."

"Kathleen didn't call you?"

"Nope. Word on the street has it that Kathleen is pregnant. A little birdie whispered the news in my ear on Wednesday."

"How reliable is your source?" Tiny asked.

"I trust my source like I trust my crew." Felicia, the only consistent female associate I have had since my freshman year, has never lied to me. Felicia told me how Kathleen came into the nurse's office complaining of morning sickness. Kathleen never noticed Felicia in the adjoining room. I respected Felicia's honesty and the fact she always smelled like Juicy Fruit chewing gum.

"Is the baby yours?" Tiny joked, which forced me to laugh.

"My mother would kick me in my booty." I pictured my mother telling me not to bring home any snotty nosed babies.

"I know that's right. Let Kathleen go. Now, you have your pick of whoever you want to see anyways."

"I wrote out my priorities for this upcoming year. It doesn't include any girls until after the SAT and after I make it to the Thanksgiving football game without getting kicked off the team. I need to finish out this season. I need to prove to myself I can do it." I went back to reading the note. Tiny put his headphones back over his ears.

The note I had written to Kathleen was simple. It went right to the point. I wrote the note so only the two of us could decipher it. The note read:

Sometime a girl
Will come and go.
You reach for love
But life won't let you know.
That in the end
You'll still be loving her
But then she's gone.
You're all alone.

I never learned
To forgive myself.
I been a fool
But right now I need someone else.
Just like Boy Blue
I blow my horn here for you.
Just lead me home.
Baby, I should have known.

Two verses was all I had written down. Kathleen would know the song "Love don't love nobody" from the Spinners. She would also know that what she was reading was the last note we would share.

A chain is only as strong as its weakest link. We held hands looking across the field as both teams waited for the coin toss. I caught myself wondering if this were similar to what Homer envisioned when he wrote the Iliad. We all had our war bonnets on our heads. It was almost show time.

Tiny Baby was on my left and Jizz was on my right. Jizz kept nudging me.

"K, Tasha Simms is holding up a sign with your number on it," he said. "The sign says, 'Show me what you got #15.' I think Tasha wants you to hit her tonight." I never told anyone other than Sparrow and Fellis about my hairy experience at Tasha's house.

The bleachers were packed. The cheerleaders led the school spirit as they performed on the race track. A quarter of the stands were taken up by the Pep Squad, predominantly girls who all wore purple sweatshirts on game day. I could pick out a few faces in the purple sea. Tasha Simms stood next to Felicia because they were best friends. Poison and Tanya were together waving in my direction. They had become out-of-their-way friendly to me ever since the day when my friends from Castle Gate Road came to summer school. Once I even found a pair of pink laced panties folded up inside a note inside of my locker. Through a process of elimination, I figured there were only two bubbled backsides that could fit those panties and both suspects were now waving in my direction.

My eyes continued to scan. I saw all of the brothers from our clique. I didn't see Kathleen Preston. I was a little disappointed, but I wasn't surprised. Before I turned my head back, my eyes locked onto Nina Mercado.

Nina stuck out because she and her two girlfriends, who had attended every one of our after-school practices that year, weren't standing in the stands with the rest of the Pep Squad. Because we were a city school, we didn't have our own practice facility. We tackled it each on the dirt on a daily basis. Then when it rained, we tackled each other on top of the rocks in the mud. Nina watched as we practiced running our plays on the side of the building. Every day, Nina was there.

"K, we won the toss. Coach wants the ball first. This is how you like it, baby! We are playing on the primetime stage!" Tiny Baby yelled. I hated when he started smacking me upside my head, but I let him go through his ritual of getting his blood pumped up.

We came together as a team in a brief huddle. The captain said something but I wasn't listening. I was too ready to play.

I remembered from the film we watched of the Acton-Boxboro team that their kicker could boot the ball into the end zone. I stood on the left hash mark and Winston took his place on the right. The referee blew his whistle, beginning the game.

The kickoff was a line drive down the middle of the field. I beat Winston to the spot, catching the ball on the run at the ten-yard line. I liked to pretend that I had just caught a bag of money from off the back of an armored truck and the police were chasing me. It gave me more inspiration to let my instincts take over and get the hell away.

Sparrow blocked in front of me as everybody else on the team made contact with someone on the opposing team. My forty-yard dash is strong—I covered this one in 4.6 seconds. There were fifty yards to go. Sparrow stayed directly in front of me as I ran across the middle of the field. He took out the kicker, who fell into another would-be tackler. I kept running down the right side line to the orange touchdown marker with no one in front of me. It was going to be the perfect crime.

I saw, out of the corner of my right eye, Nina Mercado running along the outside of the football field stride for stride with me. Nina's arms were flailing as she cheered hysterically while she kicked up the dirt bordering the football field. To be honest, I can't say for sure if she distracted me for that split second. I can't say if I thought I was all ready in the end zone scoring a touchdown. I can't say if I just ran out of gas. All of a sudden I felt the back of my shoulder pads being pulled backwards to the ground. I was tackled two yards away from scoring the longest kickoff return in our school's history.

The crowd was going wild. Fellis and Tiny Baby were running at me as the offense took the field.

"How did you let that white boy catch your black ass?" Tiny yelled as he ran past me, slapping me upside my helmet, towards the huddle.

"I set you up!" I yelled at Fellis.

"You always set me up! And you know I'm about to take it home! The crowd is chanting for me to score! I can't disappoint the fans!" Fellis yelled back.

I didn't even turn around to watch Fellis score his touchdown. Being the rising star made Fellis feel confident in his own skin. Everyone from our crew knew Fellis was insecure with 100% of his body covered in freckles. When Fellis put his uniform on, the crowd was forced to see instead a young man who could run with a football.

I walked over to hug Sparrow for making the key block. Judging from the roar of the crowd, I knew Fellis had scored. I stood, catching my breath, with the rest of the defense, getting ready to knock someone's block off when we take the field. But part of me kept scanning the stands. My eyes couldn't find the girl who matched me stride for stride running down the field.

Redemption is the best word to describe how our team felt about traveling so far even to play against a high school that had all of the plush amenities a football team could ever want or need. Meanwhile come Tuesday, our group would be right back to walking our practice area removing rocks and broken bottles before we would start tackling one another. We understood that, in that moment of play, our team collectively epitomized the inner-city struggle against the well-to-do. We were given the opportunity to compete in battle. Whenever we came out victorious, it was the cherry on top of the ice cream sundae.

We won the game on the Friday night of the Columbus Day Weekend by two touchdowns. The bus ride home had us reliving the game play by play. Coach was so happy that he treated the team bus, the bus carrying the cheerleaders, plus the other two buses carrying the Pep Squad and the fans to McDonald's.

Tiny Baby and Jizz ordered first. I didn't have much of an appetite. I was exhausted in a good way. One of the players from the other team had to be carried off the field after he caught the ball and I stuck my helmet into his hip. I heard his bone crack on impact. I couldn't remember too much since I had damn near knocked myself out again. All I could recall was the crowd wincing as I made contact.

I watched as the buses of people filled the restaurant. The third bus had everyone from the Pep Squad on it. The mention of free food made students order even if they weren't hungry. Sparrow and Fellis stood next to me. Tiny, Jizz and Chico were eating.

"Jizz, answer one question for me."

"Don't start, K!" Jizz just put a handful of fries in his mouth.

"How are you always the first person to eat when you didn't do anything tonight? Then when you got into the game your big ass didn't want to hit anybody because you have that pink damn cast on your hand. Tell us for the last time why you are wearing a bright pink cast?" Everybody busted out laughing. It was time to play the dozens.

"Fuck you, K. My cast is fuchsia. I told you already, this was the only color coating the doctors had for my cast."

"Jizz is lying. His sister told me she was with him when he picked out that hot pink cast. Jizz was given an alternate choice of black or blue.

His sister said this fool bought himself a hat to match his cast." I loved busting Jizz.

"Jizz, don't tell me you have a hot pink Kangol?" Tiny stopped eating long enough to ask his question.

"K, doesn't know shit! I had already bought that hat before school even started!" Toby-Jean was starting to get mad.

"Jizz, are you saying, you bought yourself a hot pink, I'm sorry, a *fuchsia* hat for yourself before school started?" Fellis was inquiring.

Jizz jumped up, walking away from our table. He stuck up his middle finger as he got back into line to order dessert. We all fell out laughing.

We were all slapping hands when Nina walked off the bus with her two friends. Nina talked to Sparrow for a minute before he motioned over to me.

"Kamaul, I didn't know you never met Nina?" Sparrow asked.

"I noticed her at our practices," I replied, meeting her eyes. "I've never had any classes with her so we were never properly introduced."

"Let me handle that for you. Nina Mercado, this is my really good friend, Kamaul David." As soon as Sparrow said my name, everyone standing around us got up as if on cue and relocated.

"You almost scored a touchdown tonight. But I thought it was more exciting when the other team threw the football and you caught it so our team could get the ball back." Nina had a nice smile. My eyes wandered to her hands. As I'd said to LeBaron, she did indeed have very even, manicured fingernails.

"I had a decent game. We all did our part for the team to win. I was just happy to see Fellis score."

"How bad did you hurt your neck when you fractured the other boy's hip?" Nina appeared genuinely concerned.

"My neck is sore, but it comes with the territory. How do you know I fractured that boy's hip?"

"My girls and I were standing next to the ambulance when he said number fifteen on the opposing team speared him. What is spearing?"

"Spearing is when you tackle someone and you lead into the impact head first." I answered honestly.

"Is that the reason your neck hurts now?"

I shrugged my shoulders. "I only know how to play football like I live my life. I either give all of myself or I give nothing. At the end of the day, someone is going to be carried away and someone is going to walk away. I like to make sure I'm the one walking away.

"I have a question for you, though. You appear at all of our practices. You come to all of the games. Don't you have a boyfriend to take you to the movies on Friday nights rather than you watching us play such a barbaric game?"

"I have school spirit, that's why I'm out here on a Friday night. The boyfriend topic is an unresolved issue for me." I could tell by her body language I had touched a nerve.

"I'm not going to waste your time," I said. "I think it's better to be upfront with people. That way the cards are spread out for them to see. I think you're a pretty young lady. I would like to get to know you better but right now is bad timing. I'm studying for the SAT exam. I'm trying to get the best grades possible. I work on the weekends. I'm playing football during the week.

"Those are the items on my plate. If your boyfriend situation is resolved when my plate clears off after Thanksgiving then maybe we can get to know each other a little bit better. But I can honestly say it was nice to meet you tonight." I took Nina's hand inside of mine for the first time, and kissed the back of it lightly. Uncle Deek taught me that one enduring kiss can last much longer than a heartless hour of doing the deed. There was nothing more to say tonight.

Nina walked away with a smile on her face. Tanya came over and asked if I got the note with the "surprise" folded inside. She wanted to give me a ride home in her mother's Mercedes after the game if I needed a lift, whispering that she wasn't wearing a bra or panties tonight. As Tanya walked off, it was Poison's turn to join me. She handed me her phone number and whispered that her house was going to be free for the weekend. She kept telling me how she was a virgin and she wanted to give me her womanly gift. Nice as that sounds, it pissed me off. Sparrow and I, all the members of our clique, were like brothers. My loyalty would never allow me to turn my back on any one of my boys for a second. I knew I would never be the reason our crew split up.

We all piled back onto the bus. The bus driver turned on the radio, but all that came through was static. Tiny Baby gave the bus driver a cassette tape. The speakers started to blare Soul II Soul's song with the words, "Back to life, back to reality." Every one of our teammates chimed in because we were going back home. We were going back to the city, our reality of life, but this time with a sweet victory. Sparrow turned in his chair as we continued to chant. He handed me a slip of paper. It was Nina's phone number.

"She's one of the good ones, K." Sparrow gave the confirmation head nod.

I slapped Sparrow's right hand in a handshake, pulling him close to me so he could hear me clearly. "I could tell when I looked into her eyes, Sparrow. Actions speak louder than words, partner. Let's wait to see if she's still standing when the dust settles after Thanksgiving. We all still have a lot of work to put down. We can't allow ourselves to become distracted, not here, not now. Today is just a taste of what's out there waiting for us. This, today, was just one battle. We have to stay hungry long enough to go get everything we've worked hard to receive. I want all of my spoils of this war. I'm ready to feast."

Then I just let myself get carried away by the words soaring out of the speakers.

Twenty-three minutes was how long it took for Mr. Matthews to return with my turkey sandwich.

"The small deli downstairs was crowded. Kamaul, where are you?"

"I'm over here." I was sitting on top of the toolbox.

"Are you still working on taking apart the bed? Jacob would love to hear that." Mr. Matthews had the sound of laughter in his voice.

"I finished taking apart the bed five minutes after you left. Look what I found underneath it"

"It would not surprise me if you found a rodent under there. Is it alive?" Mr. Matthews unloaded the sandwiches, juices and chips from the bag.

"No. It's definitely not alive."

"What did you find?"

"Hilda. I found Hilda underneath the bed." My voice sounded exasperated.

"What?!"

I held the brass urn containing Hilda's ashes with both hands, not sure how to handle it.

"How do you know that's Hilda? This urn has a lot of foreign inscriptions engraved on the front," Mr. Matthews asked.

"The inscription is in her native language. Hilda was Greek. Her maiden name was Hilda Athena Pappas," I answered with my head down.

"Do you speak Greek?"

"No."

"How do you know what this inscription says? Or was that just a lucky guess?" Mr. Matthews looked puzzled.

"I have been studying the ancient Greek language and culture for years. I can read and write the language pretty well. I just have a problem trying to carry on a conversation."

"Wow, that's pretty impressive. I would have never pegged you as someone who could translate, of all languages, Greek. There's a lot about you that's interesting, Kamaul. You should let people know more things about you."

"I told you, we are co-workers, Mr. Matthews. I just want to be respected as a co-worker first. If a piece of who I am outside of work becomes relevant while we are working together, I won't hesitate to place my information on the table. "

"So what does the inscription say? Because it's all Greek to me," Mr. Matthews smiled as he passed the urn back to me.

I read him a rough translation of the inscription.

The flowers will always remain bright and beautiful in my heart. I find myself missing you even more as the seasons change. I will never give up on life because helping others is my calling. You helped me realize my true calling. Thank you for entering my life, becoming my soul mate and my inspiration. My soul remains full of hope for the moment we meet again. I love you from this earth to the moon, past this galaxy to all of the celestial bodies and beyond. Our love is infinity times two. A love like ours only comes along once in a lifetime. I miss you.

We sat in silence for a moment.

"Here Kamaul, eat your sandwich. I'll take Hilda and package her up for the move."

I handed over the brass urn. I wasn't as hungry anymore.

"Mr. Matthews, is this what it's all about?"

He smiled a little. "It all depends on how much you care about helping the person whose doorbell you ring in the morning. Ask yourself, 'What means the world to me?' every day right before the customer opens the door. Would you entrust that world into your hands? Do you think your customer deserves any less service than what you would want to have yourself?"

K. DAVID

THINKING ABOUT YOU...

Even with eyes closed,
Tight, tighter;
My mind never goes absolutely void.
You are too deep in my head.

Trying to paint black over
These images are impossible.
There are too many subtle sensations,
Uncontrollable feelings and thoughts
Which are continuously etching new images.
Each one a little brighter,
Definitely clearer than the last.

Have you ever thought?
If we spent more time together,
Would we be much more?
I have.

Laying down most nights
It's hard not thinking about you.
I can't bring myself to suppress
The days we've spent together talking.
Shoes off, eye to eye, laughing, sharing,
No masks, no camouflage, all so real.
True intimate moments.

Intimacy on this level
Can only be surpassed by us
Going to my special place.
A place where shooting stars carry answers.

These stars levitate from the river's floor
To a height which must be heaven's door.
When we're there,
Underneath the haze of the largest star
Give me a moment to sit on the crown of the bench
Where I've longed for your companionship.
Allow me to give thanks for being answered, tonight.

Please join me,
This moment is just as much yours.
Place your arms around my broad shoulders
Let me cup your hands inside of mine,
Hold me.
Press your soft cheek close against mine
I don't want the wind to inhale more of
Your sweet scent than I.
Let's just sit here, aglow, in nature's ecstasy.

Why are we so compatible?
Connected at times by more than the physical,
Yet we remain apart?
When will our paths cross and become one?

Is our lives
That love story on a bigger screen?
Where the woman and man
Realize at different times,
Maybe they should have been
More than just friends.
I can't help but hold you here and ponder.

Listen?
I hear someone on the outside yelling at us now.
"Can't you two see
How much you really care for each other!"

In a good love story
The lovers always unify before the end, somehow.
But in a classic romance
The two part, knowing the truth within their hearts.
An ending is inevitable.
The true question is what type of ending,
Love Story or Classic Romance?

My biggest fear is
You will think I do not care.
But I do,
That's why these words are dedicated to you.

If you have an inkling whether or not these verses
Were meant for you
Ask me?
I may smile
But I have been holding in this desire
Too long not to tell the truth, now.
Ask me?

Before we part company
I want you to know
I've grasped tight to the memories we shared.
I know the true beauty your heart possesses and
I respect it.
I will always respect you.
You are my friend.

Sitting beneath the stars some time ago,
When I foresaw Time's chariot drawing near,
I asked Destiny to travel along with Time
To reunite us someday?
Somehow?
Somewhere?
Then I saw two shooting stars.

We finished moving Dr. James Spriggs into his new residence just after seven o'clock. It was a successful move. Nothing was broken. None of the floors were scratched. More importantly, Mr. Matthews made sure he left the priceless picture cartons off to the side, away from the other boxes. Mr. Matthews left the one solitary box containing Hilda's remains on top of his bed. So it didn't appear as though it were just some random box, Mr. Matthews asked me to write the English translation of the engraved inscription on the box's side. I was honored to be asked.

But there was still Jacob to deal with. I'm not a big fan of delaying the inevitable. Mr. Matthews made sure he kept the two of us apart after lunch. Jacob packed the truck. I shuttled everything to the elevator from inside the house on four-wheel dollies. Mr. Matthews kept at least three people between Jacob and me throughout the move.

Now we were on our way back to the warehouse. I knew I had to be ready for just about anything.

"Why are you so quiet? I have never heard you go without singing to Stephanie Mills before." Leroy and I were the only ones riding back in our truck. The orange-red sun was starting to set.

"I was just thinking about how much money I have saved for the upcoming school year." My voice sounded very raspy and low.

"How much do you figure you need to cover your expenses for the entire year?" Leroy squinted into the orange-red glare.

I opened up my wallet. Reading off the now worn slip of paper, I said, "I need to pocket ten thousand dollars. I have six thousand, three hundred and seventy-five dollars after taxes since I started working here. I haven't spent one cent of my paycheck yet."

Crowds of people walked on the Massachusetts Avenue bridge as we drove into Cambridge.

"So you need ten thousand dollars for the school year, right?"

"Yeah."

"You have more than enough time to make it to your ten thousand dollar goal."

"Yeah, right." I could hear the uncertainty in my own voice.

"I bet you're thinking, if you get into a fight with Jacob then you won't reach your goal." Leroy's eyes stayed on the road as we drove.

I nodded. "Something along those lines. I was just starting to get used to working here. I haven't had issues with anyone else on a personal level until today."

"I have an idea. You could always just let Jacob beat you in a fight. Let him just beat the living piss out of you. Then he gets his retribution. You no longer have to worry about getting fired. Then I can win the bet I made with Brian at lunch. This way every body can go home a winner." Leroy smiled, knowing this was out of the question.

"I can truly appreciate your diplomacy," I replied wryly. "But I have to be able to hold my head with some dignity when I look into the mirror in the morning, sorry." I couldn't help but smile at the impossible mental image of someone physically beating me until I urinated on myself.

"It's okay. I never really pictured you as the type."

Less than a mile away from the warehouse my pager started vibrating. Pressing the display buttons, I saw Nina's house phone number. She usually called after she got home from her job at the bank. Nina Mercado's timing never failed to make me smile even when life's weight became a little too heavy for my shoulders.

Having a job on the road was so inconvenient. I wasn't working out of an office, so I couldn't call her as much as I would have liked. Every day I was in a different customer's house in a different part of the state. Nina constantly paging me was her way to let me know she was thinking about me. And, I needed to speak to her at that moment more than she knew. I needed to hear her voice.

I dug my hand in the front pocket of my backpack for loose change to use the pay phone in the warehouse lobby. Leroy nudged my elbow. Barney ran frantically towards our truck as Leroy took the turn into the parking lot. He covered the fifty yards remarkably fast with his long six foot, eight inch frame.

"We have a couple of late jobs we need to get off." Barney was breathless from his sprint but we could still hear the excitement in his voice.

"How many men do you need?" Leroy asked.

"Well, we need one man to go out with Tom on an estimated five to six hour job over in the North End. Then both of the other two jobs are estimated two to three hours each," Barney answered back.

"Kamaul can go out there with Tom. You are going to need his fresh, young legs to run the tight stairways over in the North End. I'll do one of the other jobs," Leroy answered.

Barney looked over at me to confirm Leroy's assessment. I nodded my head "yes." What else did I have to do? Barney jumped down from the driver's side of the truck where he had perched to talk with us. His whistle caught Tom's attention. Tom Dolan started up his truck and began to drive towards us.

"Working a late night tonight should help you get a little closer towards your ten thousand dollar marker," Leroy encouraged. "Remember, don't let one man, one situation veer you off your path towards your goals."

"Thanks, man." We shook hands before I jumped out of his truck and into Tom's.

"Are you ready?" Tom asked. "It's just the two of us. We are moving two sisters from a fourth floor apartment to a second floor." The green shamrock tattoo over Tom's right ankle and the Irish flag on Tom's left calf caught my attention as I stepped up into the truck. I had counted six different tattoos in the span of ten seconds.

"Yeah, I'm ready—can I ask you a question? The tattoos, did they hurt?" The distorted look on my face indicated how much I truly dislike self-inflicted pain.

He laughed. "The tattoos hurt a lot less than most of the injuries we sustain while we're working. Getting a tattoo is like peeling a scab off your body. It has that same sensation. After you get the first tattoo, you almost feel incomplete without a second." Tom began driving the truck back towards Boston.

Tom and I passed the truck carrying Mr. Matthews, Jacob and Liam on First Street. Brian had immediately jumped on the train to go home and shower the dirt off his after we finished moving Dr. Spriggs. The two passing trucks honked horns in recognition. Jacob's eyes stayed locked on mine as everyone else waved to one another in passing.

Tom picked right up on it. "Did you see Jacob's face? He looked pretty pissed off. Didn't you work with him earlier today? Did something happen out on your job today?"

I shrugged my shoulder noncommittally. "All I remember was a discussion about baseball right before lunch. Maybe he's upset that the Red Sox are trailing the Yankees in the American League East by six games."

"Some people take baseball way too serious." Tom was a rugby player not a baseball fanatic.

"It's just a game." I shrugged again, then turned to watch the people standing in the crosswalk.

Our destination was 24 Thatcher Street in the North End of Boston. The North End is richly influenced by the Italians who immigrated there decades ago. The red, green and white Italian flag is either hung inside the window or outside the doors of most businesses. But ever since I was a young boy going home on the Green Line trolley, it was always the smell that attracted me to the other side of Interstate 93.

I was eleven years old the first time I ever crossed under the highway. I was looking to buy fireworks. The purchasing and distribution of fireworks has always been illegal in the Commonwealth of Massachusetts. Many adults I knew ventured to New Hampshire to purchase theirs. I didn't know any adults that would be willing to take me that far north. Andrew Tardinnico, my Italian pal in grade school, had a cousin who had a friend over in the North End who could get whatever we were looking to purchase.

Andrew and I left school at 11:15 on one of the Fridays when parochial schools were let out early. I had my empty blue school bag on my shoulder, having left all my books inside my desk. I had sixty dollars in bills wrapped around my right ankle held tight by my sock. I had no idea how much sixty dollars would buy me in fireworks, but the possibilities seemed endless.

We didn't talk much on the trolley ride to Haymarket Station. Instead, we played Blackjack-21.

Our school house rules were: at any point when the loser exceeds the twenty-one dollar marker, he had to pay a minimum of half the money before play could continue. I implemented this rule to slow guys down from constantly betting double-or-nothing wagers. I was always a ring leader as far as gambling went. Most of the girls in our parochial school were disgusted by the boys gambling during lunchtime. We were viewed as sinners. I always told the girls that we would stop playing blackjack when the church made Bingo a part of our lunch menu.

Andrew, pissed, was down twenty-four dollars to me when the conductor called our stop over the intercom. He handed me twelve dollars before we reached street level. As we walked over Cross Street into the North End section, my nostrils started to flare. The smell in the air was heavenly.

There were pizzas, calzones, potato balls and a host of other foods in each of the windows we passed. It smelled as if the restaurants were cooking everything right on the sidewalk. Then there were the bakeries with the fresh cakes, pies and breads. It was hard for me to keep walking because I have such a sweet tooth.

The mission that day was fireworks. Sixteen people had given me their orders for the kinds they wanted. We walked about five minutes to Andrew's cousin's house, then the three of us went to an alley where an older man had one of each available kind laid out in the back of his green station wagon. We gave the man our orders. He walked over to a curb level window where he quietly spoke through a white curtain. Out came the fireworks after a couple of minutes.

Quick and easy. We headed back to the trolley with full schoolbags, right past the restaurants. I couldn't feel any more paper currency against my ankle. I had spent my entire sixty dollars buying fireworks. It was well after lunchtime and the aroma in the air made my stomach growl.

Andrew and I waited on the corner for the traffic light to turn red. Then, we could cross the street, walking underneath the highway en route to Haymarket Station. I stuck my hand in my back pocket and was surprised by the rustling of the twelve dollars I won playing cards. I ran right back down the street, coming back three minutes later with a white bakery box tied shut with string. I didn't open it until we were back on the trolley riding home. I felt like my name should have been Noah. I had two of every pastry and slice of cake that twelve dollars could afford me. I traded Andrew whatever he wanted so I could eat the second cannoli with chocolate chips underneath the powdered sugar.

I have never left the North End without buying something from the bakery. Yet still, there will never be another moment like the first time I opened that white box with the thin string. It was the best lunch I ever had.

The sun was still lingering in the sky. I figured there was probably a little more than an hour and a half of daylight left before we would be fully blanketed by the night. I guessed the temperature was still in the mid-eighties. The humidity of a Boston summer didn't let up even this late in the evening, but at least I was still working.

It only took us fifteen minutes to reach 24 Thatcher Street from the warehouse, so we got there just about seven thirty. There was barely enough room to maneuver the truck down the narrow street.

Parking was only permitted on the left hand side of the street, and we were driving a twenty-four foot truck. The only available parking to accommodate the truck was at the far corner of the street. This meant we had to walk an additional one hundred and twenty yards to get from where the truck was parked to the front door of the apartment, then up four flights.

I had seen Tom Dolan in the gym many times. He worked out religiously every morning before work. If Tom's day happened to end before five o'clock, then he would spend an additional hour in the gym before he went home. Tom requested stair jobs every day. It always seemed as if he wasn't satisfied unless he was sweating. Every muscle on his six foot, one inch frame resembled a chiseled statue.

I had been working out at the same gym around the corner from the warehouse for almost seven years. Barney paid for ten memberships for the year, and if we wear our green moving company T-shirts inside the gym, we can work out for free.

Tom pressed the top button on the short column of apartment buzzers. Waiting there with him side by side, I began to feel a little fat. But I laughed to myself because I knew Tom had a totally different body type than mine. Tom was tall with leaner muscle density. I was about four inches shorter with a bulkier frame. This thought helped to ease my mind a little. I also made a mental note to eat a little more chicken and fewer servings of beef. And, to add an extra one hundred sit ups to my daily routine. Like everyone else, I have to combat my own insecurities. Plus, I knew if we just so happened to get into a foot race for some inexplicable reason, I would smoke Tom like a pack of cigarettes.

The buzzer opening the outside door sounded. I followed my statuesque partner up the four flights to the top of the stairwell. The door was unlocked and slightly ajar. Tom rapped lightly on it with the knuckles of his left hand.

"Come on in," a female voice called. "I hope you ate your Wheaties this morning."

"We're two movers who can't eat Wheaties," Tom responded once we stepped inside of the living room. The boxes were stacked from floor to ceiling along the far wall to the left of the loveseat. Every box was a recycled liquor box. There were more than two dozen of black airline suitcases piled in the middle of the floor.

"Explain why you two movers can't eat Wheaties," said the voice. We still couldn't see the person.

"At least not with milk. We're two movers who just happen to be lactose intolerant," Tom said.

The explosion of giggling from adjoining room informed us there were two people in there.

"We'll be right out. We're just taping up the last of the boxes." said the first voice, still laughing.

Meagan and Tiffany Winters emerged from the bedroom showing their perfect teeth. Their young attractive smiles genuinely complimented their personas. We all shook hands while introducing ourselves. Both sisters seemed to have extremely outgoing personalities. Tom and I were soon informed they were both airline stewardesses. This was the reason for the plethora of traveling bags in the middle of the living room floor.

The only true difference between the sisters was their hair color. Meagan had blonde hair. Tiffany seemed to be a more natural brunette. Tiffany also gave the impression she was slightly older by her demeanor.

The humidity had forced Tom and me into our green tank top T-shirts before we came upstairs. We were not the only ones wearing tank tops. This was not all we had in common. Out of the four of us standing in the living room, not one person was wearing another item of clothing under their respective tank top. I had to keep reminding myself to keep eye contact, but it's difficult when the two people standing across from you appear to be pointing directly at you four times over. I would personally like to thank the manufacturers for white ribbed cotton tank tops that absorb perspiration.

I spent the next two hours and twenty minutes running the items in the fourth floor apartment down to Tom. Tom was loading the truck. Each trip down, I could catch a clean breath of fresh air. The air inside the hallway was dense and heavy. There were no windows in the four-story building so the air could circulate. A step or two outside the door, Tom ran towards me to take the items from my hands back to the truck by sprinting the one hundred plus yards to where it was parked. Then he still had to pack the items he was carrying from the apartment.

I concocted a game to occupy my mind while we worked. First, I sprinted up the stairs to the apartment. Then, I made sure that at least one of the two sisters pointed at me like the two forefingers of Isaac the bartender from the *Love Boat,* saying "He-e-e-y!" before I ran back downstairs with my arms loaded. I had to make sure I got at least two fresh breaths of air in my lungs before Tom, the bionic man, took the relay away from me. The goal was to maintain this pace and never stop to drink anything. I wanted to see how far I could push myself to exhaustion. Sometimes you need to know your own breaking point.

I have been seen at the gym on the Stairmaster for hours. The equipment in the gym would be recess to the hell I was putting my body through. After we had loaded the truck, I realized how much my stamina had increased since the first day that Fast Eddie and I worked with Paul Cavanaugh, the road driver from out of town. I actually felt proud of myself.

It was a short drive over to the offload. Meagan and Tiffany only moved a couple of blocks away to 68 Hanover Street, still within the North End. Access for the truck was definitely better at the new location. Meagan had parked her car at the parking meter in front of the handicapped parking spot, which was directly in front of the building. Once Meagan moved her car the two parking places were enough room for the truck to fit.

It was ten minutes past ten o'clock. I could see the blue and yellow clock from the Custom House just across the way in Faneuil Hall Market. This was turning out to be one of the longest days in my summer moving career.

I wondered how many calls I had missed on my pager, so I went to the truck to take a peek. There were thirty-two calls missed, twenty-six calls of them from Nina. I knew she was pissed because twenty of her calls were made by inputting the house phone number, followed by the star key, then she inputted consecutive numbers from one up to twenty. Granted, all of these twenty calls were made in the time frame of three minutes. But what could I do? I didn't work at an office. There were no pay phones in sight. And I didn't think it would be professional to ask the customer if I could make a personal call on their time. All things considered, I decided to call Nina after I left this job if it wasn't too late.

I followed Tom up to the sister's new second floor apartment. The idea of it being only two floors up was a huge relief. The hallway smelled edible. When Tom and I got upstairs, Meagan and Tiffany had two pizza pies waiting for us. They had their wine glasses full of Pinot Noir. I hadn't eaten since Mr. Matthews bought me lunch at Dr. Spriggs' place, but Tom didn't want to slow down by stopping to eat. Tom wanted to get the job completed. However, Tiffany wouldn't accept his answer. The pizza pies were deep dish, reminding her and Meagan of their hometown of Chicago.

"A true deep dish pizza has to be consumed hot to truly appreciate it," Tiffany exclaimed as she handed over a plastic fork, knife and paper plate to us.

"So what really brings you two pretty women to Boston?"

Tom's question was our only contribution to the conversation. Tiffany and Meagan shared the time talking and sipping their wine. One sister would talk while the other sister would sip. The one question Tom asked had an hour long answer. Since I was not the crew chief, all I had to do was follow Tom's lead. While Tom sat there pretending to look intrigued by the life stories he was hearing, I kept eating. Tiffany was absolutely right about how good deep dish pizza is.

Tom took the opportunity when Meagan went to uncork the second bottle of wine to restart the job we had begun almost four hours ago. The upside to offloading the truck is it is always faster than loading.

We went right back into work mode. We had everything from the sisters' apartment reconfigured into their respective places in less than an hour's time. I was sweeping out the back of the truck when Tom and Tiffany came walking outside the front door with their arms interlocked. The clock chimed from the Custom House. It was midnight. I didn't say anything, I just listened.

"Kamaul, Tiff can't seem to remember which box has her checkbook. I'm going to walk her over to the bank machine, over in Faneuil Market, so she can get the money to pay for her move. Do you mind going upstairs and putting Meg's bed together for her?" I smiled because Tom seemed to be the only reason Tiffany could actually remain standing.

"Kamaul, maybe you can put my bed together first so Tom and I can test it out when we get back." Tiffany's slurred speech erupted into a slurred laughter.

I raised my eyebrows and went back upstairs. Meagan and her friends were still pointing in my direction. I took the toolbox into Tiffany's room first, but actually didn't need it. The metal frame was easy to assemble. I wasn't quite sure about Tiffany's intentions with Tom, but if it involved this bed, she was all set.

Meagan had a canopy bed that the girls had disassembled before we reached them at seven thirty. I wasn't quite sure how to reassemble a canopy bed since this was the first one I was ever attempting. I asked Meagan for her help after I had the bottom of the bed frame erect. Together we reassembled the bed.

I was underneath the bed tightening up a couple of screws when Meagan opened the door, walking back into the room. I watched her freshly pedicured, French tip toes saunter towards the foot of the bed.

"So why are you so quiet?" From my position, it was almost as though her toes were talking to me.

"I'm always quiet. It's been a long day. Plus I have a couple of things on my mind." I found myself checking to see if Meagan had been born with any extra toes. But, there was no surgical scarring in the foot region.

"I'm a great listener if you want to talk. It would help me stay awake since I have to leave for a red-eye flight to California in a few hours." The cute toes were talking to me.

"Sorry, I'm not one to start a conversation I won't have time to finish. Tom mentioned he wanted to take off once he returned from the cash machine." I was tightening the last screw.

"Tom and Tiffany came back a couple of minutes ago."

"Oh, so is Tom ready to go?" I crawled out from under the bed.

"From what I could hear, he sounded like he was just getting started."

"Excuse me?" I was confused.

"If you stay quiet, you can hear for yourself." The toes replied in almost a giggle.

I stayed quiet for a few seconds. I placed my ear to the wooden floor boards. "Are they testing out the bed?"

"Yes, yes they are."

"Well, how long can that take? I give Tom about ten minutes at the most." I was standing in front of Meagan. She had both hands behind her back.

"What's going on in that room has nothing to do with Tom and everything to do with my sister's needs. You will be waiting a minimum of an hour. That's even if Tom's completely horrible. But from what I can hear, I think Tiffany likes Tom." Meagan was all smiles. Her hands were still behind her back.

"So what do I do?"

"You have options, too." Meagan licked her lips. She could definitely hold her liquor better than her sister but she was still saucy.

"My options are?" I had a smile on my face from being pointed at.

"Your first option is you can leave. You might be able to catch the last train home if you run. But you will have to leave at this very moment to make the train. Leaving now would deny you the opportunity of listening to the last two options. Tom left the keys to the truck on the table if you need to grab your bag from inside the truck."

"My second option is?"

"First I want to reemphasize, you do realize you are going to miss the last train?"

"My second option is?"

"I need to stay awake for my red-eye flight. Like my sister, I also have needs. I like what I see. I think we should see how stable my bed is?" Meagan waited for my response.

I tried to be reasonable. "You just met me not more than five hours ago. You know absolutely nothing about me. Yet, you want me to test out your mattress with you, interesting. I'll tell you this about me because you don't know me.

"My sexual appetite is insatiable. That is probably due to the scorpion in me. But from my perspective, we already have a problem. You are trying to stay awake. I want you to know, when I'm done I can guarantee you will go to sleep and miss your flight. I'll hook you up and rock your ass fast to sleep. So please, tell me about my third option. This way we can both lay all the cards on the bed, so to speak?"

"Option three is we can talk. You can tell me what seems to be troubling you. You can tell me what keeps you so quiet. I have some coffee brewing in the kitchen. I also have some fresh pastries I picked up from the bakery before it closed." Meagan pulled the white box from behind her back. The white box had the thin white string holding it closed.

"I don't drink coffee. I'm already too wired up."

"I'll grab you a glass of water then."

"Do you have any cannolis in this box?"

"Two regular and two chocolate chip." Meagan handed me the water when she came back into the bedroom. "Kamaul, are you really a Scorpio?"

"Yes, yes I am." I stood at the foot of Meagan's bed.

"So what's your most enduring trait as a Scorpio male?" Meagan never dropped her alluring eye contact.

"Loyalty." I answered without hesitation.

"Interesting. I too am a Scorpio. I was born on November the first. But the question I really want to know the answer to is; do you choose option two or option three?" Meagan climbed backwards up to the head of the bed. She untied the white box and placed it strategically between her outstretched shapely legs.

I was a grown twenty-year-old man. I knew it was going to be option three, but given the situation, I said the first thing to cross my mind.

"Meagan, do you play baseball?"

Every night went the same, since we moved to the condominium. My sister was in the bed by nine o'clock. My father usually followed suit and fell asleep just before ten o'clock—he usually woke up early in the morning for a five-mile jog before he started his day.

I tried diligently to finish my homework by ten o'clock at the kitchen table. I knew once ten o'clock rolled around the atmosphere in the small apartment would change.

"Are you done with your schoolwork?" Mom would ask.

"I'm just finishing up now." I always told my mother I was finishing up even when I wasn't.

Ten o'clock was Mommy's time to relax. She and I had been staying up after ten o'clock since we moved there to watch "Nick-at-Night" together. She would take her place in the floral armchair across from the pullout sofa. Mommy needed me to pull out the bed part of the sofa so she had a flat surface to cut out the pattern she was currently sewing. Of course, I lay across the middle of the bed since my cousin had destroyed the bed frame.

My mother very rarely purchased clothes from the department stores. When she was fifteen and Aunt Baye was twelve, Grandmama gave them a sewing machine for Christmas. Grandmama told them if they wanted new clothes, they had to learn to make clothes for themselves. Mommy and Aunt Baye worked after school. Half of their money went towards helping out Grandmama and the other half was theirs to spend. My mother spent most of her money in the garment district downtown.

My mother took me down to Chinatown from when I was a baby. She spent her leisure time buying patterns and fabric. Her closet was full of outfits she made. She could visualize an outfit just by holding a yard of fabric in her arms against other fabric. By the time she left the store, she had enough pattern, fabric, thread, buttons, zippers and elastic to keep her occupied for the next three days.

My mother sewed well enough to complete an outfit in a day. At the time of this story, though, it usually took her three days because of her first and second jobs, on top of caring for the family and making sure she was taking at least one class towards her degree.

No matter how many people begged her, no matter how many people pleaded with her to make them an outfit, Mommy always refused. Sometimes people would call the house offering her more for an outfit than the department store price. But her time sewing was simply her time. And anything after ten o'clock was our time.

"Did you finish washing the dishes yet?"

"Yeah, I did them when you went to go shower."

"Please don't let that man wake up and see one dirty dish in the sink. You know he will wake your butt up to wash one dish. Then he'll wake me up talking about you." She rolled her eyes as she spoke.

"The dishes are done." I laughed because she was dead right about my father. Daddy had indeed been known to wake her up out of a sound sleep to discuss dirty dishes. He was a Marine. Discipline is his life. Laziness is not tolerated.

Mommy pulled a paisley silk scarf out of a plastic bag. The scarf's dominant color was blue with a touch of burgundy scattered throughout. It would well complement the burgundy skirt suit she was making.

"This suit is going to be fierce," Mommy went on to say. "Everybody is going to love this outfit." My mother believed that people at work saw her as well-to-do because she dressed nice, she was married, she was taking classes to get her degree, she was paying for her children to go to school and she had self-confidence. She knew that just because you haven't eaten in a few days, you didn't have to look hungry. My mother was the greatest illusionist I've ever known.

My mother has always worn her emotion on her sleeve. I could tell from her face just what she is going to do or say next. If she ate food she really enjoyed, she'd start humming. If my father talked to her about the bills, she'd turn away from him to roll her eyes to the back of her head. When ten o'clock rolled around, her shoulder blades always seemed to pinch together.

"Kamaul, you need to scratch my back."

"I hate scratching your back."

"Boy, get your butt over here and scratch my damn back!"

We went through the same routine every night. Mommy would turn in her armchair so I could pull up the back of her shirt, unhook her bra and scratch her back. There was nothing weird about this, we'd done it for years.

"Why do you need your back scratched every night?" I asked, as I started to scratch away.

"Up, up, to the left. A little more left. Right there, that's the spot. Damn it, you. Let me see your fingernails."

I started laughing. "What's the problem?"

"You think you're slick. You think by biting your fingernails down to the nub you don't have to scratch my back, but you're wrong. Go in the bathroom and get my hair brush."

"I hate scratching your back!" I sucked my teeth as I went into the bathroom.

"Don't make me swear at you. Hurry up. Don't pretend like you have to go to the bathroom either. Grab the lotion while you're in there so you can moisturize my back after you scratch it. You know how dry my back gets."

"I still hate scratching your back!"

I actually didn't mind massaging her back. I knew she had tough days. I just didn't want her always asking me every day to scratch and massage.

"So, you are going into your third year of high school. Are you excited?" Mommy faced the television as I rubbed the cocoa butter on her back.

"Yeah, I finished all of the book reports so I can play football. I decided I'm going to try harder to focus on my school work this year. I know I didn't do so well before but I promise to make a change."

"I have always known you to try hard at whatever it is you're doing, so I believe in you. I just want you to go to college and finish your education. You don't realize how important that degree is to you now, but I do know. Not having my degree has limited me in ways I hope you'll never know. All

I ever truly ask of you and your sister is to get that degree. See, once you have that piece of paper, nobody can take it away from you. So just promise me you'll get your degree."

"I promise to get my degree. The day I receive my degree I'm going to hand it right over to you."

"Your father and I have invested a lot to give you opportunities many of your friends won't get. I don't want you to become distracted by what street life has to offer. Everything moves so fast when you're outside these four walls. You can get caught up in it all before you can turn around and walk away from it."

"I know."

"I can't tell you how you as a man should conduct yourself outside this house. That's your father's job to teach you. However, I do know I don't ever want to hear about you physically doing violence to any woman, ever. It's a punk who places his hands upon a woman. A punk knows there is no way that a woman can physically beat him. I didn't raise a punk. Did I?"

"No. What do I do if a woman puts her hands on me in a physical way?"

She nodded in understanding. "See, I know it's confusing sometimes. Women are confusing. Some women want their man to become confrontational with them so they can see how far they can actually push his buttons. They want to see how far it takes for their man to show his emotions. Then the same woman will say she was only playing when he happens to knock her upside her damn head.

"I don't want you to ever get to that point of hurting a woman. It will only lead you to the penitentiary behind some old bull crap. When that moment comes where you know you are at that point of causing harm to a woman, show her you have more control. Walk away. Even if it means you never acknowledge her again. If things get too bad, then you call me. I will personally come and beat a woman down."

We both laughed. My mother has been fighting for Aunt Baye and her other girl cousins since they were all kids. Since my family is heavily dominated by women, my mother has done more than her fair share of fighting. I watched her clean house on three women about to jump on Aunt Baye one afternoon on Blue Hill Avenue. All three women left from Blue Hill Avenue limping slowly, nursing one another's wounds as the crowd standing heckled them for not being able to beat one woman. Everyone around the block knew my mother has skills. She doesn't take mess from anybody, especially when it came to protecting the family.

"What else do I need to know?"

"I can teach you about staying away from fast-ass girls."

"What's a fast-ass girl?" I couldn't help but laugh as the phrase passed my lips.

"Don't laugh!" she warned. "A fast-ass girl is a girl who always wants to be surrounded by men. She usually has way more male friends than female friends. The male attention she seeks is compensation for feeling insecure. She is usually looking to validate her self-worth by affiliating with whomever she feels is going to be the next best name around. She always wants to be involved with the success of others. She has never put in any of her own work other than lying down on her back."

A mental picture of Poison and Tanya popped into my mind. "How am I supposed to know what she looks like?"

"Be observant. Pay attention to every girl you meet. A girl's actions will relay more information to you than she will ever tell you. More important, be choosy. Go with your gut feeling. If it doesn't feel right then it usually isn't right. Listen to the voices within you, don't second guess them. Decide what individuals are truly worthy of your time. Time is the only true luxury you have been granted on this earth."

"My voices tell me I'm done with your back."

"Stop fooling around. When you meet a good girl, you will know it. I would hope she too, will be working hard towards her own independent agenda. You will know she's worth your time. So get to know her. You remember when you were a little boy how people always made fun of you simply because you wore glasses? I would always feel bad for them."

"Why feel bad for them? I was the one being tortured."

"They were judging you on how you looked, not by who you were. They were not worthy of your time, your friendship. Those people who met you in passing will never truly know the beauty your heart holds. You have an optimistic way of looking at life, just like me. You must always look for the inner qualities of others first."

"But Mommy, a fast-ass girl has inner qualities, too. Shouldn't we give her an opportunity?" I teased.

"Shamaul!" My mother called me Shamaul when she gets irritated. Shamaul is a combination of profanity and my name, without actually swearing. Mommy was good about not swearing in front of the family.

"That's not my name."

My mother's voiced raised a decibel or two. "I'm telling you right now, boy. Don't bring home no fast-ass girl. Don't bring home no loud-mouthed girl I'm going to have to curse out. And don't bring home any snotty nosed babies for me to watch neither. You know how busy my life is. I work two jobs. I go to school. You hear me."

We both started laughing. Mommy knew I had my head on straight. We had that conversation more than twenty times. Mommy and I talked about everything. There wasn't a topic that was taboo after ten o'clock.

"Kaaamaaull." Mommy had the biggest grin on her face.

"I don't have any money."

"How do you know I'm going to ask you to loan me twenty dollars until this Friday. I get paid this week." The grin was so pronounced, it almost looked drawn on.

"You ask me every night. Every night I tell you the same thing." I shook my head.

Mommy got up from the arm chair. She walked into her bedroom. I knew my father hid his money before he went to sleep at night. Hiding his money was the last thing Daddy did right before he closed the bedroom door while Mommy was taking a shower.

It's sad to say I wasn't surprised to see her emerge from the bedroom with the huge apple cider jug we all put our pennies inside. She poured the pennies onto my deformed sleep area.

"Start wrapping. Fifty pennies goes into each wrapper. Wrap enough for my morning coffee too." She tossed the penny wrappers on top of the copper mountain on the bed.

We sat there talking, watching the *Donna Reed Show* and wrapping pennies. I caught myself sneaking glances over at her. No one ever had to tell me what kind of girl my mother was. She had been with my father since they were fifteen years old. She was the type of woman that would always be ready to weather the storm. My father made the right choice a long time ago.

Mommy taught me that you cannot have a relationship without communication. I knew whoever came into my life as a possible mate would have to be my best friend. My potential mate would have to be able to talk me well beyond ten o'clock. I knew she would have to be as special as Mommy. I just hoped she would know how to manage her money.

Tom and I pulled into the parking lot of the warehouse just before three o'clock in the morning. Neither one of us said much on the drive back. It had been a long day. Tom and I both knew we'd only have time for a quick cat nap before we had to come back to work again in a few hours.

Tom's car and my father's blue bike were the only means of transportation left in the parking lot other than moving trucks. Tom jumped in his car, tooting his horn as he drove out of the parking lot. I stuck the key inside the lock that secured the bike to the chain linked fence and I threw my backpack on my back. I ran three full strides with the bike on my right side to gather momentum. Securing my left foot on the pedal after the third stride, I shifted my body weight to bring my right leg over the body of the bike. Then came the unexpected sensation of falling forward over the handlebars.

My body bounced one time off the contorted handlebars before I used my arms to shield my face. I closed my eyes just before hitting the rocky unpaved road of the parking lot. It took a couple of moments for the kicked up dirt to settle. I was in no particular rush to get up.

My arms were on fire from the momentum carrying me to a halt. The hand breaks on top of the handlebars had broken the skin on my chest and my right hip. My left shoulder had absorbed the brunt of the damage. A coaster-size patch of skin had been removed upon contact with the road. Within a few minutes, the white meat in my exposed shoulder turned to free flowing blood. Taking one of the sweaty T-shirts out of my backpack, I tied it around my shoulder as tight as I could manage.

I walked back to my father's blue bike, which laid there mangled. The rear of the bike, the frame and the handlebars were all in tact. The front tire, however, looked worse than I felt. I loosened the clamp on the quick release and held the tire close to examine it further. That's when I knew that my fall was no accident.

The tire didn't have a flat. Someone had used some form of metal cutters and snipped every other spoke at the base of the front bike tire.

I picked up my father's bike and carried it on my right shoulder with the front bike tire in my left hand. A song popped into my head to help distract me from hurting. It was that Soul II Soul song again. At that moment, all I could remember from the song was the chorus. "Back to life, back to reality...However do you want me, however do you need me." I used the next fifteen minutes to fixate my mind in that happy rhythmic place as I limped home. The words to the song kept me going as I walked, limped, bled, smiled and sang.

NOT TODAY....

You're not in the mood.
Now neither am I.
You say you want to see me smile.
Stop and think
Have you given me one reason why?
Not today.

I turned over in the bed this morning
Thinking today would be a good day.
I felt good
I wanted the day to be perfect
So naturally I called you
So you could feel the same way too.

I cooked
Even placed a rose in your seat.
I thought a candle-light breakfast
Was a step close to the extravagant.
But for you
I certainly did not mind the journey.

When you finally arrived
You turned the lights on
You said it was too dark in here.
Before I could pull out your chair
You had already sat there.
Now, I feel like that rose
Whose fullness of life was quickly put to rest.

Can I have a hug?
I'm trying to eat.
Can I have a kiss?

You'll ruin my hair.
Can you show me some affection?
Maybe later.

I would be a little more
Compassionate about your feelings,
Compassionate about you having a bad day
If it wasn't nine in the morning.
Was the traffic congested?
Was it something I said or didn't do?

So I think its best that you leave.
Call me when your attitude changes.
Maybe tomorrow?
Possibly later in the week?
But definitely
Not today.

"Kamaul, are you all right?"

"I cleaned myself up last night. My shoulders and arms took the worst of the fall. My arms look worse than they actually feel. I'm just a little bit sore on my hip."

"I saw you fall last night. More important, I watched as you got back up. It's always important that you get back up. Even though it hurts, I need you to find a way to smile. I need you to find a reason to keep pushing on towards your tomorrow."

"I'm trying out here. It's just not easy. Why are there so many obstacles in my way?"

"You will always have choices to make of how to defeat the obstacles. The answer will not always be as simple as going over, under, going around or through the obstacle. Sometimes you have to learn to play a better game of chess."

"Is it as simple as chess?

"The game of life is as simple as you want it to be. Yet, this journey for you was never intended to be easy."

"But why is this journey being made so difficult for me?"

"I can't give you all of the answers you seek today. I can tell you to believe in yourself. Trust in yourself, even if there is no one else you feel you can trust. When the day finally comes, it will all make sense then."

"If I play a better game of chess do I ever win?"

"Kamaul, sometimes when you win you actually lose. Sometimes a loss can be the most satisfying victory. Sometimes when you think you've won, it's actually a stalemate. You have to place the game of your life into its proper context."

"Now I'm confused."

"It will all make sense to you when the time comes. Never stop playing the game with all of the energy, passion, hunger and knowledge you attain. You truly only lose when you become a quitter. But I need you to get back up."

"I am getting back up. I'm not a quitter."

"That always reassures me to know. I actually meant it's time for you to wake up."

"It's already time for you to go? The time goes by way too fast."

"Yes, but I'm always with you. I promised you that a long time ago. Just keep smiling baby, just keep smiling."

"Bye, Nana. . ."

The front door slamming shut was my alarm clock. My father was going out for his morning six o'clock jog. I was caught somewhere between dreaming and waking up. The morning daylight had been shining on my closed eyes for the last half hour. It always astounds me, how the colors resemble a blazing fire when light shines on your closed eyelids. Laying cozy on the sofa would have been nice if I could have continued to sleep a full eight hours. But I had never heard of anyone earning any money while sleeping on a broken sofa. I admitted I probably wouldn't be the first person to pull off this feat either. The work schedule at Barney's had me due in at seven o'clock. I just needed a little push to wake me up.

The telephone rang. I reached over my head for the receiver. Small heads of sewing pushpins scratched my right arm as it stretched. My mother used the sofa—my bed—as a huge pincushion when she sewed. But she didn't always get all of the pins. She had a tendency to leave a few small, pointy, sharp pins wherever she was sewing last. Apparently she had recently been sitting where my head was right now. She had four tomato-red pincushions somewhere in that two-bedroom home, yet I was constantly being stuck. Believe me when I say there is no feeling like being stuck in the leg by sewing pins as you're rolling over, trying to get comfortable in the middle of the night.

I still managed to pick up the receiver on the first ring. I didn't want to wake up my mother and sister.

"Hello?" My voice was barely audible. I could smell my own morning breath ricocheting off of the phone receiver.

"And where were you last night? I paged you!" Nina's Puerto Rican accent came out full force when she was upset. I could usually tell how upset she was with me by how heavy her accent sounded. Judging from what I heard, I knew the woman on the other end of the phone was well past upset. It's ironic how Nina speaks without an accent the other ninety-five percent of the time.

Now, I was awake. "I got your pages after I finished up last night," I explained patiently. "It was just too late for me to call your house."

"Who is she?"

"Who is who?" I was confused

"Who is the whore you were with last night, because you definitely were not with me. You didn't even think to call me last night."

"Are you crazy?" I already know the answer to this question.

"So who is she?" I could hear the huffing and puffing on the receiver.

"I already told you I was working last night! The job didn't finish until after midnight. And I'm not going to call after midnight disrespecting your parent's house."

"Are you telling me you were not with any other female last night?! Nobody moves furniture at midnight! Do I look stupid to you?!"

"If you are wearing a red nose and you have on big pink Easter Bunny ears with pink high heel shoes to match, you might look stupid to me." But then I paused. "Wait a minute, that might actually look cute if we playing dress up." She snorted. "How about if you are wearing a motorcycle helmet with the clear visor while carrying a skateboard, when we both know you take the train to work every day. Then the answer would be yes." I reckoned it was in my best interests not to tell Nina about the two sisters and their four pointy friends. There was no reason to add fuel to the fire.

"*Mira*, don't play with me!" I heard a slight chuckle.

Nina has been this hot tempered crazy young woman since I met her. She carries a butterfly knife on her hip for protection. One day Nina proved to me while we were wrestling that she could flip open her weapon while taking a one-step lunge towards me before I had the chance to extend my right arm in an attempt to strike her. Baby Girl was smooth with the butterfly knife her father taught her to open. She always promised me she would never fly her knife open on me as long as I didn't give her a reason. I figured my best bet is never to give Nina a reason to reach for her hip.

I had been anticipating her phone call on some strange level. I could count on one hand how many days have gone by where we haven't exchanged any words at all since we got together. I also knew she really called because she worried about me. Nina just wanted to know that I was all right. She just had a dramatic way of expressing herself. It was a piece of what made her special. But not the short, yellow bus type of special.

"Well, unfortunately, I was. Then on my way home my front bike tire gave way and I fell over the handle bars. So I had to carry the bike all of the way home last night."

Nina started laughing on the other end of the phone. "Are you okay? That's what you get for not calling me back last night."

"Don't start laughing at me getting hurt! It's too early in the morning." I couldn't resist cracking a smile myself although I was telling her not to laugh.

"You are the only person I know to have more crazy stuff happen to you." Being with me has definite entertainment value. Nina has watched complete strangers go out of their way to start conversations with me about their most personal topics. Because I like to listen to people I will usually engage them in whatever subject they want to discuss.

"Baby Girl, me flying over the handlebars into the dirt is not even funny. When I stood up I looked Pigpen from the Charlie Brown cartoon. I think I know who messed with my front tire though."

Baby Girl's mood changed from laughing to serious in an instant. Her accent mysteriously disappeared. "Oh no, you said you *think*. If you think then you are not 100% positive that someone messed with your father's old blue raggedy ten speed bike. Kamaul, you know your father's bike is a piece of junk. They don't even make ten speed bikes anymore. You need to take advantage of the situation and trade that thing in to get your father a mountain bike. Promise me you won't start any fights when you go to work, promise me."

"You know I can't make you that promise. You're not the one who went flying into a pile of dirt late last night."

Nina must have been imagining me flying through the air into a dirt pile, because she laughed again. But then she said, "Then, promise me you will have 100% confirmation that someone tampered with your bike before you get into it, okay? Promise me."

"I promise to find out who messed with my bike before I do anything."

"Don't forget why you're working at the moving company in the first place. You are trying to save enough money to pay for your tuition. This is also the only reason I let you break so many dates with me on Friday and Saturday nights because I know you don't want to ask anyone for money towards supporting your education. So don't blow it all on fighting."

"I hear you."

"Don't forget we are leaving to go to Six Flags in New Jersey on this Friday night for the long Fourth of July Weekend. You will be the last pick up on our way out of Boston."

"I have to go get ready for work."

"I love you," said Baby Girl.

"*Te amo.*" I hung up the telephone.

Nina and I started seeing each other a month after the Thanksgiving football game. She cheered on as I hobbled through the entire game with a badly sprained ankle. I had set my goal on finishing the season off by playing in the finale game against Boston English High School. Whether it was running or hobbling, I had my mind set. I have to admit that I'm pretty stubborn when my mind is made up.

Nina actually kept a scrapbook of every football game we played during the fall of 1989. She gave me the scrapbook the week after Thanksgiving. I was impressed how much time she spent creating the album. She went through both local newspapers, using a yellow highlighter to show not only when I made the newspaper but when any member of my crew made the newspaper.

The Valentine's Day of my junior year at Boston Latin, I wanted to do something creative and original for Nina. Walls and I won enough tickets the night before so I could surprise her. The next morning when Nina opened her locker, one hundred and seven stuffed animals tumbled onto the hallway floor. We had officially been dating one hundred and seven days. One little monkey remained, holding a yellow rose in his left and small yellow satin bag in his right. Nina opened the bag to see her new gold anklet. It made me happy to see her so ecstatic.

Nina was the first girl to hang with the crew who could play the dozens. I watched as she traded insults with Tiny Baby and Sparrow even when it came down to "Yo Mama" jokes. Nina was one of the crew.

Although we were together, it took me awhile to tell Nina I loved her. It took me two years after we started dating to express my love. It was when we were up at Amherst in 1991. It was the moment I hated myself the most; it was the moment I knew I truly loved the crying eyes which stood in front of me. Nina cared more about me than I think I cared about myself up in Amherst. But that's another story.

It was closing in on six thirty, so I got dressed quickly to get to work. The ten-minute bike ride was about a thirty-minute walk. I threw on a long-sleeved shirt to cover the fresh wounds on my arms and shoulder. I didn't want to give Jacob the satisfaction of seeing the results of his handiwork. I also had to hurry up to leave the house because I knew my father would be looking for his blue bike, which I had hid in the basement of the building until I could get it fixed. My father has a tendency to do nothing but ask questions when things are out of place. Me not riding his bike to work or the bike not being in the apartment at night would definitely raise his left eyebrow before the rapid fire questions began. So, I waited for my father to jog to the back of the building before I sprinted out of the front door.

The fifteen-minute jog woke me up. My sweat felt like rubbing alcohol on my injuries. Jacob was one of the first faces I saw while running onto the dusty parking lot. He had the same angry scowl on his face from the day before. Well, maybe it was less intense since he probably found out that his girlfriend did not know me from a hole in the wall. His remaining anger was probably due to all of the other information I had picked up about his lady. No man wants another man to have too many facts about his woman. But when all was said and done, Jacob didn't have the surprised look in his eyes saying, "You should be hurt. Why are you here today? Where is your bike?" Jacob's eyes were still simply saying, "I want to kick the piss out of you so bad."

Nina's words danced in my head about being 100% sure. I had to back off from the thought that it was Jacob who had cut my front tire spokes. It had to be someone, but out of the warehouse full of workers, I just couldn't pinpoint the right person yet. Yet the tingling of my street sense was a definite indication the culprit was within my scarred arm's reach.

I strongly dislike jogging. Actually, I hate jogging. My father used to wake me up, when I was around ten years old, to ride my bike while he jogged. Daddy figured it would be good quality time together. I volunteered two days later to clean the bathroom on the weekends instead of going out early in the morning with him. I cleaned that bathroom until I got my first job.

Now, I found myself jogging to work for the next couple of days. I let my father know his bike was at the bike shop getting fixed. Daddy was happy about me paying to tune up his bike. There was no need to tell him what happened for me to put the bike in the bike shop. I disliked the thought that I had given someone the opportunity to ruin property that I didn't own. I figured by me running to work, if someone has a personal issue with me then it forces them to come deal with me directly.

Wednesday I decided to push myself a little bit harder by turning my jog into a sprint. Short sprints mixed into the jog shaved four minutes off the time it took get there. It felt pretty good to push myself. My body has always responded well for me. I tend to treat my body like a machine. It gets a little stronger and little tougher with each push I give it towards the edge. I'm still looking to find my breaking point.

Running with a back pack was uncomfortable, and made it take a little longer for my body to cool down. Jogging in a long-sleeved shirt in the summer morning made me sweat double. I decided to switch shirts in the second floor bathroom. There was a conversation going on between two sets of unidentifiable feet in the closed stalls. They were doing their necessary business—it wasn't easy changing shirts while holding my breath. I made a point of spraying the air freshener a few extra seconds before leaving the bathroom.

The days were beginning to run into one another. I honestly couldn't remember what day of the week it was, other than Sunday because that was the only day I didn't have to get up to go to work. I was glad the daily job corkboard displayed the date as well as the day of the week. I found my name on the board underneath crew number twenty seven. My name was first with the initials B.M. underneath. The paperwork had two men going to an assisted living facility in Newton. We had to switch around two of the residents' rooms due to a change of flooring at the facility.

"Excuse me, Dominic, who is B.M.?" I asked.

"B.M. is Big Man. We don't use his legal name around here."

Ah, Rhino-man. I threw my hands open as the words passed my teeth, "Why not?"

Dominic pulled me over to the side. He was just audible enough for the two of us to hear, "He doesn't exist. B.M. is a ghost to most. He doesn't legally work here because if he did then he would have to report the income to the courts. The courts would give more money to both of his ex-wives.

"Once in awhile his ex-wives get together to follow him around to wherever they think he works before he drives the local bus for the night shift. If one of his ex-wives catches him working at a moving company for cash and they bring it before the judge, then Big Man quits. He moves on to another moving company that will pay him cash no questions asked. He currently works for five local moving companies. That's the reason he usually rides his bike into this office. Then there are days like today where he's going to meet you out at the job in his van."

"So Big Man is the crew chief?"

"No. We don't allow him to collect payment. Years ago, we tried Big Man as crew chief. He had the customer write the checks out to cash. The office never received the payment. Do you think you can handle being crew chief?"

"Yeah, I can handle it." I could feel my grin stretching from ear to ear.

"A couple of the older veterans said they believed that you were ready. So I'm willing to give you a shot."

Dominic showed me the three places where I needed to have the customer sign. The first place gives us permission to begin physically moving the furniture. The second place was the signature with regards to insurance. The Commonwealth of Massachusetts automatically gives each customer we move sixty cents per pound on any article that is damaged. For example, if we were moving a priceless framed letter from President John F. Kennedy to his brother President Robert F. Kennedy in which we accidentally smashed the case and tore the letter rendering the paper worthless, the owner would only receive sixty cents per pound of the letter. In contrast, customers also have the right to take out full replacement coverage on the entire shipment that we are to handle. In the case there is something damaged, the item is replaced with no questions asked. The third and final signature is to say that the customer has received a complete moving experience.

Dominic had given me a lump of information to digest that morning. I asked him to use a yellow highlighter on the areas where I needed signatures on an extra bill of lading. I also wrote down in layman's terms the explanation for the times I needed signatures.

I drove the truck. I practiced my speech at red lights as Dominic had explained the paperwork to me. I couldn't stop smiling on the way to the assisted living facility.

It was just after seven thirty when I parked the box truck in front of the main building. I saw Rhino-man's white van with the purple trim parked across the street. His van always looked like it was in getaway position for a bank robbery. Rhino-man liked to park in the best position to disappear. If something was to happen and the police were called, Rhino-man was ready to go.

Rhino man walked out of the main lobby as I closed the driver's side truck door.

"Hey, Kamaul, the resident coordinator says we can't start moving anything until eight thirty. They need to feed the residents breakfast." We shook hands when we were arms reach of each other.

"So, what do we do for the next hour?"

"The old people are eating. Let's walk around the corner to grab a cheese danish at the Au Bon Pain."

Au Bon Pain was set up in the cafeteria fashion, so you serve yourself. There are trays available to transport your food. You pay at the register before you sit down.

One of the two workers in the store, the older white woman, was behind the counter making deli and breakfast sandwiches. The other, the younger black lady, manned the cash register. She would periodically walk around wiping down tables and clearing off debris for the next customers to sit down.

I by-passed the pastries since I wasn't hungry. I grabbed a cranberry juice. I took two steps towards the cash register to pay for my juice when Rhino-man grabbed my arm.

"She's cute—talk with her for a couple of minutes at the register while I pick out my breakfast." He spoke in a whisper.

There was no one in line behind me. Starting a conversation was easy. The name tag on the cashier's shirt read Elizabeth. My baby sister has the same name. Rhino-man stood off in the corner of the store, out of view of the two store workers. I watched out of the corner of my eye as he stuffed cheese, cherry and blueberry danishes into his mouth. He took sips of coffee between each outrageous bite just to help wash the pastries down. Then he wrapped an apple turnover in a napkin before he stuffed it into his pocket. It was hard trying to maintain a conversation let alone a straight face. A burst of laughter almost escaped when Rhino-man licked his fingers clean. Then he walked over to us at the cash register.

"If my friend takes your phone number, do you think you can give me a discount on this small cup of coffee? The prices you guys ask for a cup of coffee are outrageous." Rhino-man said with a guttural laugh.

Elizabeth was looking me in the eyes, "If your friend promises to call me than you can have the cup of coffee for free."

I took Elizabeth's phone number. Rhino man got a free breakfast. I paid for my cranberry juice. Rhino-man spent the remainder of the time until eight thirty trying to convince me how each item he ate is already precalculated into the company's daily profit/loss. Today, apparently, Rhino-man had felt it was time to make a personal appearance. He didn't appreciate being merely statistical data.

Sabrina Gordon, the residential coordinator, walked us to the westernmost of the three building complex. It was easy to see that the west building was the first constructed. It was in desperate need of a fresh coat of paint. As we walked, Sabrina pointed out that all of the residents from the west building were temporarily being relocated to the east building, the newest on the grounds. The renovations were scheduled to be completed over the next four months. Therefore Mrs. Gordon wanted us to take the personal effects of two of the residents to a corresponding room in the east building. She asked if we could set the rooms up so they would be identical to the rooms they had been living.

The first room the three of us reached belonged to Davis Jones. Davis was an older gentleman in his mid-seventies. Mrs. Gordon introduced us to him and informed us on the way to the new room that Mr. Jones didn't have too many visitors. It was sad to hear that most of his sons and daughters lived less than ten minutes away in the town of Newton.

Rhino-man and I walked back to the truck after we parted company with Mrs. Gordon. We grabbed two large empty bin boxes and four four-wheel dollies. The long walk from room to room, then back again, was just over five minutes.

Davis Jones' bedroom had just the essentials—one bed, one triple dresser with an attached mirror, a taller dresser also doubling as a television stand, and one rocking chair. The living room area held a sofa, one reclining arm chair, one side table, one coffee table, a kitchen table with two chairs, and, in the middle of the kitchen table, sat a chess board. Mr. Jones sat at the kitchen table studying the pieces.

Rhino-man suggested we move the bedroom set first. He pointed out it would give one of the nursing assistants an opportunity to make Mr. Jones' bed while we were moving the rest of the living room.

"I heard about the run-in you had with Jacob," Rhino-man said while pushing the triple dresser to the new location.

"Yeah, it was no big deal. How did you hear about it?" I walked the higher dresser down the hall.

"This is a small company. These bitches, who work on the trucks with you, gossip more than women. So be aware of what you say. More importantly, be aware of to whom you say it." We were entering the main building.

"Leroy already pulled my coattails to most of the ass-kissers working amongst us anyways," I said. "Me being new this year, I just been working hard while trying to get my bearings." I found myself speaking a little louder. Rhino-man was in the lead.

"So, have you been working a lot of hours since Barney had his last meeting?"

"I've been averaging about forty hours every three days. The lack of sleep is starting to take a toll on me. I'll catch up on sleep when I'm back taking classes in the fall."

"See, ever since Barney had his little meeting, he's been using you newer guys to take hours away from the guys like me who have been around since the inception of this bullshit company. Instead of everyone working more hours, I've noticed my working days have been getting cut back. Barney knows I rely on working here to take some of the pressure off from working a full-time job where I only see a quarter of my check after everyone else eats. I love my kids. I just hate the fact that my ex-wives reap the pleasures of me working while they sit on their asses watching soap operas every day."

"I thought you just worked here just to put extra money in your pocket."

"I move furniture because it's the only way I can survive. I learned early in my years, if I work overtime then my ex-wives get a raise. They would make more money with each extra bus route I drive. So I said screw it! I'll give them the minimum the court requires. Any extra money earned is money that has to remain hidden. Now, Barney wants to take away my hours. But I'm way smarter than him. I already made the necessary adjustments that leave him no choice but to call me to work the next day." Rhino-man's evil laughter filled the desolate corridor.

"How can you make sure Barney calls you to work?" I was curious.

"Let's just say I'm guaranteeing myself more work on a daily basis." The smile was all I needed to know the conversation had come to an end.

Rhino-man and I moved Davis Jones and then his next door neighbor to the east building. We finished up minutes before noon. The hallways were beginning to get packed with the residents on their way to the cafeteria for lunch.

I did a double-take, because Rhino-man had an oversized johnnie gown to fit his large frame. He motioned to let me know he was going to lunch with the other residents. He fit in perfectly with the flowing crowd on their way to the cafeteria. All I could do was laugh.

I passed by Davis Jones's door and saw him studying the chess board again. I started to believe this was the extent of his day. I stepped into the room and hovered over the board.

"White wins in six moves." It was the first thing that came to mind.

"Black wins in three moves." Davis turned his head in my direction.

I had to take a second look, but Mr. Jones was correct. "Do you want to play a game?" I asked.

"Are you sure you have time? No one seems to ever have time to indulge an old man."

"My partner went to the cafeteria to have lunch. I watched him eat earlier today. I figure we have about a half hour before he completely fills himself," I smiled.

Mr. Jones talked while we played. He had been born and raised in the Newton Highland area, and had four children and nine grandchildren. The doctors had diagnosed him with early stages of Alzheimer's disease at sixty-seven. He showed no sign of it now, and he'd been in the facility for maybe ten years.

Mr. Jones's children had stuck him in the assistant living facility because no one wanted to take him into their own homes. The irony was Mr. Jones paid for all four homes outright when each one of his children married. Instead of the care and attention he deserved, Mr. Jones was stored away from his home as his kin waited for him to die. Mr. Jones figured they were waiting to split up his estate. Not one of his family members had come to visit him in more than five years. Every three months his oldest son would call the resident director to find out if Davis had died—he needed to know if he should send a check for his father's living facility for the following quarter.

Mr. Jones beat me in two games before Rhino-man finished eating lunch. We still had another small job to do before Rhino-man had to report for his full-time job. I promised Mr. Jones if I ever found myself in the neighborhood I would stop by for a rematch game.

I left Mr. Jones sitting there staring at the third game we had begun. I made a mental note to myself to never let my elder family members die alone.

The second job was quick. The three hours floated by as we moved a lady from the twentieth floor of her apartment building down to the fourth floor of the same building. Most of the time was spent putting all of the contents of the cupboards away. The lady hadn't packed a single box. We transported most of the contents in her apartment with our big bin boxes. The lady was nice, so we didn't mind.

I drove back to the warehouse after the second job. Rhino-man left to go do his best impersonation of Ralph Kramden, the bus driver. As I traveled along the highway, I counted two of Barney's green moving trucks in a movie theater parking lot. I jumped off of Interstate 93 South at the next exit, which brought me about a mile from the warehouse.

My first impression was that of a giraffe running in my direction. Barney Lynch's long, enthusiastic strides had him reach the driver's side window of the truck before the front tires had a chance to kick up some of the dirt in the parking lot. I shifted the truck into park but let the engine idle.

"How was it out there for you today?" Barney's face was flushed red from the exertion.

"Both of the jobs were accomplished within the estimate. I suppose everything went fine. I brought back the checks." I handed Barney the paperwork with the payment folded inside.

"This is great! I knew you could crew chief your own jobs. You are a great company asset. Kamaul, we need you to be a team player here. We still have fourteen jobs that desperately need to happen today. We promised our customers we would be there. We should have more crews and more trucks back by now, but every one of the morning jobs are still out there. Do you think you can manage to do another job?"

Barney looked so humbled begging. I realized at that moment why those trucks were parked in the movie theater parking lot. Those other crews were done with their morning jobs. They were probably hoping that all of the afternoon jobs would be off the corkboard by the time the movie's credits ran. Most of my co-workers had started to look worn down over the last few weeks. I was tired, too. On the other hand, I needed to keep grinding. I would get all of rest I needed after Labor Day.

"I don't mind going back out."

Barney's face lit up. He reached through the driver's side window and beeped the horn twice. I was surprised to see Fast Eddie swing the building's front door open. Eddie carried the paperwork in his hand for my third job of the day and smiled when he saw me behind the steering wheel. I hadn't worked with Fast Eddie in about two months. Eddie had emerged as one of the favorite rookie movers by the veteran crew chiefs thus far this summer.

Another green truck was making the turn coming down the street towards us. Barney didn't say a word. He patted my shoulder before he took off running. I could see his long, lanky body become smaller and smaller through the driver's side mirror. It was the other truck's turn to hear the whole team player spiel.

Eddie shook my hand once he sat down in the truck. He handed me the paperwork while he looked up the address in the yellow Metro Boston map book. The job was a four to six hour estimate. We were moving a second floor apartment to a single family house in Brookline Village. After seeing the 20 Homer Street address, I didn't need to see the map book. I shifted the truck into gear, turning the steering wheel counter clockwise until we made a quick u-turn.

"Do you know where you're going?" Fast Eddie asked.

"Homer Street is a one-way street that intersects onto Harvard Street. I spent grades five through eight of my parochial schooling at St. Mary's School of the Assumption. Then I used to go back to pick up my sister who also went there," I answered back.

"You went to Catholic school?" Eddie seemed surprised.

"I went for eight years. I wanted to go for twelve years but that didn't happen."

"Are you Catholic?"

"No, I was never baptized."

"Then why go to a Catholic school?" Eddie had a legitimate question.

"My father always figured the parochial school system was a more disciplined, structured environment. Meanwhile, I was being taught the Bible, without being force fed. My mother's family has a heavy Baptist influence. We also have family who are Pentecostal and Jehovah's Witnesses. I've gone to worship with all of the different denominations. I also enjoy sitting down and eating a bean pie while talking over the teachings of the Koran. My father figured whenever I was old and wise enough I would be ready to decide which religious path I wanted to take. I consider myself a nondenominational God-fearing student of the truth."

We then had the most intelligent conversation I had had since working at Barney's. It felt good going to work shoulder to shoulder with someone who was willing to hang in there until the job was done. I couldn't help thinking of the first day Eddie and I worked together with the road driver moving the couple in from California. We were the blind leading the blind on that first night. Today, we were both running a job together. We were still small fish in the big pond. It didn't matter to me that we were given our opportunity out of desperation—I was just glad to be given the opportunity. The rest was up to us.

We took the left off of St. Paul Street and the quick right onto Homer Street. Judging from the garbage cans in front of number 20 securing the parking place, it was safe to assume we had the right place. The pair sitting on the steps had the grandest smiles on their faces as they jumped up to remove the parking barriers from the street.

Steve and Marjorie Charlotte is what I consider to be a "Ten Couple" as I watched them take a step back onto the curb. Steve stood on Marjorie's left. They were both around five feet, five inches tall. Steve was thin as a rail, looking as if he weighed about one hundred pounds. Marjorie filled out her numerical digit weighing close to triple Steve's weight. I-0. They appeared to be in their early thirties. Steve wore his hair long in the back, which highlighted the premature thinning on the top of his head.

Fast Eddie and I parked the truck and followed the couple upstairs after a brief introduction. The Charlottes were definitely a chipper couple, and I needed to be around upbeat people after the assisted living facility. All those lonely people made me think of an orphanage for the elderly. That's why working with Fast Eddie was a plus.

The heat wasn't too bad for six o'clock. I still wore a fresh long-sleeved shirt and wasn't sweating too hard. One detail troubled me—I couldn't help noticing a crimson red flush on the left side of Steve's face. Steve's pale red face was ornamented by transparent tape holding the two halves of his glasses together. Steve didn't speak much nor did he make much eye contact for a man in his early thirties. Marjorie did most of the talking. Marjorie was so bubbly.

"I had Steve take apart all of the furniture," she said. "Every box has color-coordinated stickers on them so you know where the boxes are going. I had Steve measure each piece of furniture. Steve also sketched out the furniture setup for each of the rooms of our single family house. There is a taped drawing sketch over the door frame of each of the rooms."

Steve nodded his head in agreement as his eyes watched the ground.

I asked for the signatures I needed so we could start the move. Fast Eddie and I carried one box apiece downstairs as not to go outside to the truck empty handed. The first rule of Big Barney's was never make a trip to the truck empty handed. Eddie asked if he could pack the truck. He wanted to use the fact that we were together to gain some experience packing a truck efficiently without being bombarded by the likes of a bigger truck job. With the bigger jobs, when there are five men shuttling the truck packer boxes, it's tougher to gather your thoughts fast enough because the beginning of the job is in rapid fire mode. I have seen truck packers become backed up by a wall of boxes in less than a minute. Inside the truck the packer plays a live game of Tetris, the computer game where different shaped blocks have to fit into each other in rapid fire succession. I could tell Eddie wanted to be known as a good game player.

I started shuttling Eddie boxes first. We were in a nice rhythm. A lot of the colored stickers the Charlottes had placed on the boxes were peeling off, probably due to the humidity. I made the suggestion when I picked up the next box that it might make it a little easier if the couple also used a marker to write down each box's destination on the side of the box. Marjorie agreed.

As I began walking back down the stairs, I heard a thunderous crash back in the apartment. No one yelled, so not thinking much more of it; I continued to carry the box out to Eddie. I told Eddie he might have been a mason in his previous life the way he built his wall of boxes. Eddie laughed as I ran back upstairs.

I counted a total of twenty-two stairs from outside to the second floor landing. It took me four seconds to reach the second floor apartment. There, my eyes caught on a shiny piece of glass next to the apartment door. I realized you could only see the glass while standing in the hallway. The small piece of glass was actually an eyeglass lens. I picked it up.

"Are you aware that you have an eyeglass lens underneath the door?" I asked.

Marjorie was the only one in the room. "Oh, thank you for finding it! Steve was trying to move some of the boxes. He tripped over his own feet carrying the box of books. The weight of the box broke his glasses." Marjorie laughed at Steve's clumsiness.

Steve emerged from the bathroom wearing basketball goggles. I hand-ed Marjorie the eyeglass lens and picked up a box. Eddie was right behind me so I passed the box off to him. After taking the box down to the truck, I went to sprint back upstairs but I stopped short on the outside steps before entering the building. I thought about it for a minute. Turn-ing around, I could see my old seventh grade classroom window from the steps. I couldn't help but laugh to myself.

Sister Geraldine was our seventh grade teacher. Although by nature the sweetest woman, she a strict disciplinarian when it came to her daily curriculum. I never had a problem with any of my assignments because I was an A student. Wednesdays were the only days I dreaded. Every Wednesday we read together, as a class, from the Bible.

I have never been the type to read for fun away from the classroom. If I had to go to the library to read a book to complete my assignment to receive an A, then I did it. But I was always an active child. I played every organized sport known to man since I was eight years old. I didn't have time to do much more. And, reading out loud just wasn't my thing.

I managed to break my glasses playing Nerf football against the eighth graders during recess one afternoon. It was hard to play football while wearing penny loafer shoes, hard to keep your footing while sliding around on the asphalt. I didn't mind wearing the standard school shirt and pants. I wore my burgundy loafers for a little flare. Every week, I put fresh, shiny dimes in the tongues where other people put pennies. The dimes were good just in case I needed to make a phone call.

It wasn't a problem for me to repair my glasses. I carried bonding glue in my pocket every day along with my house keys, Grandmama's house keys and my bus pass. I could have easily been the poster boy for a bonding glue company. I managed to glue the break over the left lens before Sister Geraldine had us all take out our Bibles.

"Today we will read from *The Gospel According to John*. I want everyone to read ten verses. I want everyone to stand up when you read the verses." Sister Geraldine spoke in her shaky voice.

Sister Geraldine pointed her arthritic finger to the first girl in the first row on her right hand side. Since we sat in alphabetical order I counted out where I was supposed to start reading when my time came. I found my place in John, Chapter 3 verses 14—23. It was just my luck that my verses were all four to five lines long.

My anxiety started on cue when the first person in my row stood up. I was third. The beads of sweat didn't waste any time formulating. The sweat slid my glasses down bridge of my nose. I went to push my glasses up on my face when I heard the cracking of the bonding glue. I could see the separation of space on the frame. I didn't have time to add more glue. I was next.

"Kamaul, could you please continue with verse number eleven?" I knew Sister Geraldine could see the sweat running down my shiny forehead.

My chair slid back. I stood up. I pushed my chair in before I started. I held the Bible close enough to my face where I would be comfortable reading—about three inches away from the tip of my nose. I began reading from verse fourteen.

"Sister Geraldine, why is Kamaul reading verse fourteen? You just told him to begin reading from verse number eleven." I didn't have to turn around to know who was talking because she was always talking. Sylvia White was the biggest loud mouth in our class. She never held her tongue for one minute. Sylvia was always the last person to read due to where she sat according to the alphabetical order.

"Sylvia, please stop talking. Kamaul, could you continue with verse number eleven?" Sister Geraldine had a calming shaky voice for an older woman.

"Why does Kamaul have to hold the Bible so close to his face since he's wearing bifocals anyway? He should be able to read his Bible from three rows away. Don't be mad at me! Every one else knows they're thinking the same thing."

"Sylvia, please stop talking. Kamaul, continue."

I wanted to walk over to the last seat in the back row so bad just to punch Sylvia dead in her forehead. I knew if I threw the first punch there was a good chance the rest of my classmates would join in behind me. But, I had promised my mother never to raise my hand to a girl. Maybe, if I explained myself, my mother might give me a free pass when it came to Sylvia White. I had to shake the happy thought off. I needed to focus.

I began reading from the correct verse. I could feel the eyes in the class watching me. I pulled the Bible to an arm's length away and managed to get through the first four verses slow and steady.

"Sister Geraldine, why is he reading so slowly? He's stuttering so much the school bell might ring before I get my chance to read."

"Sylvia, please stop talking. Kamaul, continue please."

I started to read the fifth verse. I was holding the Bible with both hands when my hands and my head began to shake nervously. The shaking was too much to stop gravity from taking over. My left lens fell into the crease of the book. I brought the Bible back to within three inches from my nose so I could see. I closed my left eye. I tried to read with just using my right eye. When I get really nervous I have a tendency to add and subtract words that either may or may not appear on the page. This nervous habit reared itself while I attempted to read verse seventeen.

"Oh my God, now he's making up words that don't even appear in the entire book of John."

"Sylvia, I am not going to stand for your blasphemous talk in this classroom!" We all knew Sylvia finally had gone too far.

"Sorry, Sister Geraldine, I didn't mean to be a blasphemer." Sylvia's apology was far from sincere.

"Sylvia, please stop talking."

"Sister Geraldine, I'm just saying we all know Kamaul is not stupid. He was one of ten students sent to represent our school in the spelling bee last year."

"Sylvia, please stop talking."

"Sister, maybe Kamaul is a functional illiterate? Look at how much he's sweating. He can't even manage to get through with reading half of a page out loud. I think you should inform his parents."

"Sylvia, please stop talking."

Sister Geraldine finally realized I was only able to see out of one eye. She nodded to me to stop. I pulled my chair out, sat back down, and reached in my pocket for the bonding glue.

"Joseph, could you please continue where Kamaul left off?"

Not being a confident reader pushed me away from reading even more. I couldn't help but wonder if my reading slower than the rest of the class didn't classify me as a functional illiterate.

Most of the class hated the fact that Sylvia was so outspoken at times. Everyone disliked how Sister Geraldine truly allowed Sylvia to be so boisterous. Yes, Sylvia definitely embarrassed the hell out of me in front of my peers. But for the life of me I could not stay mad at Sylvia for speaking the truth as she saw it.

Sylvia and I always had an unexplainable bond. Maybe it was the fact that our birthdays are only twenty-four hours apart. I always stood by Sylvia's side even when most of the girls, and some of the boys at times, wanted to fight her. I knew she could handle herself. She had better be able to handle herself with such an expressive mouth. No matter what, we always call one another on our birthdays. Sylvia and I are probably the only individuals from our grade school class to remain in contact since we were ten years old.

I went to purchase my first pair of contact lenses two weeks after my lens fell into the Bible.

Eddie and I followed the Charlottes over to their new house. There was no reason to look up the address in the map book—I knew the Brookline area fairly well. Four lefts and three rights later, we pulled up in front of a nice little blue one-family house. The walkway was a longish. That was the only issue I could see from outside of the house. The neighborhood was filled with adolescent kids riding bikes and skateboards.

Marjorie and Steve walked us through their two-level home. Marjorie made it a point for us to set up the rooms according to the sketches Steve made. I let the couple know the best plan was for bigger pieces of furniture to come in first. Marjorie made a sarcastic gesture, indicating I should learn how to read the drawings. Steve nodded his head to agree with his wife. I wondered what happened to the chipper, upbeat couple I met two hours ago.

I followed Eddie out of the front door back to the truck.

"Did Marjorie just transform into a royal bitch right in front of our very eyes?"

Eddie turned around facing me, looking down towards the ground while nodding his head yes. We both burst out laughing at his dead-on impersonation of Steve Charlotte.

"You keep it up, Eddie, and you might be the next Benny Hill."

Eddie took umbrage. "Benny Hill was English. I'm Irish."

"Benny Hill was funny. It doesn't matter where you were born. My motto is: funny is funny. You mean to tell me you never laughed while watching the Benny Hill Show?"

Eddie couldn't manage to keep a straight face. "Of course, I laughed at Benny Hill! But I liked watching the models run around during the program far better."

Three of the neighborhood women came onto the walkway as we approached the white picket fence. The women were holding one dish apiece.

"Are you our new neighbors?" The women spoke in unison.

"Your new neighbors are in the house." I smiled as we kept walking.

The women walked onto the front porch of the house. The doorbell rang before the introductions commenced.

Eddie and I began to shuttle in the big items of furniture first. The way Eddie packed the items on the truck, each item of furniture was to enter the house to be set up before the boxes could be properly placed.

The Charlottes entertained their neighbors while Eddie and I matched the furniture to the appropriate room according to the sketched diagrams outside of each room. We carried in the triple dresser while the three neighbors walked by us on their way down the walkway. The dresser was the last of the bulky furniture before we began to run the boxes into the house. We carried it up to the master bedroom, then scratched our heads..

"Excuse me, either Steve or Marjorie!" I called out. "You will want to come upstairs to take a look at the layout of your bedroom. This triple dresser doesn't fit properly into the space alongside the closet door, according to the sketches." No big deal. I was matter of fact.

We heard the couple immediately stop laughing downstairs. Steve Charlotte raced upstairs first. I figured Steve had less of an issue climbing the stairs to the upper level since he seemed to only weigh a third of his wife's weight. Marjorie was on her way upstairs, judging from the thudding sound on every step followed by a pause to catch her breath every fifth step.

"What do you mean the furniture doesn't fit properly? I measured the distance of the space." Steve appeared unsettled.

Eddie spoke up, "Sir, the dresser barely fits into the space between the wall on the right hand side and the closet on the left side."

"So, it's a little snug but the dresser does fit." Steve's forehead was beginning to perspire. Marjorie was standing in the doorway catching her breath.

"Steve did measure the space. The dresser does appear to fit the space the way the sketch shows. So what's the problem?" Marjorie's sarcasm was worse than the sound the teacher makes when she runs her fingernails down a chalkboard.

I raised my hand to have Eddie let me tell them. "Do you plan on using this closet?"

"Of course, we're going to use our master bedroom closet. Do you think we would walk down stairs to get dressed in the morning? Do you think we would bathe in the kitchen sink?" Marjorie had obviously managed to catch her breath.

I could feel my blood pressure rising. I wanted to play the dozens with Marjorie just so we could both see who had the sassiest mouth in the room. Four insults were right on the tip of my tongue. All I had to do was open my mouth. But this was still my first day as crew chief, so I used actions rather than words. I walked over to the closet door to open it. The bi-fold closet door didn't get an eighth of the way open before it ran into a dead stop.

"You should probably pick out the clothes you want to wear the night before work," I couldn't help saying. "You don't want to end up late to work because you have to keep running up and down the stairs to get dressed in the morning."

"I measured the distance from left to right but I didn't take into consideration opening the closet door." Steve voice seemed deflated. His body language looked as though he were pleading his case before the judge.

Eddie and I were watching with smiles on our faces when Marjorie took one step in Steve's direction and raised her right arm. Marjorie's open hand descended like axe. The movement of the wood splitter was short, swift and efficient. Steve bounced off of the closed closet door onto the floor. Steve was wearing his goggles around his neck.

"For Christ sakes!" Eddie's three words said a mouthful. (Sister Geraldine would have been upset at Eddie's blasphemy.)

The cocky smirk had long left my face. My eyes were open so wide my contact lenses almost popped off of them. I was shocked.

"You better get up! You better not say another word for the remainder of this night!" The scowl on Marjorie's face was priceless.

Steve managed to get to his feet. He held onto the dresser to keep from falling down. The hair on the right side of his head was standing up the same way I had noticed it at the Homer Street apartment. Steve's hair was the same way right before he came out of the bathroom wearing the basketball goggles.

I finally spoke. "Eddie and I are going to give you two some time to think about the changes you may want to make in this room. We are going to keep bringing in the remainder of your items." Eddie had started down the stairs as I was getting the last of the sentence out of my mouth. I wasn't too far behind him. As I reached the front porch I heard the sound of something falling up on the second floor. This time I instantly knew what had made that sound, better yet whose body had made that sound.

"Can you believe she just knocked him down for getting the measurement wrong?" Eddie was stunned as he stood pacing in the back of the truck.

"I think Marjorie hit him earlier today, too. I found the lens to his glasses underneath the front door at the old apartment. Maybe that's the reason why he's wearing those goggles. Basketball goggles are shatter proof."

"I can't believe that bollix takes a bashing from her regularly!" Eddie was getting wound up.

"Eddie, let's hurry up and empty this truck. I have this mental picture of Steve bouncing off of the closet door after getting chopped in the head. I might not be able to look at him straight after this."

Night fell fast. Eddie kept running the boxes to me to place them in the proper room of the house. I hadn't seen Steve for more then a half hour. I finally saw him in the basement when I carried a box to the laundry room. His face was crimson red. Tissue was stuffed into his left nostril to stop the bleeding. There was still dried blood in the corner of mouth.

"Are you okay?" Standing there looking at Steve's condition, I had no desire to laugh.

"I measured every room properly. I never took into account the closet doors opening," Steve whispered.

"It was a mistake. Mistakes happen." Trying to find the words to soothe my customer was difficult.

"How did I miscalculate the door opening? This is my fault. She told me to measure everything properly." Steve spoke softly to himself.

I could hear the heavy thudding footsteps on the first floor directly above where we were standing. It almost sounded as if Marjorie was attempting to sneak up on us. I realized Steve was hiding in the basement.

"Are you down in the basement talking, Steve?! I can hear your little mouse whispers through the vents. Get up here!"

I followed Steve up the basement stairs. Steve removed his goggles. There was some wet substance on the basement step—I couldn't tell if it were sweat or a teardrop. Then I saw the trickle running down the inner side of Steve's leg into his sock.

Steve hadn't set his second foot on the top step before the human axe blindsided him from the right. My contact lens almost popped out of my eyes for the second time that night. Steve fell somewhere to the left of the doorway. His shoe was the only item remaining from his person lying in the doorway.

"Didn't I tell you not to speak for the rest of the night?! You think you can go into the basement to talk behind my back? Get up! Stand up like a man!" The happy, chipper Marjorie I met hours ago needed an exorcism.

I found myself standing in between Marjorie and Steve once I reached the top of the stairs. Steve was attempting to get up. He had made it as far as being on both knees and was feeling around for his shoe.

"I'm sorry," I said, "but I can't watch you hit him anymore today. Not while we're here working."

"Excuse you?! You are the mover. You have nothing to do with what goes on in my house." Marjorie looked like she wanted to swing the axe on me next.

"Exactly! But I didn't volunteer to referee a Mike Tyson fight either. If the tables were turned and Steve had hit you in front of me, I would have instinctively punched him square in the mouth. I wouldn't have even bothered to ask him to go out back to see how well he handled himself against another man. That would have been after the first time he assaulted you."

"I'm actually ashamed of myself that I had to witness Steve being knocked to the ground for a second time tonight before I even thought about reacting." I helped Steve to his feet. Eddie had never stopped running boxes into the house. Eddie was moving so fast I felt a draft strong enough to blow a candle out when he passed by with the last box.

"You can't stop my husband from getting what he deserves. Steve has to come up stairs to sleep tonight, unless I make him sleep on the sofa. Better yet I might just make him sleep inside of the closet he didn't measure properly." Marjorie's sarcastic laugh penetrated my ear drums.

"Marjorie, you can do whatever your black heart desires when we drive away. We have less than an hour's worth of work left in your house.

Steve will be outside sitting underneath the moonlight where I know he won't be touched. I suggest you leave him outside if you want us to finish the job."

Eddie was running like a race horse wearing blinders, trying to get the hell out of Brookline. I couldn't blame him. I walked Steve out to the curb in front of his house.

"Thanks." Steve started to sob as he sat down.

"I'm sorry it took me that long to say anything."

"No, I meant thanks for making this that much worse for me tonight." Steve changed the tissue in his nose to the other bleeding nostril.

"You have the nerve to become sarcastic after you just got knocked off of your feet for a second time tonight? She knocked you out of your shoes, man."

"You didn't stop Marjorie from hitting me because you wanted to help me. You stopped Marjorie from hitting me because it made you feel proud of yourself. Did you ever consider what she will do to me once your truck drives away? You won't even take a second look back after you leave. I still have to go inside. You just postponed my fate. If I would have just measured the space properly none of this would have happened. Then you came down to the basement and started talking to me after you heard Marjorie tell me not to speak anymore tonight. You're doing all of this so you can laugh at me."

"Now you want to blame me for your wife giving you a bloody nose. She really has your head messed up." I felt bad to hear those words coming from my mouth, but they were true.

Eddie never broke stride. The truck was empty within the next thirty minutes. I calculated the bill to present it to Marjorie and she wrote the check. She signed the paperwork stating the job was completed using my blue ball point pen. I stood up to leave.

"Could you tell my husband to come into the house? It's getting late outside." Marjorie laughed her sarcastic laugh.

I went out of the front door. The stroll down the brick walkway felt endless. I stood over Steve but couldn't bring myself to say anything. Steve looked up at me. We both knew it was time for me to leave. Unfortunately, it was time for him to go get axed.

I got into the truck without saying a word. I heard my pager go off. Reading the numbers 194 upside down I knew it translated into "H.G.I.—

He Got It." I knew the phone number where the call was coming from by heart.

Steve was just getting to his feet as we turned the truck left. I took the first left turn at the corner. After taking a right hand turn, I found myself back in Brookline Village in front of the pancake house. There was a pay-phone in the lobby of the restaurant so I grabbed a handful of change from my backpack and let Eddie know I needed to make an emergency phone call. I had business to handle. Eddie was just happy to be far away from seeing Steve getting bashed.

I dialed the phone number from memory. "One Thousand and One Games, can I help you?" came the answer.

I hadn't been back to the arcade where I had fallen through the glass counter since I started working the moving job. I had just been too busy doing the moving thing to gamble. But former gambling acquaintances were still there, although my Jamaican friend Walls wasn't any longer. To get a call, though, meant there was money to be made. The grind didn't stop

"What you want?" I responded in my usual way. "What you need?"

"Yo, Kamaul, I got this redheaded *blankito* saying he went to school with you back in like the fifth grade. He's here with two other guys about the same age. They're looking to score some nose candy. From what I heard, they want enough to party for a while."

I knew the Latino voice of one of the Dejesus brothers from the day I lost my eyesight. He was the one who found me and got Walls.

"You know I don't play in the drug game," I said. "What do you want me to do, vouch for him?"

"No, a situation went down a little while ago in the back alley. Your man was trying to buy an eight ball to test out the product from the weed dealer. Turns out your man bought some foot powder. No one around here can get him the weight he's trying to buy within the next hour without thinking he's undercover. You are the only person I can think of to pull the rabbit out of the hat tonight."

"Ask the redheaded white kid to name our seventh grade teacher."

I heard Dejesus ask the question, and knew he was saying it through the Plexiglas of the booth.

"Sister Geraldine," the answer came back.

"Last question, what was the nickname of the boy you picked on every day in school? And what was it that you did which finally made him want to fight you?"

Some muttering on the other end, then: "The boy's nickname was Boogie because I caught him eating from his nose in the fifth grade. Boogie got mad at me in the seventh grade for sliding a wooden ruler through the belt loop of his pants and the metal chair he was sitting on. When we all got up during a fire drill Boogie stayed attached to the chair until Sister Geraldine took the ruler out. Boogie started crying and throwing punches."

"Pat down everyone including the redhead before you brings him into the booth and give him the phone. I can vouch for him."

"You don't trust him?"

"This is business. I don't trust anyone."

I heard a small commotion on the other end of the phone. The receiver was finally picked up after about a minute.

"Kamaul, this is Tim." Tim's voice was deeper than I recalled.

"I heard you have athlete's foot. Good thing you bought some expensive foot powder. How can I assist you tonight?" I couldn't resist.

"I'm trying to buy some blow for the Fourth of July weekend. I want enough to party for the next four days down on Cape Cod. We plan to take off in about an hour so that's why I was trying to get things together. I remembered you were over in Cambridge. I mentioned your name down at the pool hall near Harvard Square. Someone said I had a good chance of finding you at the arcade. Now, I'm down a couple of hundred dollars from buying foot powder."

"It's funny that you called me. I was over on Homer Street working today. I could see our old seventh grade classroom from where I was working. Now here we are, I'm talking to you on the phone. This has been a nice little trip down memory lane."

"It's funny to be talking to you to after all these years." There was a faint laughter.

"Tim, I'm not a drug dealer so I can't complete your transaction. But what I'm going to do is give you a phone number to call after we hang up. You are going to walk over to the pay telephone across the street at the bus stop. Your friends will continue to play pool. Your friends can't leave the arcade or your deal is off. I want you to wait exactly eight minutes from the time we hang up before you dial the phone number. When you call the phone number you will say, 'Little Marvin told me to call.' You will speak to someone who will address your needs.

"Tim, before I give you the phone number I need you to take fifty dollars from your pocket. Hand it to the gentleman who called me so he can write down this phone number as I tell it to you. He knows the fifty dollars is for him for getting ahold of me. Next, peel off one hundred dollars. Give it to the same gentleman. He knows the one hundred dollars goes to me."

"One hundred and fifty dollars, I thought we were friends! We've known each other since the fifth grade." Tim's voice raised about two octaves.

"Tim, I haven't spoken to your ass in more than six years. You mentioned my name because you have already been burned once tonight. Your boys were already nervous about this whole transaction going south. Now they are probably starting to believe you can't come through with the goods. Am I right?"

The phone was quiet on the other end.

"You mentioned my name because you need someone you can trust. You will pay for my services because I stand by my word. But you already know this, otherwise we wouldn't be speaking now. You will pay one hundred and fifty dollars if you really want to party on the Cape with your friends. Last of all, you will pay a small amount because this game is to be sold not told. Pay your toll right now or I'm hanging up!"

"I'm handing him the money right now." I could tell Tim didn't want me to hang up. Tim was desperate. Tim knew I had nothing to lose by hanging up the phone. I gave Tim the phone number.

"Kamaul, what should I do about the weed dealer who sold me the foot powder?"

"You can go and try to find him. Or you can take my advice and charge your loss to the game. Either way you look at it, you stand to lose more by pursuing the issue. Let me make my phone call so you can drive down to Cape Cod tonight. "

"So I should just suck it up?" Tim didn't like his options.

"Tim, let me give you some advice for the future. You wouldn't go to the bakery to buy lamb chops. You should only buy marijuana from a weed dealer. You should only buy heroin from the smack man. Make sure you call the candy man the next time you want to fill up your nostrils. Tim, for the future, you should know I don't have any friends. Friendships get in the way of business. You have eight minutes after I hang up. I need to call the candy store."

I held down the hook in the phone cradle for a moment, and deposited another dime. I dialed a seven-digit number over in East Cambridge.

"Who is eet?"

I always laughed when I heard the French voice trying to sound gangster tough. Not to say the individual on the other end of the phone wasn't crazy enough to drive his car over anyone he had problems with.

"It's me!" I have a tendency to be short with everyone when I'm on the phone.

"I know a lot of people by that first name."

"It's Little Marvin." I have been known as Little Marvin by my Roosevelt Tower Crew since I met them on the basketball court at Donnelly Park.

"How can I be sure this is Little Marvin?"

"*Map krave ou!*" I spoke in the native language of my road warrior.

"This is why I don't like teaching you Americans my language. Anybody can learn to speak French Creole phrases. You probably only know curses in my language anyways. So, how did Little Marvin escape from my treacherous Haitian headlock?"

"I bit your crazy ass in the ribcage. Your only rule was that I couldn't punch you to escape. You said nothing about biting." We both laughed.

"No one has seen you for a while, brother. We were starting to think you were dead."

"I'm still on my grind. It's just a new day with a new j-o-b. I need to make the same old tissue for my same old issues."

"Why can't you just say you're working for school money? You could always come work for me. Isn't it late for you to be calling me?" That was the code phrase for me to speak business in code.

"I just got a phone call from the aquarium where I used to play." The arcade always reminded me of an aquarium from the other side of Mass Ave. The windows at the arcade stretched from the floor to the ceiling.

"You mean the place where you broke one of the fish tanks and ended up with the scars?"

"That's the spot. Well, they have three exotic fishes over there that they said they need to sell by the time the store closes tonight. They turn off the lights and lock the doors in an hour. They already have the fish bagged and ready to go."

"What size bag do they need to transport the fish?" He's asking how much nose candy the new boys are looking to buy.

"They put the three fishes in one bag, which should last at least four hours. One more thing before I go. There is one piranha floating around the aquarium eating up fish food that's not his. So his belly is full." This means the weed dealer needs to be taken care of. Tim mentioned my name. Tim should have been given a pass.

"What's the price I'm being charged for your three exotic fishes?"

"You know I don't eat seafood. We can exchange fish food later." I let him know I don't want drug money. I would rather have a favor at a later date. Favors last much longer than money.

"Is there anything else I should know?"

"You have five and a half minutes before the 'Bat Phone' rings. I suggest you hurry up."

The Bat Phone was the pay phone on the corner of Donnelly Park. There were payphones on each corner of the field. However, there is only one corner where the little flying rats linger during the night waiting for prey.

My work was done with regards to answering my pager. I hung up the payphone. About fifteen minutes had passed since I left Eddie in the truck. I just needed to make one more phone call.

"9-1-1 Brookline emergency dispatch operator speaking, how can I direct your call?"

"I was walking down to Brookline Village with my wife and daughter to the pancake restaurant when we passed the green residence on Park Street with the white picket fence and the long walkway just near the corner of Auburn Street. Well, the three of us witnessed a vicious domestic assault ensuing. It pained my ears to hear the wretched screams coming from the inside of their house."

"Could you please hold the line, sir, we have a patrol car in the area." I pictured the operator sitting down while speaking into her headset. I wasn't surprised to hear there was already a car in the area.

"It looked as if the couple has just moved into their home. There was a green moving truck out in front of the house earlier. I also took notice of a couple of the neighborhood women bringing over house-warming treats earlier in the evening. This is a good neighborhood where the kids go out to play. I don't want to see my neighborhood turn into a danger zone. I just want to make sure my family can walk down the street together at night." I was pretty amazed at how good I sounded using my nervous white guy voice.

"Yes sir, we have two police officers knocking on the door of Steve and Marjorie Charlotte. From what they see the wife does not appear battered. She says her husband walked down to the store. What is your name sir?"

"Tell the police officers that I watched the husky man beat up his skinny wife with the receding hair line."

"Sir, we would like for you to remain where you are. We are sending a cruiser down to your location so you can verify your claim."

I was barely able to turn the key in the ignition just as the police cruiser pulled into the parking lot of the pancake house. I left the pay phone receiver dangling by the cord for the officers to see. I managed to maneuver the truck out of the town of Brookline in three minutes. The rest was up to Steve.

I hoped Steve would use the opportunity to save himself from the pain of the domestic beatings. I got the impression Steve had been under this stressed roof for a while. I hoped the police officers would do a clean sweep of the Charlotte house. Maybe they would find Steve hiding in the basement. He might be sleeping in the closet. It was out of my hands now.

It was around ten thirty when I turned the corner to the warehouse. There were still cars parked in the parking lot. Bicycles were scattered and locked along the fence. It was good to know we weren't the only crew still out working.

I didn't see the headlights coming towards me until my tires reached the parking lot. The vehicle was coming toward my truck pretty fast. I locked eyes with the driver before I noticed it was the white and purple van. Our vehicles came to a screeching halt. I put my truck in reverse while rolling down the window.

"Kamaul, you're just getting done working?!" Rhino-man said. "This is crazy! You're going to need a new backpack with all of the money you're making! I would throw all my money away if I had yours." The guttural laugh was a bright change to a long night.

"Barney gave me a third job after I left you earlier. I thought you went to work after you left me earlier today?"

"I did. I'm just getting off of work. I'm on my way home. I was just taking a moment to guarantee I would be working with this moving company tomorrow. Barney is trying to work all of the new guys fresh off the plane. He wants to work his new boys more hours at a cheaper rate than he pays me, so he figures he can wean my hours away. Barney forgets when it comes to me, he doesn't have the power when the sun goes down. I dictate my world." Rhino-man burst out laughing again.

"I guess I'll see you tomorrow then?" I said as I shifted the truck into drive.

"See ya."

Two more trucks turned the corner as Rhino-man drove off in his white and purple chariot. Eddie and the other three guys who had their bikes locked up against the fence were ready to take off for home. As I started to walk my paperwork to the warehouse door and to deposit my truck keys, I understood.

I grabbed Fast Eddie by the shirt before he had a chance to mount his bike. "Check your front bike tire."

Eddie and I both watched as his flatmates fell like dominoes. It was shocking to watch someone else take the same spill I had a few days earlier. I wondered if I looked that bad when I went flying over the handle bars. One of new boys landed face first, breaking his nose.

"How did you know?" Eddie asked surprised.

I removed my long-sleeved shirt. Eddie saw my shoulder. I showed him the bruise where the handlebars caught me in the hip.

One of the veterans drove the new boys to the hospital to clean their injuries. I started jogging home. Rhino-man had mentioned earlier how convenient it is was for him to live one town away from the bus depot where he works. For Rhino-man to come to the warehouse, he has to travel three towns south. There was no way he was on his way home from work when our vehicles passed. Rhino-man was guaranteeing his hours. With Fast Eddie's roommates on their way to the emergency room, Rhino-man was sure to work tomorrow.

I didn't interfere. I had held Fast Eddie up from getting on his bike because I didn't want to see him take the fall countless others had taken. Although I know tomorrow has never been promised to any man, I also know you can't stop a man from taking the necessary steps of preparing for tomorrow either.

I kept on jogging home. This day was finally over.

REMEMBER ME...

Will you remember me
Long after the sun has set,
The clock has chimed
For the twelfth time
Bringing this day,
Bringing our day
To an inevitable end?
What will you remember?

Will you remember
The first day we encountered one another?
The conversations and advice we exchanged?
All the times I made you smile?
The first time I caught you
Staring at me lost in thoughts?
Precious moments, unforgettable moments.

Will you recall
The days I tried my best to surprise you?
Making every day we spent together
More significant than the last.
I remember a special person once telling me,
One of the best feelings in this world
Is when someone goes out of their way
For the sole purpose of filling another with joy.
Never wanting,
Never asking for a thing in return.

Will you admit
That the attraction which exists
Between us is a touch more than physical?
That when we are together

LOOK WHAT I FOUND UNDERNEATH THE BED...

When you are looking into my brown eyes
You are engulfed by an unexplainable feeling of comfort,
Where harm could never find you?
Where everything worth dreaming is worth attaining?
I am like no one you have ever met before
Or anyone you will ever meet in the future.
But you already know this.

I will never forget
The time we have spent together.
It may have felt like seconds
Compared to that of a lifetime.
But all it truly takes is a second
To make a moment,
Timeless.

Will you remember me
When I'm gone?
Chances are
The next time
We look into one another's eyes
Smile and say good-bye
It may in fact be our final good-bye.
Remember Me.

It was just after seven in the morning on the second-to-last Saturday in August—the day of the Third Annual Family Reunion Cookout. I had been awake since the crack of daybreak, around four thirty in the morning. Anxiety never allowed me to sleep too long for fear I might actually over-sleep. Today was like my first day of school all over again. I had laid out the outfit I wanted to wear the prior night. I forced myself to relax before I took a few hours of needed rest on the mangled sofa bed.

The only question on my family's mind for a week was whether rain would soak the Boston area on the Saturday of our reunion cookout. I had been watching the weather forecast all week long like everyone else. It wasn't until Thursday night when the meteorologist finally said the rain was moving south of us into the Atlantic Ocean that most of the family could officially do their food shopping for the cookout. The weather fore-cast called for sunny skies with an expected high close to ninety degrees. There was always a nice breeze rolling off of the Charles River especially on those extra hot days.

It was a good thing the Magazine Street M.D.C. pool area along the Charles River in Cambridge was less than two miles from our apartment near Central Square. I was always the first person out at the park. The area I wanted to stake out was closest to the open space where my family would have enough room for our four barrel grills, games and socializing. This is the only day each year in which we all come together as a family.

It took me three trips stuffing the eight ten-foot cafeteria tables in the trunk of my mother's grey Oldsmobile compact car. I had the radio blasting the Saturday morning program "Time Tunnel," on WILD on the AM dial. "Time Tunnel" played classic rhythm and blues for three hours. Each week the disc jockey highlighted one featured artist. Today's artist is none other than the beautiful Stephanie Mills. I belted out songs as the DJ played them. The last song on the play list tribute was "Home" from the musical The Wiz. This song reinforced my feelings for the simple gather-ing I was planning for that day. Just hearing the first three chords of the song was enough to make me just shut up and listen. I sat in my parent's car envisioning the day I hoped to have.

The first cookout was back in 1991, about two weeks before my head-ing up to UMass Amherst for my freshman year. I was only eighteen at the time. I had a strong desire to see all of the family come together for one day without everyone all dressed in black with tears in their eyes mourning a lost loved one. Plus I realized at the last funeral, I hadn't even recognized most of the family outside of my immediate circle. I spent the time before and after the service being re-introduced to family I obviously should have known but I didn't. Just the thought of sitting on the bus or train across from one of my blood relatives without recognizing them made me uncomfortable, so I decided to do something about it.

Years ago, the family would get together at least twice each summer. On the Fourth of July, we would all meet at a designated relative's house at the crack of dawn. Once everyone arrived, all of the cars would create a convoy to an amusement park away from the city. It was always fun during the convoy to keep passing each others' cars on the highway, cheering on the driver of your car as you made silly faces at the carload of family you were passing. We also played games on the highway, such as pointing out the better vehicles and exclaiming, "That's my car!"

Once at the park, we would ride on the rides we were tall enough to get on from opening until nightfall. We would convoy back home to the city in the pitch black, with most of us young kids falling asleep because all our energy got left at the park. We would always wake up the following day holding a newly won stuffed animal.

The family reunion cookout for 1993 that year went great—truly exhausting but a lot of family fun. Now, it was time to man-up for the last push of a mover's summer—Labor Day.

The college students swarmed back into Boston as the Labor Day weekend approached. The week before Labor Day was pretty intimidating from my viewpoint. Extra caution was needed in driving Barney's big green trucks throughout the city. Most streets had double-parked cars with their hazard lights flashing. Students emptied the cars of clothes and other necessities they had raided from their parents' homes. Rental trucks stretched from Beacon Hill all the way down Beacon Street to the Boston College campus.

The influx of students moving throughout the Boston and Cambridge areas challenged our workload even more. Barney told the office staff to keep booking any and all work that was called into the office.

We became shorthanded very quickly. Barney preferred to hire college athletes, specifically rowers. Many of the young rowers hired for the summer months worked their last day on Monday of that week so they could begin training with their team. Some of the other students who worked with us attended universities out of town so they had to leave. Out of the ninety workers who had come onboard in the spring, we were now had only sixty-eight remaining. My own classes at UMass at Boston started the following week.

Barney forced many of the men from his sales staff onto the trucks during the last week in August, including Barney himself and the four foot, nine inch assistant who had interviewed me when I was hired. Barney looked like a fish out of water wearing his short shorts—they may have shrunk a little since the last time he wore them, or maybe he got bigger.

Barney began the company moving refrigerators and sofas by himself. Doing solo jobs is how Barney built his referral base of clients. Barney's big six foot, eight inch frame started the company when he was a student. But that was years before my time. Everyone was convinced Barney could do the work. I just prayed I didn't have to work with him.

Every day that week didn't end until after midnight. Some crews didn't begin their final jobs for the day until ten o'clock at night. Some of us wondered why those same jobs couldn't just be shifted over until the following day. The answer was actually simple. Most people's leases expire at the end of the month, so they have to be out of the apartment before the first of the next month. Each day leading up to Labor Day was inundated with more jobs than the day prior. No one was allowed to go home until every job was off of the corkboard.

There were some three-man crews that would go out to a job after five o'clock in the evening. The job would be a total nightmare once the crew arrived at the house. For example, the crew chief would call back to the office saying the job was not a five-hour job for three men. The job would be better suited for six men and another truck. That phone call from the crew chief would result in Dominic, the dispatcher, categorizing the job as an S.O.S. distress job. It was not unheard for two different crews to show up to complete an S.O.S. job. It felt great to pull up to a job with extra energized guys who were charged and excited about coming out so we could all go home together. It was pretty exciting to be a part of the camaraderie every evening. It was also exhausting.

I had already worked forty-eight hours by Thursday morning. Getting dressed in my green T-shirt, sweatpants and sneakers took five minutes longer than usual. There was no more jogging left in my tired legs. I contemplated riding my father's blue ten-speed bike into work—I knew Rhino-man was getting more then his fair share of hours. But then again, I couldn't be sure that he wasn't carving another notch into his van's wooden headboard marking the young movers he had personally eliminated from his little mental game. I could hear his evil guttural laugh just thinking about him.

I left the apartment in a slow stroll. One of my co-workers noticed the green work shirt on his way into the warehouse. I accepted the ride gratefully. This would have been the first day I was late. To be honest, I didn't care that much. My body was well past feeling physically spent. I needed sleep badly.

But, I was very close to reaching the dollar figure I needed to pay for the fall and spring semesters in cash. I just had to get through the last three days of work. I just had to keep grinding until Saturday night. Then it would all be over.

I still made it into work before the rest of my crew. The two men and I were to move a single-family home on the Fells Way in Medford to a two-family home in Malden. The paperwork said the job was supposed to be straightforward with the possibility of moving an office if we had the space on the truck.

I went ahead to prep the truck with the standard equipment of furniture pads, tape, wardrobe boxes, a few extra empty boxes, etc. Beeman and a brand new Boston University student named Joe were slated to work with me. Beeman had that habit of being thirty minutes late every single day. I didn't quite understand why he couldn't just wake up thirty minutes earlier to cancel out his tardiness. But, God help me if I said anything about it because I knew he would start calling me an anti-Semite. I didn't have the patience to hear that crap that day.

We left the warehouse at seven thirty. Beeman let it slip that if our job happens to finish early maybe we could catch a movie or venture up to Walden Pond for a quick dip. It hadn't dawned on me until that moment why Beeman never looked as tired as everyone else. His crews never came back to the warehouse until late every night, yet they always appeared so well rested. This son of a bitch had a tan comparable to my skin tone.

Now, I understood why. And he still had the nerve to show up thirty minutes late every day.

It ended up taking us until five o'clock to load and offload the truck. Just when I thought we were done for the day, Beeman came outside to inform Joe and me that our customer wanted to go to his office to pick up a few items.

None of us knew our customer was a teak cabinet maker. Another full truckload of unfinished cabinets, wood, sawing tools and office furniture needed to get moved. Since our office staff was already shorthanded, the three of us decided to bite the bullet and finish this job ourselves.

At three o'clock in the morning, the three of us found ourselves hoisting a sleep sofa through a second floor window. One of the neighbors called the police around two o'clock. The two police officers watched from their cruiser until we finally finished at the crack of dawn. Twenty-two hours had elapsed since I had left the warehouse the morning before.

Beeman and Joe went to sleep in the back of the truck. There were only two hours left until we had to come back anyways. They pleaded with me to stay so Dominic could find all three of us asleep in the truck. But there was no way I was going to work again in the same sweat drenched, funky clothes from the day before. I needed to shower, brush my teeth, change my underwear. I needed to change my shoes. I needed to put on deodorant. There was no way I would want any movers showing up to my house in the condition I was in. I gave them a half-hearted smile before I started my jog home.

On my way home, I saw a familiar face jogging towards me. His face looked just like mine.

"Where are you coming from?" Daddy never broke his jogging stride.

"Just finished working from yesterday morning." I continued jogging as well.

"Are you working today?"

"They put me on the schedule to be in by seven."

"I guess I'll see you tonight? Maybe?" We both smiled as we passed by each other.

The Boston Magazine September issue was released on Friday evening before Labor Day weekend. Saturday morning most of the workers couldn't resist thumbing through the many pages naming "The Best of

Boston." The magazine named their top rated customer service industries throughout the Boston area. The industries highlighted ranged from auto care, dry cleaning, restaurants, to wineries—every category imaginable.

Sadly, Big Barney's Moving Company was not selected as the Best Moving Company in Boston for 1993.

There was an unbelievable amount of chatter on the warehouse dock in the morning. Barney hadn't been seen in the office since the issue appeared. A couple of guys testified they heard Barney sobbing as they listened outside his closed office door. Some of the men said Barney's injuring himself while out on the moving trucks on Friday morning was the reason he hadn't been seen. Barney's body was no longer conditioned to the rigorous abuse of working on the trucks. Others said Barney limped back to the warehouse early Friday, favoring his left ankle. These grown men gossiped more than women.

All I knew was that day was my final day moving furniture for the year. I had never been so happy to go back to school in all my years. My focus was on finishing the day without injury. An injury-free day would be enough for me to walk away from the moving experience with my head held high. But, I tried not to put the cart before the horse.

Looking at the work board, I saw my name underneath Mr. Lawrence Matthews's name. We had three jobs scheduled for the two of us, moving three different pianos. I had never moved a piano with just two guys before. The usual protocol while moving a piano is to have a third person along for security. More than half the jobs on the board were going out understaffed.

I stocked the fourteen-foot box truck with the necessary supplies—a piano board, power straps, a good toolbox, furniture pads, a four-wheel dolly, a piano block, and tape. I hadn't placed keys in the ignition of the miniature truck since I had crashed it into the tree back in the early summer. I had wrecked the truck earlier in the year because I was driving tired. I was one hundred percent sure I was way more exhausted now then I was the day the tree assisted in decapitating the truck. I was not getting behind the wheel today. After I stocked the truck, I climbed into the passenger side and fell asleep until Mr. Matthews arrived.

"Do we have everything we need, Kamaul?" The strong baritone voice awoke me out of a deep sleep.

"Yes, yes, I do believe we have everything we should need for all three jobs." I was trying to refocus my eyes. My contact lenses almost popped out of my head while I tried to adjust. According to my watch, I was only asleep for four minutes.

"Do you want to drive?"

"If you want us both to live to see tomorrow I would suggest you drive."

"Hmmm. I have plans for Labor Day weekend, so I guess I will drive."

We were all tired. Have you ever heard the phrase, "I can fall asleep on a dime"? I used to think I was the only one who could take a dime out of my pocket, place it on my thumbnail, use the resistance from my index finger and flip the dime into the air, meanwhile falling asleep before that dime hit the ground. But that summer, I worked with drivers who would take advantage of a red traffic light for a quick catnap. They would wait for the cars behind them to honk and wake them up. I sat in the passenger seat wondering how anyone could fall asleep so fast. I didn't have to wonder anymore. I was no longer the sole anomaly.

We drove out to Tewksbury to pick up the first piano. I fell asleep on the hour ride up north of Boston. Mr. Matthews let me sleep, only waking me up when we were a few streets away. It was great to sneak in the catnaps. The catnaps continued for the second piano as well. I finally fully awoke when we reached the house for the third piano job.

The third piano pick-up was in Brookline. The piano was another upright, but with an automatic player attached. It's one of the old style pianos that you see in black-and-white movies that usually appear inside a saloon playing itself. I used to think a ghost was playing the piano when I watched old westerns as a child.

From a mover's perspective, player pianos are about the heaviest kind manufactured due to the built-in self-playing attachment. The moment we lifted the piano and sat it on the four-wheel dolly I guessed its weight at close to eight hundred pounds.

Getting the piano out of the house was easy enough after it was rolling along on the dolly. But the drop off for the player piano was a two-family duplex in Winchester, at the home of Dianne Parker. The living room was on the first floor. We were relieved because 90% of pianos are staged in the living room.

"So which wall in the living room would you like the piano along?" Mr. Matthews asked with his sincere smile through his beard. It was funny watching the mound of hair on his face part when he talked.

"Oh no," Mrs. Parker said. "The piano will go upstairs in the second bedroom to the right. I bought this secondhand piano for my granddaughter. My daughter's family will move in upstairs next month. Let me show you the way to the bedroom upstairs."

We followed Mrs. Parker back out onto the front porch. She continued to the door on the right leading up into the second floor apartment. I counted first sixteen steps before the stairway turned sharply to the left for an additional seven steps. It seemed too narrow to me for the piano to make it up. Looking at Mr. Matthews' face, I could tell he was thinking the same thing.

We took the piano off the truck and rested it on the front porch. Mr. Matthews pulled out the tape measure from the toolbox. I started stretching out my body. Good thing I had slept a little before this moment.

"Kamaul," he said finally, "this is the deal. The piano is just going to barely make it upstairs. But we have to take the piano off the piano board because the extra four inches of height and length won't make it when we get to the top of the stairs to turn the piano to the left."

"What am I supposed to hold onto as we take the piano up the stairs?"

"You're going to have to muscle up the front end. I'll be muscling up the back end."

"Are you serious?" I couldn't believe it. "You want me to pick this piano up and walk backwards up the stairs? Did you forget this piano weighs close to eight hundred pounds?" I could tell by his face that Mr. Matthews was as serious as a heart attack.

"Let me walk you through how I envision us moving the piano up the stairs," he said patiently. "This way we can share the same vision."

"By all means, share your vision with me, please. I feel like the fourth blind mouse at this moment." I followed Mr. Matthews over to the first step.

"The stairs are made on about a thirty-degree angle. The ceiling is also on a thirty-degree angle. The piano stands a little over five feet in height. The measurement from the step to the ceiling is just under six feet, that's why I have to stay bent down so I don't hit my head against the ceiling. After we reach the eighth step, the ceiling is no longer a factor because it becomes closer to ten feet in height. You should be close to the fourteenth step just as I reach the eighth step.

"Listen close because this is where it gets complicated. When your back reaches the wall, we will need to take the piano off of its feet and stand it up on its side. The piano is longer, left to right, than it is tall. Once the piano is on its side, we need to carry it that way so we can make the sharp left turn at the top. You are going to have to keep a shoulder press on the piano until we clear the corner and make it to the top of the other stairs.

"We will have less than eight inches for the piano to sway from side to side. Keep in mind, if this heavy piano smashes into the wall there is a good chance the piano will make a huge hole. Let's finish off the day without any damage."

"Would you prefer me to throw my arm between the piano and the wall as a bumper as we turn the corner?" I couldn't help being facetious.

"That would be great if you can manage it!" Mr. Matthews beard parted in a smile.

"I need a minute to sit down and process your vision. I need to mentally walk myself through that scenario a few times before I'll be ready."

Mrs. Parker was standing behind Mr. Matthews as he walked me through the plan. She had the same bewildered look in her eyes that I had.

"Excuse me, Mrs. Parker," I asked, "could you direct me to the bathroom?"

I followed Mrs. Parker to her apartment on the first floor. I needed a few minutes to sit down and get ready. According to Mr. Matthews, there was no room for any accidents. Before moving this heavy damn piano, I felt it necessary to eliminate any possible accidents of my own from the equation.

I returned back to the second floor staircase after a few minutes. Mr. Matthews had already stripped the furniture pads, power straps and piano board away from the piano. The four-wheel dolly still remained in the middle underneath. The piano appeared impossibly boxy in shape once the covering was removed. It looked heavier now that I could see its solid natural wood.

"Are you ready?" Mr. Matthews asked as he descended down the stairs taking the last measurements.

"I'll give you everything I have to give. I just hope it's enough." I had my game face on.

"Can I be of any assistance?" Mrs. Parker asked in a nervous voice. She stood out on the front porch staring at us.

"You can help us out greatly by changing your mind. Deciding you don't mind after all having your grandchild come downstairs to spend quality time playing the piano for you. Think how it would provide those special moments for you both to recollect as you become older. If you want, we can roll this piano right into your living room right now." Mr. Matthews made his last plea.

"Sorry, but I'm too old to listen to a young child banging away on ivory," Mrs. Parker replied as she cracked an odd-looking smile. I got the impression she accidentally promised her granddaughter a piano in the excitement of the moment when she made the suggestion for her daughter to move in upstairs. After her daughter accepted Mrs. Parker's offer, she didn't want to break her promise. Hence, the reason for our impossible task.

"Well, then, I guess you've answered the question regarding assisting us," Mr. Matthews replied. "You may not want to watch us move this piano upstairs."

Mr. Matthews and I knew Mrs. Parker wasn't budging from the front porch. The more I looked at her face over the crown of the piano, the more Mrs. Parker was reminding me of a chicken hawk wearing a dress. She had front row seats to this main event. There was no way she was going to miss out on the excitement.

I got into position at the foot of the stairs. Mr. Matthews was on the other end of the piano. Since we still had the dolly underneath it, we could tip the piano up at the same thirty-degree angle as the stairs. We rolled the piano up on the two rear wheels closest to Mr. Matthews until the dolly could roll no more.

I squatted down. From my angle on the stairs, I tipped the piano high enough from the bottom so Mr. Matthews could remove the dolly from underneath. I continued to tip the piano higher and higher until I finally heard the blessed phrase, "The dolly is out." I sat the piano back on the stairs.

My lower back was already starting to throb. I knew I initially had the tough job of picking the piano up while walking backwards. But I also knew that Mr. Matthews had the toughest job of moving the piano up the stairs while also fighting against gravity. Once the piano has moved up a couple of steps, it will naturally want to roll back down. If Mr. Matthews slips there is the good chance he will be steamrolled by the piano, which outweighs him four times over.

"What step are you standing on right now, Kamaul?"

"I count the fourth step."

"I can't see you from my position because I need to stay low on this end of the piano. You are my eyes okay?"

"I copy that."

"Communication is the key."

"Believe me I won't hesitate to communicate." I had to try to remember to avoid cussing.

"I will lift and bring the piano up one step at a time on your count. I'll yell, 'Lift,' then you bring it to me. The weight of the piano will want to sway either left or right, so try to stay in the middle of the stair. Are you ready?"

"It's show time." I don't smile when it's show time.

I had a brief mental image of picking the piano up from the bottom the way I had when we tipped it up to take out the dolly. My mind's eye kept showing me the piano tipping forward and Mr. Matthews jolting the piano towards me at such a force that my hands, my wrist and my forearms would be rammed into the next step. I honestly didn't like what I was seeing.

"Wait a minute! Wait a minute!" I shouted. "I can't pick up the piano from the very bottom because I won't be able to cleanly back up the next step before you bring it towards me."

"What do you want to do then?"

"There's a handle on my back left side. I'll grab the handle with my left hand. I'll place my right hand underneath the section where the piano keys are. It's a solid area to lift from. I just hope I can take my step backwards before you jam the piano into my legs." There was way too much to think about.

"I'm ready. We'll go on your call."

Once I got my hands into place, I tilted the piano backwards towards Mr. Matthews so as to get its front edge away from catching the top of step behind me. I had to hunch the piano up as high as I could and I stand on the tips of my toes.

"Lift!"

The piano came toward me so fast. The body of the piano smacked me square on the side of my head, hard enough that I knew I could definitely not allow my head to absorb another blow like that. I wondered if this was how a boxer felt after a solid shot to the head. Then again, they're not being hit with pianos.

I could feel fire in every muscle in my skinny legs. Despite this, I repeated the same maneuver. I waited until I was at the very top of my toes and reminded myself, *Move your head this time.*

"Lift!"

This time I managed to turn my left shoulder into the piano's impact. It still hurt. I just didn't want my face taking anymore smacks from pianos. I could really have gone for three pain relievers right about then. A headache was looming from the initial head shot.

"Lift!"

The sweat came off my body so fast you would swear I had taken a shower. I was so glad I had used Mrs. Parker's facility. The last time I got up on my tiptoes I couldn't hold my butt cheeks tight enough.

"Lift!"

The piano slammed into my shoulder once again.

"Wait a minute! Kamaul, was that you?" It sounded as if Mr. Matthews was trying not to inhale as he spoke.

"Sorry about that. You can't ask me to pick up my end of an eight hundred pound piano and try to hold my stomach together, too." I hid my face behind the body of the piano. The embarrassing grin stretched from ear to ear. I was glad I was too high up on the stairs to be able to make eye contact with the chicken hawk. But I knew she was down there standing on the front porch listening to every word we spoke. How embarrassing.

"Do you need a moment to check your underwear?"

"To be honest with you, I would be too scared to check my underwear right now." We both couldn't contain our laughter. The minute we took joking around made me realize how sore my body was.

"Are you ready?"

"Yes! Lift!"

The last slam of the piano into my shoulder sent a sharp pain throughout my body.

"Lift!"

I knew I was hurt from the last shoulder slam. The grunt that I made from the piano hitting me this time echoed through the staircase. I didn't want to say that damn word anymore, but we were too far up the stairs to turn back now.

"Lift!"

The next slam jarred my hands clean off my grips. I found myself bouncing off the wall behind me

"Stop, Mr. Matthews! I think I injured my shoulder." I didn't hesitate in taking off my green T-shirt. I was wearing a white tank top underneath. The area of my shoulder the piano had consistently slammed into had already turned a dark plum color. But I knew I would rather my shoulder and chest looked like the outer skin of a plum than my face.

"Are you all right?"

"No, but I'll give you everything I have left."

"I'm ready whenever you are?"

I readied myself. "Lift!"

Slam!

"Lift!"

Slam!

"Lift!"

Slam!

"Stop, Mr. Matthews! We're on the fourteenth step. My back is nearly against the wall."

It was now time for phase two of the initial plan. We needed to tip the piano up on its side to stand it vertically and make the turn at the sixteenth step.

Mr. Matthews stabilized his end, the bottom edge of the piano, back down on the eighth or ninth step. My mind had trouble focusing on anything other than the original plan. I needed to lift my end of the piano from a thirty-degree angle up to ninety degrees. It took all the strength I had left to lift my end.

It was time for phase three. Mr. Matthews wanted me to shoulder press the piano up the stairs. With the bottom of the piano now facing me, I needed to push the piano clean in the air as Mr. Matthews picked up his end somewhere near the piano's crown. We are supposed to lift and carry, going one step at a time. The piano was leveraged on the eighth step. There are still fourteen steps to the second floor.

"We'll go on your count. Are you ready?"

I was so far away from being ready, I think I might still have been waiting for Mr. Matthews in the passenger seat of Barney's green miniature truck.

"Lift!"

At least there was no more slamming into my chest. I managed to press the piano up for a second and a half before my left shoulder completely gave out. The piano started rocking towards the wall on my left side. Mr. Matthews must have felt the weight shift and set the piano back down onto the last step.

"What happened?" Mr. Matthews asked in a calming voice.

"I tried. Believe me, I tried. I cannot physically press this piano up step-by-step for fourteen more steps."

"Why not?"

"Do you have a handle on the piano?"

"Yes!"

"Look at me on the right side." I knew the chicken hawk was not able to see me from that angle.

Mr. Matthews head ducked into the area between the piano and the wall like a turtle coming out of its shell. My skin complexion is close to a caramel color. With the white tank top on, the bruise appeared far worse. It now extended to the left half of my chest as well. There was a good possibility the bruise was deep enough to have hit the bone.

"Did that happen from the piano?"

"Yes."

"Okay, I understand now. Just give me a minute to think."

"I have no other place I have to be."

Mr. Matthews's turtle head eventually reappeared.

"Since we already have the piano up on its end," he said, "it makes more sense if I just 'dog walk' the piano the rest of the way."

"Excuse me? Did you just say you need to go walk a dog, right now?" I wasn't sure if I was getting delusional.

"No, I'm going to 'dog walk' the piano."

"What's a 'dog walk'?"

"Since the piano is already on its end, I'm going to set my body on the step below." With his one free right hand, Mr. Matthews demonstrated the procedure. "I'm going to make my back as flat as a board. We will take my end of the piano out to the very edge of the step. Kamaul, I need you to slide the piano from the step all of the way onto the square of my back. I'll have all of the weight on my back. I will use my legs to keep the piano level as I use my arms to crawl up the stairs one by one. I will literally look like a dog crawling up the stairs.

"The piano should appear from where you're standing as if it's floating up the stairs. Make no mistake about it. I'll be underneath this heavy mother. Believe me when I tell you there is less of a margin for error once the piano is on my back.

"I can see you're injured. Moving the piano this way places all of the pressure on me. Kamaul, I do need you to navigate the piano's top weight up the stairs. There is a possibility the piano may want sway from side to side. You cannot allow that to happen. You have to still be my eyes in the sky. Kamaul, it's just you and me here today. Let's finish this together." Mr. Matthews ducked his head back into the shell.

We backed the piano off to the edge of the eighth step. I could see Mr. Matthews's head kiss the step below. The piano's weight shifted entirely over to Mr. Matthews's back. Everything he explained to me about the "dog walk" was all in total theory until this moment.

"Kamaul, slowly tip the rest of the weight of the piano over to me. Easy!"

I always try to be a good student—try to give the teacher exactly what he's asking for. This was no time for independent thinking.

"The piano is totally on your back now, Mr. Matthews. I'm watching the top weight. I'm your eyes in the sky whenever you're ready."

"I'm ready."

Without saying abracadabra, the piano started to float up the stairs. The movement was nice, slow and controlled.

"Oh, my good God, I can't watch this!" The gasp came from the Mrs. Parker, a.k.a. the chicken hawk.

I felt absolutely the same way. Not looking, however, was not an option for me. I held my emotions on the inside. There was no need to talk or say anything to distract Mr. Matthews's focus. I counted to myself as I walked backwards up the stairs—eleven, twelve, thirteen.

It occurred to me there was not a dog created capable of walking this piano up those stairs. The fourteenth step was where the turn came into play. Just as smooth as the piano had floated up the last six steps, the piano turned the corner and kept going. My hand never touched the piano again until Mr. Matthews reached the top step of the second floor.

"I can't believe what you did to get the piano up the stairs. I'm going to tell everyone I know the impossible feat you did to get this piano up here." Mrs. Parker just became a groupie.

We placed the piano in the bedroom where it was supposed to go, in between the double windows. The exhaustion must have hit Mr. Matthews the second after we touched the piano down for the last time. He looked how I started out this Saturday morning.

"Are you okay?" He looked across the piano at me. His eyes were fixated on my shoulder.

"Are you okay?" I asked him right back, dumbfounded at what he had just done.

There was no need to talk about what just happened, we were both there. I was awestruck as my mind continuously replayed the piano floating up the stairs. I knew even if I were not injured I could never in a million years have done what Mr. Matthews had just done. Well, at least not in this lifetime.

Mr. Matthews stopped at the liquor store on our way back to the warehouse. He bought a case of beer, a large bag of ice, and a cranberry juice for me.

Smoke could be seen as we made our way down the street toward the warehouse. More than half of the trucks that went out earlier in the day had already returned. We could see another two green trucks making the turn onto the street.

The smoke was two barbecue grills in front of the warehouse loading docks. Two tall grey trash barrels brimmed with iced beer. I counted fourteen full cases stacked close to the barrels—beer waiting for its chance to get cooled before being swallowed away.

The drinking and eating meant all of the jobs were off the board. Every crew was either done or on their way back to the warehouse. Dominic was manning the grills. The guys waiting for food didn't care what they ate. Burgers, hot dogs, sausages and chicken were all on the grill. Some of the older guys wanted steaks, so a few of them were making a run to the grocery store. Some of the guys didn't care for food at all—they were on liquid diets, with a menu of any and everything stacked next to or inside the two trash barrels. A few of these same guys tried to pry the cranberry juice from my hands and replace it with an aluminum can.

I walked over to Leroy, who was yelling at a couple of guys taunting him about his height. Leroy was giving it back as good as he got. Everyone was in a good spirits. The summer was officially over.

"For a little guy you are the biggest damn trouble maker I think I've ever met in my life," I said. Everyone in the small circle started laughing.

"Burgers, dogs and sausages are up!" Dominic exclaimed while fanning away some of the smoke. Everyone made a mad dash to form the grill line, except Leroy and me.

"So did you make all the money you needed for school?"

"This check's overtime should place me where I need to be."

"I'm glad you stuck it out." Leroy gave one of those proud fatherly smiles.

"I'm glad, too." I extended my right hand. Leroy slapped my hand away and gave me a hug.

I guess Barney was making his way around the dusty parking lot. I didn't see him until he was standing between Leroy and me.

"Kamaul, I just wanted to say thank you for everything you did this summer. You were a great addition to the family."

"Thanks, Barney." We shook hands.

"I hear that you're going back to school for the fall. Have you considered being a weekend warrior, maybe working Fridays and Saturdays? A couple of days' work would give you a few extra dollars in your pocket during the school year. Or maybe we'll just see you next summer. I hope we definitely see you next summer. I want all of you guys there when we win the Best of Boston Award."

I smiled at his continued ambition. "My focus is on school for the moment. I'll see what happens after my finals. I'll call Dominic either way."

"Does Kamaul make more money if he decides to come back next summer?" Leroy asked the question I had been thinking but didn't think it was the right time to ask. Obviously, Leroy thought otherwise. I couldn't help but grin.

"Leroy, you would ask me that right now. Kamaul the answer is yes, I will give you more next year if you decide to return." Barney shook my hand once again while thanking me. He gave Leroy a disappointed head shake as he walked away.

"Why did you do that?" I asked.

"Barney's a manipulator. Don't trust that snake for a second."

"What happened?"

"Remember when he was making the announcement about there being more work because he was going for the best mover of Boston honor? He also said that everyone was getting pay raises."

"I remember I got a fifty cent raise."

"Well, Barney likes to play favoritism. Those workers who he personally likes, those who kissed his ass, received two dollars. The workers he felt were on the faster track all received a dollar or more. The movers he felt did a fair enough job all received fifty cents."

"So what did you get for a pay raise?"

"That big dickhead gave me twenty-five cents!"

I busted out laughing because I could tell Leroy was pissed. I also knew Leroy had a mission to prove to the newer guys like myself why he and Rhino-man treated Barney the way they did.

"Burgers and sausages are up!"

Dominic had already motioned for Leroy and me to get in line before he made the announcement to the rest of the savages. We placed the fixings on our burgers and made our way over to another small circle of co-workers double-fisting beers.

The chatter was about naming the best rookie for the summer. A few names were tossed into the ring but it was the clear choice of our peers that Fast Eddie should be the winner. Believe me, Fast Eddie had proven himself on a daily basis. Then everyone began traveling down memory lane telling their funniest moving experiences. The common thread from most of the stories was the fact that Rhino-man was out on the job with them.

I stayed around another hour, waiting until the last of all of my co-workers returned to the warehouse. The crowd cheered for the last truck to arrive. The crew was given food and drinks right away. By then, they had the choice of steak or chicken breast.

I shook hands with a few more of the guys I hadn't had the chance to talk to like Dominic, Beeman, and Fast Eddie. Then, just like a thief in the night, I took off my green T-shirt and white tank top and jogged home.

My body was starting to shut down but it wasn't quite there yet. A shower woke me up. The summer didn't feel complete to me yet. There was one thing more I needed to do before getting ready for school.

I drove my parents' grey Oldsmobile for the ten-minute drive out of Cambridge into Newton. I walked into the building and made my way up the flights of stairs to the door on the seventh floor. I gave my customary three knocks.

"Come in," said the voice on the other side of the table.

I opened the room door. "Are you up for a visitor today? Or are you going to spend the rest of your night studying your chess board?"

"Since you seem to be the only visitor I ever have," Davis Jones said, "I'll take your visit. And then I'll beat you in chess. Then I'll spend the rest of my time studying my chess board." He smiled at me from across the room.

I have been dropping by to see Davis since we had moved him to his new room. We played chess together. I had made myself a promise to visit Davis if I were ever doing a move in the same assisted living facility or if he just crossed my mind.

I sat across from Davis at the kitchen table. We played chess. I told him all about the piano "dog walk." I told him whatever was on my mind. I talked, he listened. He talked, I listened. The day would come soon when, after a stroke, he'd only be able to tell me where to move the pieces rather than move them himself. His kids never did come to see him. I was glad to be there. I hoped to let some sunshine in for a man who never walked outside, who never even opened the curtains covering his windows.

I was dead to the world as the rest of Labor Day 1993 passed before my closed eyes. My body completely shut down ten minutes after I walked through the front door at my parents' house Saturday evening. In that ten minutes, I took another shower and managed to wash down two glasses of orange juice with a bowl of oatmeal. Then I hit the sofa. I didn't even have the energy to pull out the deformed sleeper. I slept for the next sixty hours, excluding bathroom breaks. My body needed the rest.

I sat alone on the gold crushed velvet sofa in the familiar apartment. Daddy put me in my blue shorts with the white half inch border along the seam before we left our house. I guess my clothes sort of matched if you looked at me while squinting both your eyes hard. I preferred it when my mother dressed me. But Mommy was going down to Chinatown to the fabric store. Today, Daddy wanted me to go with him.

The rest of my attire consisted of my three tiered multiple-blue shaded shirt. The white tube socks with the three blue rows on the calf coordinated with my red, white, and blue Captain America sneakers with the Velcro fasteners in the shape of the superhero's protective shield. I didn't mind wearing the Velcro sneakers since I was having trouble remembering how to tie my shoes properly. I was lucky if my feet weren't aching at the end of the day from wearing my shoes the wrong way around. I really did prefer it when my mother dressed me.

My legs were still too short to reach the floor when I sat all the way back on the sofa. They kept sticking to the plastic slipcover. Daddy told me to sit still until he was done. He didn't want me getting in the way while he and his three brothers moved the furniture out of his sisters' apartment on the seventeenth floor on Babcock Street near Boston University. Daddy's two sisters had decided to remain in the same building but they needed to change to another apartment three floors down.

My outlook on life was unusual for a couple of reasons. I had just been fitted with my very first pair of eyeglasses. The harsh, teasing comments made about me wearing my new glasses brought me to tears because they were mainly from the people who knew me. They didn't seem to see me anymore. They only saw the little boy wearing these thick damn eyeglasses.

When people make foul comments to little kids, it hurts more than they know. Kids have an uncanny ability never to forget the mean words said to hurt their precious hearts. I know I never forgot. I spent more days with my head down than I did smiling since the day my mother brought me home wearing my eyeglasses. There have been days—weeks—that have gone by where I just couldn't find it in my heart to smile.

However, I was excited about starting first grade. I was going to Mission Grammar School. Daddy said I had to wear a uniform with a shirt and tie like a grown-up. I liked the idea of being like a grown-up. Maybe no one would pick on me and make me feel sad. No one knew me at the new school except my cousins Bird, Fayfae, and Tess. They would be going to the same school with me in September. They have to wear plaid dresses every day like little ladies.

You never truly miss what you had until its gone. I remembered why I missed being in this apartment. I smiled. This was the first time I had been back to this apartment in almost two years. Everything was still where I remembered it. This was also the first time I could see the picture of the two men clearly without squinting. I couldn't help but smile.

"You see those two men in that picture, Baby? Look at the way they're both smiling in the photo. They appear as if they were best friends, yet they only had the pleasure of meeting each other just that once. Nonetheless, this one photo has appeared in more Black homes than any other photograph in our short history.

"Those men were very important in your history. I am grateful to have been present to witness them become who they were blessed to become. Each had very different stories to live. There were many men before these two individuals with similar agendas who were edited out of America's history books. The history books you will read as you get older may never give those two men the credit they so notably deserve, but I will.

"Maulie, these two men were on special journeys. Neither man was aware where his path was leading him. Their paths lead them in completely opposite directions from the time of their conceptions. The roads they traveled were on American soil but they were both in search of human acceptance. The road to finding social change, equality, justice, self respect, and opportunities was filled with peaks and valleys—more valleys than peaks. They both found out that all of these roads lead to one major road called the truth. America hates admitting to its own distorted truths.

"Ironically, each man's search for the truth led him down similar streets at different moments in time. Both of these men sauntered through the streets of Boston at some point in search of their individual truths. A major part of their education was attained here in Boston in totally different institutions.

"It takes a powerful individual to teach someone how to love himself. There is a power there that is immeasurable. Although these two men didn't believe they shared the same ideology, the respect they shared was one of love. They first made sure love was established at home before they could spread love to their individual communities and then to people as a whole. The fundamental love they found for humanity worldwide was the same love they realized was lacking between the Atlantic and the Pacific.

"It's amazing to know it took them both years later at the United State Senate debate of the Civil Rights Bill on March 26, 1964, to realize that both of their roads led to a finish line emblazoned in mutual respect. That was the day when this photo was taken. Shortly afterwards, both men met similar fates at the same young age of thirty-nine.

"Baby, your opportunities exist today because of men like them. You will wake up one day and realize your journey is also one in search of equality, opportunity, justice, and, most of all, truth. Know that your quest also has a finish line filled with the power of love. Use the power of love for good. Too many men abuse love for selfish means.

"Never become complacent with any achievements you may reach in life because tomor-row is coming. You can always hope for more achievements, but they are not guaranteed. There is only one guarantee granted to you as a man. One day your time will expire on this earth. Just keep your feet moving towards a better, changed tomorrow for those who will follow behind you. Make the most of every day you wake up. A change is coming.

"Let me see those teeth, Baby? Smile one time for me."

Daddy's baby sister KiKi opened the front door and came in. I never broke eye contact with the photo. I could hear the refrigerator door open. The glass ketchup bottle wobbled for balance as it knocked up against the mustard jar. The refrigerator closed before the ketchup bottle could catch its balance. Auntie Kiki sat down next to me on the sofa in the apartment she and her sister had lived in since Nana passed away.

"That was your Nana's favorite photograph in this house aside from those of the family. She said seeing Martin Luther King and Malcolm X smiling like that give her the energy she needed to see tomorrow. I miss her so much. Sometimes I hear her talking in this apartment when I'm all by myself." Auntie Kiki handed me the bag of cold clementines.

I peeled one. My face automatically puckered as I bit into the tart miniature fruit. I hadn't eaten clementines in almost two years.

"I hear her too."

There is no better feeling for me than to meet a personal achieve-ment. I had earned the tuition money I needed for the entire school year. According to my calculations, I had actually exceeded my marker by three hundred dollars. While speaking with a family member at the reunion, I heard that one of my cousins, who was starting her freshman year of col-lege, still was waiting for her financial aid package to come. I went over to her house to see if she had everything she needed to get her college experi-ence off on the right foot.

We talked for awhile. She relayed to me that since her mother was a single parent, their savings were limited. They had already maxed out her mother's credit cards just to buy the essentials a freshman needs for living in the dormitory. I knew my cousin was a hard-working young lady. Her mother raised her in the church since she was a baby. So I was 90% sure this young freshman would lose her mind once she moved down to Con-necticut and was without a chaperon. I just prayed she had enough com-mon sense to remember what she is truly away at college to pursue.

Before I left her, I handed her five hundred dollars—my three hundred extra and two more. She was overwhelmed. I made her promise to use the money solely for buying books. I remembered, since I had traveled down this road already, how stressful it was trying to keep up with the curriculum when books were the one expense you hadn't covered. Then after a couple of weeks, when you finally get the money you need, you're playing catch up to where you should be with your class.

Giving her the money felt good. I decided that I would contribute five hundred dollars every time one of the younger family members decided to pursue higher learning. I just wanted to give whoever needed it the opportunity to start their journey without having to play catch up.

When you're going through life's changes, sometimes you just need someone to hold your hand for a second. I got that helping hand throughout my life. Now, it's time to be that helping hand in return.

AFTERWORD

A week after resuming my classes at UMass at Boston I moved in with Grandmama. Living with the "Woman," as I liked to call her, was a formula that had worked for me in the past. I had moved into Grandmama's two-bedroom apartment during junior year of high school because Uncle Deek, being her youngest child, moved out. This move finally gave me my own bedroom. More importantly, it gave me a place where I could concentrate on my schoolwork. It also kept Grandmama from being alone.

Grandmama was now living in the Morton Village apartment complex in Dorchester. Building 95, apartment 204 is a one-bedroom with an adequate kitchen, big enough to fit a two-chair kitchenette set. I spent the majority of my time at the bigger dining room table with my books spread out. When it was time to sleep, I just spread out the foam bed that folded up into a sofa during the daytime. It was comfortable enough for me. I have learned to never complain about too much.

I gave my Grandmama sixty-five dollars a week to help out. I always gave her money even though she never asked for any. It was no big thing since I had been paying rent on a weekly basis to my father since I became a teenager. Somewhere in the back of my mind, I always thought the money I was paying my father for rent over the years was going into a savings account that he would eventually give back to me when I left to go to college. I knew I was just fantasizing because in reality my family was still broke. My father always said it was better to get in a habit for paying for your own keep. He felt it instilled a sense of responsibility making payments on time.

I knew the money helped out my Grandmama a little bit. She worked a full-time job anyways. But what Grandmama really relished was the companionship of having me stay with her. The thought of Davis Jones's loneliness crossed my mind—time for another visit.

At only fifty-seven years old, my Grandmama was young as far as most grandmothers are concerned. Grandmama had my mother young and I'm my mother's oldest child.

Grandmama's bedroom door opened as I sat at the dining room table. She always closed the door when she was on the phone gossiping. She and her sister Beatrice were good for staying on the phone for hours talking about folks, especially their co-worker named Mary-Ellen. I had never met Mary-Ellen but I could tell you more about that woman than her own husband knows about her. Many late nights I would pick up the other line of the telephone to hear both Grandmama and Beatrice snoring into the receiver.

"That doesn't look like schoolwork to me," Grandmama was standing directly behind me reading what I had written.

"Woman, why are you reading over my shoulder?"

"Man, I can read over your shoulder because this apartment's lease is in my name." We both started laughing as she slapped me lightly in the back of my head.

"I was writing down this list. I was answering the question, 'What would I do if I had all the time in the world, if I had all the money in the world, and if I had all the opportunity in the world.' This is my personal list of goals and dreams I want to achieve one day. I figure if I work hard towards everything I write down, maybe I can cross off the listed items once the goal is accomplished. "

"How many dreams to you have listed now?" asked Grandmama.

"I am on number seventy-two." I had been working on this list since I was seventeen years old. I had already crossed off eight items.

"Did you add anything on there for me?"

"Yeah, my goal for you is my number forty-six. I want to buy a house so you never have to move again."

She pursed her lips. "House prices are way too expensive in Boston. The only way number forty-six is going to happen if you hit the lottery. It would be nice to live rent-free by the time I retire." Grandmama has always been a pessimistic person.

"If I am able to buy a house, without hitting the lottery, you will still have to pay rent."

"I'm not paying you any rent."

"How do you expect the mortgage to get paid if you don't pay rent?"

"I'm not paying you any damn rent!" I could hear the stubbornness in her voice. My Grandmama barely stands five feet tall. Her personality is comparable to an upside down tack. As small as she is, Grandmama can cause more mental and physical pain to anyone who doesn't handle her properly. She will sink in a leaking boat just being stubborn. Before she sinks, I can guarantee everyone else inside that boat would rather take their chances overboard than go down listening to Grandmama. The sad truth is people would rather jump overboard than hear her tell them the honest truth. We all know it's not what Grandmama says that rubs our skin like steel wool, it's how she says everything. Grandmama spits fire.

"Woman, you are telling me you are willing to pay every month to lease this one-bedroom apartment but you are not willing to help me out so you never have to move to another apartment again?" I tried to remain monotone.

"Boy, you can put your college spin on it anyway you want to. I still ain't paying you no damn rent. See, you owe me. You owe me from the day I stopped you as a baby from eating chocolate. You were walking around in your diaper with your mouth covered in chocolate. You brought your little chocolate bar over to me because you wanted to share. See I was smarter than you, I didn't take the chocolate. I let you hold the chocolate while I held your wrists. I sniffed that chocolate. That was not chocolate. Boy, you don't get chocolate out of the back of your own damn diaper. Therefore, you owe me and I'm not paying you no damn rent." Grandmama slapped me again in the back of the head.

"First of all, that eating from the diaper thing was Bird not me." I have been blaming this incident on Bird for years. Four months separate Bird and me in age. Grandmama has babysat both of us since birth. The family didn't find out until years later that Uncle Deek, Grandmama's youngest child, had been cutting holes in the seat of me our diapers until we were potty trained. Deek was no longer the baby in the house when Bird and I came through the doorway. Deek found great humor in being a menace.

"I have been cleaning your dirty backside from the day your mother bought you into my house. I know a boy from a girl. You are the nasty little chocolate eater." Grandmama was scrunching up her face like something stunk.

"Second of all, you honestly think I be listening to you, Woman? But I want you to know I don't be listening to you. Third of all, I want you to know you are getting crossed off the list as goal number forty-six." I threw my hands up to protect my head, laughing. I got smacked in the back of the head again.

"Your mother called when I was on the phone. She says she wants you to call her back as soon as I was done."

"I'm not loaning her any money."

The smack came before the words this time. "You only have one mother in this world. I don't care how much you don't like giving her twenty dollars whenever and how frequent she may ask you. You give to your mother because you can. Whatever you give her will never amount to even a fraction of what she has provided for you since you were born. So call her back and see what she wants. And if she asks you for money, you better take it over to her tomorrow.

"I told your mother a long time ago she should have made you pick a switch off a tree and beat you way more than she did. She felt so bad, not wanting to whoop you because you wore those glasses that were bigger than your whole damn head. She wanted to talk to you kids. I told her, 'Damn that talking mess.' She should have talked to you while she set your ass on fire, then you would have paid more attention. If she would have whooped you damn kids I wouldn't have to keep popping you in the back of your fat head now."

The telephone rang again before I had the chance to get up from the dining room table to call over to Cambridge to speak to my mother. It's amazing how Grandmama could make all of her offspring feel in a matter of seconds. Grandmama was a seasoned veteran at making everyone around her feel like they were on the wrong side of right. She was the alpha dog, and that was never going to change. Even when you knew you were right, she could tie you up in knots. There was a lot of love there, but she was truly formidable.

My Grandmama went to answer the telephone in her bedroom. Two seconds passed before the door to her room closed shut.

My pager vibrated on the top on my text book. I grabbed it and pressed the display button. 5-0-5-3-8 was the code I saw. Flipping the pager upside down I could read the Spanish word for kisses. Nina was calling to let me know she tried to call the house but no one clicked over on the call waiting line. "Besos" hyphenated between each of the letters was Nina's way of displaying she was tired and going to sleep. She had been home studying all night as well. Nina had transferred over to Endicott College in Newton, a smaller school than Amherst where she could focus more.

I sat down on the foam blue sofa next to the patio sliding doors with a yellow note pad and pen. The swimming pool in the middle of the complex was closed for the season. The small boom box radio next to me could barely pickup the MIT radio station. I kept a two-foot piece of aluminum foil on standby if the radio reception needed help.

Boston only had one true contemporary rhythm-and-blues radio station. It was on the AM dial and is on the air from sun up and to sun down. Some of the colleges fill the demand for good soul music at night. That Saturday night, P.J. Porter, the disc jockey broadcasting from MIT, came on at around ten o'clock and lasted into early Sunday morning. I was getting ready.

I had been subconsciously singing along to the radio until the clock in the living room chimed the midnight hour. I had been lost in what I had written about my goals for two solid hours. Finally, the door to my Grandmama's bedroom opened as I could hear her shuffle in her house slippers her feet into the bathroom. She emerged from the bathroom and walked into the kitchen. I had already washed the dishes. She turned off all of the lights except the standing lamp where I was sitting.

"Goodnight, Woman," I said.

Grandmama didn't give her usual reply. She just said, "Goodnight."

"Are you okay, Woman?" Something didn't feel right. The vibe in the one-bedroom apartment actually hadn't felt right since the last time the phone rang.

"I'm okay." Grandmama walked into her bedroom, closing the door.

The Spinners song "Sadie" was playing when the door to my Grandmama's room opened again. She didn't walk into the bathroom. She didn't turn on any lights. I could tell from her silhouette she was looking in my direction. Grandmama's silhouette was also missing her hair wig.

"Your Uncle Teddy called tonight." Uncle Teddy was my Grandmama's second child after my mother.

"What's going on?" I asked from the sofa.

"Teddy called to say he's very sick, Kamaul." She was struggling to get the words out.

"How sick is he?" We had all noticed that during the family reunion Teddy just didn't seem energetic at all. He sat in the patio chair underneath one shaded tree all day.

"Your Uncle Teddy just told me he has full-blown AIDS. The doctors are given him less than a year to live." Grandmama's silhouette vanished back into her room

Although I felt like going to give my Grandmama a hug, I didn't. My Grandmama is not an affectionate person. I don't remember too many times where I can say I saw my Grandmama show positive emotions to any of us as we got older. But there was not a shadow of a doubt that she showed her love by making sure all of her offspring had whatever she was capable of providing to them.

Tears filled my eyes. I couldn't help but to be consumed by my own emotions. It was because of the friendship between my Mommy's brother Teddy and my father when they were just fifteen years old that I exist today. Uncle Teddy displayed the affection to us kids that he felt he was denied during his youth. He was great for rubbing his stubbly beard against all of our faces when he scooped us up in the air to kiss us. I would not have been able to travel on this journey had it not been for the pivotal role Uncle Teddy played.

The teardrops rolled of the tip of the chin hairs of my goatee onto the yellow pad of paper. I used the sleeve of my sweatshirt to dry my face. The teardrops that saturated the yellow note pad embodied the two-word phrase at the top of the page. To me at that moment, those two words were the most profound in the English language. I continuously reread—"Remember Me."

Author photograph by Special Effects Photography

Author's Note:
I thank everyone who purchased this part of my life. I hope it was as enjoyable to read as it was for me to sit down and write it. Thank you.

Please write me at:
Marathon Moving Company
c/o Kamaul David
129 York Avenue
Randolph, MA 02368

or

email: kamauldavid@yahoo.com

1118532

Made in the USA